Maik Fielitz, Laura Lotte Laloire (eds.)
Trouble on the Far Right

Political Science | Volume 39

Für Roland

MAIK FIELITZ, LAURA LOTTE LALOIRE (EDS.)
Trouble on the Far Right
Contemporary Right-Wing Strategies and Practices in Europe

[transcript]

Gefördert mit Mitteln des Auswärtigen Amts.

Bibliographic information published by the Deutsche Nationalbibliothek
The Deutsche Nationalbibliothek lists this publication in the Deutsche Nationalbibliografie; detailed bibliographic data are available in the Internet at http://dnb.d-nb.de

© 2016 transcript Verlag, Bielefeld

All rights reserved. No part of this book may be reprinted or reproduced or utilized in any form or by any electronic, mechanical, or other means, now known or hereafter invented, including photocopying and recording, or in any information storage or retrieval system, without permission in writing from the publisher.

Cover layout: Kordula Röckenhaus, Bielefeld
Typeset by Michael Rauscher, Bielefeld
Printed and bound in Great Britain by Marston Book Services Ltd, Oxfordshire
Print-ISBN 978-3-8376-3720-5
PDF-ISBN 978-3-8394-3720-9

Content: Trouble ...

... To Begin With

Trouble on the Far Right
Introductory Remarks
Maik Fielitz and Laura Lotte Laloire | 13

Europe's Far Right in Flux
Liz Fekete | 27

... At The Ballot Box

No One-Trick Ponies
The Multifaceted Appeal of the Populist Radical Right
Stijn van Kessel | 37

The Far Right in Austria
Small on the Streets, Big in Parliament
Bernhard Weidinger | 43

The Turning Fortunes of Romania's Far Right
The Rise and Fall of Greater Romania Party
Mihnea-Simion Stoica | 49

Svoboda and the Restructuring of Ukrainian Nationalism
Mathias Schmidt | 55

... On The Street

Don't Call Me Right!
The Strategy of Normalization in German Right-Wing Extremism
Holger Marcks | 65

On Patrol with the New German Vigilantes
Oliver Saal | 73

CasaPound Italia
The Fascist Hybrid
Heiko Koch | 79

Who are 'They'?
Continuities and Changes in the Discourse of CasaPound Italia on Migration and Otherness
Caterina Froio | 87

What's in the Mind of the Neo-Nazi Next Door?
A Personal Reflection on the Rise and Persistence of Golden Dawn in Greece
Angélique Kourounis | 97

... Over Cultural Hegemony

Preparing for (Intellectual) Civil War
The New Right in Austria and Germany
Natascha Strobl and Julian Bruns | 105

The Strategy of the French Identitaires
Entering Politics through the Media
Samuel Bouron | 111

Arguing with the Nouvelle Droite
Substantive Debate, Partisan Polemics or Truth-Seeking?
Tamir Bar-On | 117

Black Sheep in a Far-Right Zoo?
Fethullah Gülen's Strategy of 'Non-Violence'
Laura Lotte Laloire | 125

Women and their Rights in the Nationalists' Strategies
Abortion as a Contentious Issue in the Polish 'Culture War'
Halina Gąsiorowska | 135

... UNDERGROUND

A Warfare Mindset
Right-Wing Extremism and 'Counter-State Terror'
as a Threat for Western Democracies
Daniel Koehler | 147

Right-Wing Terrorism and Hate Crime in the UK
A Historical Perspective
Alex Carter | 155

... WITHIN

Patterns of Far-Right and Anti-Muslim Mobilization in the United Kingdom
Graham Macklin | 165

But – Where Do These People Come From?
The (Re)Emergence of Radical Nationalism in Finland
Oula Silvennoinen | 173

The Far Right in Latvia
Should We Be Worried?
Matthew Kott | 179

The Achilles' Heel of Bulgaria's Patriotic Front
Yordan Kutiyski | 189

The Changing Faces of Neo-Nazism
Militant Far-Right Activism in Greece
Maik Fielitz | 195

List of Contributors | 205

Trouble ...

The Other Side: Street sign in the German city Kassel, where Halit Yozgat, a local resident, was assassinated in his internet café by members of the far-right terrorist organization *National Socialist Underground* (NSU). (Original photograph taken by Sören Kohlhuber, edited by Deniz Beşer, 2016).

... To Begin With

Trouble on the Far Right
Introductory Remarks

Maik Fielitz and Laura Lotte Laloire

Europe is in trouble as right-wing motivated attacks have become a regular occurrence. Their targets span from religious minorities, such as Muslims and Jews, and ethnic minorities, such as Roma, to participants of LGBTQ[1] parades, civil society protagonists and sometimes even representatives of the political order. At the same time, a xenophobic discourse, especially against migrants and refugees, has gained momentum among European publics, further blurring the lines between far-right agitation and mainstream politics. Likewise, far-right actors have become increasingly influential at various levels: political parties in Austria, France and Slovakia have achieved electoral successes. Movement organizations in Germany and Italy have mobilized thousands of people onto the streets. In Finland and Great Britain, vigilante and terrorist groups have been waging an armed struggle. Last, but not least, 'illiberal models of democracy' in Poland and Hungary demonstrate the far right's capacity to transform entire political systems.

Several causes for this rightward shift are being discussed by the media and within academia; the most prominent of which are the economic crisis, the diversification of European societies as a consequence of the arrival of migrants and refugees, the post-democratic European austerity politics, and the vague disenchantment with liberal democracy.[2] While these analyses tend to focus on macro-level explanatory factors, the actual strategies and practices used by far-right actors remain largely unexamined – at least outside of activist debates.[3] This diagnosis stands in contrast to an expressed concern among policy-makers and within civil society about how to assess new forms of far-right organization and mobilization.

The contemporary European far right goes through a process of restructuring that is taking place within two distinct types of actors as well as between them. On the one hand, new far-right actors have recently emerged and gained influence in national and European political spheres. They draw on new forms of mobilization, agitation and (transnational) networking while integrating ideological components that had previously been alien to far-right ideologies and constituencies. At the same time, the scene is home to parties and movements that trace a long existence but have begun to fundamentally alter their image and political positions. The interaction between these two types of actors on the far right ranges from a division of labor to a struggle over hegemony in a contested far-right arena.

THREE CONTEMPORARY DEVELOPMENTS IN FAR-RIGHT POLITICS

Far-right activism today is being transformed by social conditions as well as by deliberate decisions by its actors, which are creating new political constellations. This has made contemporary far-right politics increasingly unpredictable and opened them to external influence. In the face of the changing landscape of far-right actors, some central research categories formerly used for far-right politics are being dissolved or hybridized. Below, we summarize three of the most striking tendencies:

First, the clear-cut boundaries between parties, movements and subcultural actors[4] are increasingly becoming obsolete. For instance, actors from former neo-Nazi subcultures have established themselves as political parties in the political mainstream of Sweden, Slovakia and Greece.[5] At the same time, far-right movements simultaneously act on different stages and, according to the respective setting, may appear as sober opponents one moment or as violent militias the next. In contrast, other actors bank on street mobilizations to distance themselves from the political establishment. *Second*, setting the far right strictly apart from the political mainstream has become increasingly difficult to maintain owing to the fact that mainstream attitudes and, in effect, the political center have shifted to the right – most visibly, for example, in Poland, Hungary and France. As a consequence, the threshold for the far right to enter mainstream politics is much lower today than it was in the 2000s, when the political center tried to keep far-right influences at the margins. This shift is also being facilitated through broader media attention and a general transformation of the media landscape. *Third*, it is hardly feasible to discuss far-right actors in purely national terms anymore. As the *Nouvelle Droite*[6], the *Identitarians*[7] and various racial nationalist groups have proven, the far right is not only capable of organizing beyond national borders, it also envisions common geopolitical strategies and sometimes even prioritizes Europe over the nation state.[8] The following three paragraphs will elaborate on these developments in further detail.

The Diversification of Far-Right Activism

Internal schisms within far-right activism as well as external shifts in public opinion have set into motion the dynamics of changing boundaries between different actors of the far right as well as between these groups and representatives of the political order. In this context, the bifurcation between the 'old extreme right' – that has little chance in elections given its positive stance to fascism – and 'new extreme right' – that is flexible to adapt to the political environment –[9] are increasingly difficult to maintain today. With the rise of neo-fascist movement parties such as *Golden Dawn*[10] in Greece along with New Right militant formations such as the *Identitarians*[11] in France, such accepted distinctions blurred. Hence, in several instances, a mix of different, and sometimes even contradictory, influences can be detected, as illustrated by the case of the ideological and organizational hybridization of *CasaPound Italia*[12]. Similarly, this process has fostered a diversified appearance within the far right, with new actors springing up and others ceasing to exist, as has been the case in Ukraine, Finland and Latvia.[13] While conflicting issues have emerged and new forms of activism have been negotiated among far-right cadres, interactions between different actors within the far right are constantly oscillating between competition and collaboration.

This development may lead to unexpected encounters and new patterns of collaboration that can even hinge on trivial factos like personal loyalty. Paradigmatically, vigilante justice has exceedingly been put into practice, especially in regions through which refugees pass, such as in Hungary and Bulgaria but even in Scandinavia. The step from local controversies about shelters for refugees to paramilitarism or right-wing terrorism is not as great as sometimes assumed in mainstream public discourse. At the same time, violence as part of the far-right repertoire is adaptable to political circumstances and can be conducted under the cover of state institutions or by other unobtrusive means. Often neglected due to a focus on the larger framework, far-right micro-politics in the form of what has been called entryism into youth subcultures, the infiltration of (un-)civil society organizations and/or the subversion of direct democratic procedures now stand to receive greater academic attention. Such grassroots dynamics reveal local strategies and practices that quickly connect with other, seemingly isolated incidences, which, taken together, are meant to produce a (self-)perceived flourishing movement on which far-right entrepreneurs can rely.

Fading Lines: The Far Right and the Political Mainstream

When comparing today's European far right with the 'third wave of right-wing extremism' from the late 1980s and 1990s[14], we are now witnessing a tremendous transformation in the constellation, representation and acceptance of such politics. Mobilization patterns are changing – such as through the greater use of social media for propaganda – and far-right issues are constantly being renegotiated and modified. Far beyond the focus on migration, a multifaceted appeal to voters is being cultivated and kept flexible to permit entry into or the take-over of mainstream discourses.[15] So as to not be blinded by far-right 'strategies of normalization'[16], this volume aims to investigate both official and hidden agendas. For example, repertoire variation and strategic re-framings of far-right claims only come across as comprehensible strategies when taking their potential for contagion of the political 'center' into account.[17] Building on wide-spread prejudices and propensity for authoritarianism and disenchantment with liberal democracies, actors on the far right function as catalysts of a gradual rightward shift taking place in European societies.[18]

Recent developments have accelerated the radicalization of the political mainstream in terms of increasingly nationalist rhetoric and measures, transforming the institutional landscape. The Slovakian parliamentary elections and the presidential elections in Austria represent two central events that are products of this inherent dynamic. In both cases, the major parties heeded the anti-migration impetus of their far-right contenders and eventually moved to the right themselves. Another example of a tremendously altered political order is Poland, where the right-wing government has begun curtailing fundamental liberties such as the freedom of press and women's right to abortion, thereby fostering authoritarian values and shifting the country's political discourse to the right.

This trend has provided space and political opportunities for more radical forces which strive to escalate social and political conflicts. In other words: far-right activism should be understood as tactically oriented in the short run; at the same time, it may also target gradual changes in mindset, discourse, values, loyalties and legitimacy in the long run. One aspect of the long-term strategy is the professionalized political appearance of many right-wing organizations, which has contributed to the gradual disappearance of a so-called *cordon sanitaire*: a figurative firewall that the political mainstream would previously use to block far-right influences.[19]

Processes of Transnationalization

Beyond the national consensus, far-right actors are joining forces at a transnational level. Discourses, ideological fragments, strategies and practices can diffuse beyond borders despite (and sometimes precisely *because of*) their nationalist outlooks. This includes on the one hand the creation of new platforms and (in)formal cooperation in the European Parliament as well as common appearances on the streets of European cities. Besides traditional party-coalitions,

New Right actors such as the *Identitarians* constitute European projects that frame nationalist sentiments in 'European' terms.

On the other hand, more subtle processes of cross-fertilization are taking place and have contributed to a collective experience in regards to specific political situations: What happens on the streets of Athens may serve as inspiration for local struggles in Great Britain; electoral gains in Austria can have ramifications for the political situation in France; members of the Latvian far right may fight alongside Swedish far-right militants in Ukraine. The increasing overlap of discourses and the mutual exchange of strategies and mobilization patterns in different places – regardless of geographical distance – prove that we must understand far-right activism in international contexts. The translation of discourses and practices from one region to another as well as the mechanisms of transnational diffusion are recurring issues throughout this volume.

Taking these three recent developments as a starting point, there is a need for broader reflection on these new forms of politics within the far right and in its exchanges with the political system. This volume discusses contemporary developments in the European far right, focusing on the actors involved and their practices in conjunction with social developments. The favorable climate throughout European societies that was caused by (deliberately spread) anxieties and resentments during the so-called refugee crisis turned the possibility of a social backlash from a remote threat into a tangible reality. How is the far right responding to this situation? More specifically: How do actors on the far right capitalize on social grievances, and in which cases do they fail to do so? Which short or medium-term strategies have been used in attempts to reshape European societies? How do far-right actors mobilize on various levels and terrains? And how do they interact with the political mainstream? These questions serve as common threads that guide the following chapters.

ACADEMIA IN TROUBLE:
CHALLENGING PERSPECTIVES ON THE FAR RIGHT

Scholarly debates on far-right politics are far from a consensus as to the use of concepts, terminologies and methodologies. Conflicts abound concerning the normative basis of research, the appropriate instruments for empirical inquiry and the relationship to the research object.[20] As the editors of this volume, we offer a pluralist framework that has encouraged the contributing authors to use different approaches. We apply a broad definition of *far right* including the margins of the center right as well as armed insurrection. For us, the far right is a political space whose actors base their ideology and action on the notion of inequality among human beings, combining the supremacy of a particular nation, 'race' or 'civilization' with ambitions for an authoritarian transformation of values and styles of government.

As in other publications, we use *far right* as an umbrella term to subsume actors, attitudes and behaviors, spanning from those which articulate dissent within the framework of representative democracy but are not geared towards the entire system *(radical right)* to those which deny the values, rules and arenas of democracy, impelling a revolutionary overthrow *(extremist right)*.[21] In contrast to conventional extremism studies[22] we do not see the state as the sole addressee of far-right actors, neither as the sole reference to evaluate their behavior. Rather, we highlight that far-right politics also operate below and above the nation state and target different constituencies, some of which are far less protected than state institutions. Without placing particular focus on this issue in our volume, we are well aware of blatant political realities in Europe at the time, such as far right representatives in office – be it in the form of illiberal democrats of the Hungarian *Fidesz*[23] or the Polish party *Law and Justice* (PiS)[24] – and far-right elements appropriated by the mainstream.

In the same vein, we find the academically established distinction between populist and extreme right as being increasingly blurred, and not only due to the hybridization of far-right politics as described above. Instead, we point to the mutability of far-right actors who may incorporate timely aspects to appear more moderate and to their steady drive towards the political center. Hence, we do not consider (right-wing) populism as a phenomenon *per se*, but rather one contemporary feature of far-right politics that varies in its form and degree.[25] In line with this approach, we neither intend to continue the academic 'war of words' on far-right definitions[26] nor fall back into simplistic schemes of plug and play designs.

Closely intertwined with these quarrels about concepts and definitions is the question of how scholars are to approach the far right as an object of study. Since academic analyses influence public debates, every researcher has to find her or his own way of communicating academic knowledge and, where necessary, actively intervene in those debates in a responsible manner. Scholars can hardly remain neutral spectators or commentators: they increasingly need to take a position on issues such as inequality, migration and citizenship. As a consequence, opinions and estimations about the political nature and impact of far-right actors will inevitably diverge on different levels among the authors of this volume. Actually we are convinced that such disagreements will be productive, that they will provide new perspectives on contentious issues and also enhance our understanding of the phenomenon. An adequate analysis of authoritarian tendencies and narrow worldviews requires a plurality of perspectives in academia – for scientific as well as political reasons.

UNDERSTANDING FAR RIGHT POLITICS – LOOKING BEYOND STRUCTURES, NATIONS AND PARTIES

Research on the far right in times of political and/or economic crisis especially cultivates demand-side explanations that focus on "socioeconomic developments such as the impact of migration, unemployment or rapid social change"[27]. For many observers, it seems obvious that this situation bears the rise of reactionary and protectionist actors and contributes to a social polarization that is ethnicized by far-right protagonists. There is ample evidence for this thesis which is exemplified by the rise of neo-fascism in Greece. However, this neither is a direct consequence of social and economic conditions nor do these changes simply advance *any* far-right agenda. The connection between social and economic circumstances and the rise of far-right groups is certainly not this straightforward. In countries such as Spain[28] and Portugal but also in Romania[29], for example, which face high unemployment and the emigration of large numbers of young people – in other words, places where demand for far-right options should be high – no such actor has thus far managed to exploit the situation.

Bringing organizational capacities back into the academic debate, a burgeoning strand of literature emphasizes the supply-side of (mainly) far-right *parties* – meaning, for example, the study of party programs and the role of leadership.[30] Influenced by the tools and insights of social movement studies, some focus on political opportunity structures and/or resource mobilization of far-right parties,[31] and others on the recruitment strategies and internal compositions of far-right organizations.[32] However, apart from a few studies that use political process models to contextualize far-right politics,[33] there is a large gap between demand- and supply-side approaches. This divide undermines a dialectic understanding that incorporates both the agency of far-right actors and processes of social change that reconfigure (power) relations between ruling forces and challengers. Through this volume, we do not argue for supply-side rather than demand-side approaches, but instead concentrate on how social and economic conditions shape – and are shaped by – forms of far-right mobilization and their potentials.

Another deficit is the oftentimes one-sided focus of far-right research on elections and numbers thereby neglecting extra-parliamentary manifestations of the far right which also have long-term influences on European societies and should be evaluated accordingly. One testament to this rising complexity are massive street mobilizations such as the homophobe *Manifs Pour Tous* rallies in France (and beyond) and the migrant-hostile *Stop Invasione* demonstrations in Italy, by the radicalization of vigilantes, and by the flourishing relations between state authorities and far-right movements, such as the Greek *Golden Dawn* and the German *National Socialist Underground*[34].

Innovation is also needed when considering the scale of analysis. Despite growing international exchange on the respective trends[35], in terms of methodology, many approaches remain trapped in a national framework and hardly discuss the far right from a European perspective. They argue that national peculiarities outweigh parallels (and differences) in far-right activism throughout Europe, and thereby restrict themselves to country-based case studies. However, we believe that an examination of the far right today demands a view beyond the national horizon. National or even local developments are hardly understandable without taking processes in other European countries into account.

In sum, this volume offers a collection of different actors' practices, strategies, and their instruments to mobilize support. The pan-European approach aims to not only identify parallels and differences of mobilization efforts or electoral performance among different countries, it also points to core ideologies, interconnections and organizational structures of the far right that have far surpassed national boundaries and therefore demand a transnational response.

In order to realize the idea of sharing scholarly research with a broader audience, we have kept the chapters short, the language basic and questions of definition to a minimum. As such, we did not conceptualize this volume as being purely academic or highly theoretical, and have instead opted to incorporate accounts by practitioners and filmmakers in prominent positions to provide in-depth insights from the people on the ground. By not setting one over-arching theoretical framework, we invite readers to use the empirical insights to draw their own conclusions.

FIVE TERRAINS THAT STRUCTURE THIS BOOK

This volume originated from an article-series that was published on the academic blog *sicherheitspolitik-blog.de*. Altogether, twenty-five international scholars and practitioners grappled with recent developments related to far-right politics in Europe and built a forum to exchange their insights. Rather than simply analyzing far-right politics through case studies for different countries, we have attempted to classify the chapters within five 'terrains' on which far-right politics take place. Though some may overlap, they abide by different logics, appeal to different constituencies and thus also demand diverse styles of inquiry. The terrains we have identified are: competition at the ballot box, action-based performance on the street, long-term (meta)strategies to prepare the cultural grounds for political change, armed insurrection underground, and changing tides of far-right constellations as an arena for internal far-right competition.

To introduce the metamorphosis within the European far right laid out here, we placed Liz Fekete's overview of recent changes in far-right activism at the very beginning, followed by twenty-one chapters that are clustered into their respective terrains.

Introduction   21

▶ **Trouble at the Ballot Box**

In the first part of the volume, contemporary electoral campaigns, voter turnout and changing constellations of far-right political parties in Europe are discussed. Populist radical right parties in Europe have been able to boost their votes – and not only by instrumentalizing the refugee issue. Stijn van Kessel shows how the populist radical right manages to generate a multifaceted appeal by addressing and combining various issues such as culture and economy. Taking a closer look at specific cases, Bernhard Weidinger discusses why the Austrian far right, in the guise of the *Austrian Freedom Party*[36], has been successful in parliament, yet not in terms of street-based mobilizations. The changing tides of electoral success for far-right parties dominate the two chapters that follow. First, Mihnea-Simion Stoica discusses the changing fortunes of the *Greater Romania Party*[37] and asks what is left of Romania's far right. Subsequently, Mathias Schmidt elaborates on the dynamic restructuring of Ukrainian nationalism by tracing the rise and fall of *Svoboda*[38].

▶ **Trouble on the Street**

Moving beyond the focus on political parties, the next chapters provide analyses that delve into street-based practices and argumentation strategies of far-right actors that have recently emerged and received much attention from the media. At the beginning, Holger Marcks examines strategies of far-right rhetoric and their reciprocity with mainstream discourse in Germany. Oliver Saal exhibits the fluent passage from vigilantism to far-right terrorism by examining the German group *FTL/360*[39] and its self-representation on social media platforms. In Italy, the neo-fascist movement party *CasaPound Italia* made headlines on account of their disruptive public appearance. Heiko Koch approaches this actor by scrutinizing its organizational and ideological hybridity. Placing the magnifying glass over a special feature of the same organization, its discourse on migration, Caterina Froio analyzes the strategic 'othering' of refugees by the self-proclaimed 'fascists of the third millennium'. Another movement party that became infamous for their direct political action is the Greek *Golden Dawn*. Filmmaker Angélique Kourounis followed its leadership as well as its rank and file for five years to understand the intrinsic motivation of the members and voter base. She reflects on her experiences in this chapter.

▶ **Trouble over Cultural Hegemony**

New Right and religiously oriented members of the far-right family have proven that its politics are not just the domain of everyday affairs. They tend to pursue strategies on the meta-level; influencing the epistemological setting and attempting to steadily shift cultural hegemony in civil society. This intellectual current within the far right has gained further influence as Natascha Strobl and Julian Bruns explain in their account of New Right politics in Germany and Austria where like-minded protagonists have entered the political stage. They argue that intellectual debate no longer precludes an action-oriented repertoire comprising street-based mobilizations, as epitomized by the expanding transnational model of the *Identitarians*. Referring to the archetype of this movement, the French *Identitarian Bloc*[40], Samuel Bouron investigates its media strategy and reveals how its actors attempt to occupy a cultural and 'meta-political' territory that was once the monopoly of the left, likewise making smart use of the Internet. After years of debating with Alain de Benoist, the leader of the French *Nouvelle Droite*, Tamir Bar-On assesses the arguments and methods de Benoist uses to convey far-right content in a seemingly sophisticated, philosophical way. Laura Lotte Laloire analyzes the different strategic means used by the Turkish Nationalist and Islamist preacher, Fethullah Gülen, who was able to mobilize worldwide followers over the course of decades before being decried a 'terrorist' by the Turkish President Erdoğan. Also applying a long-term perspective, Halina Gąsiorowska decodes the racist and sexist discourses of nationalists who frame anti-abortion campaigns resonating in a general atmosphere of a 'Polish culture war'.

▶ Trouble Underground

Analyzing 'clandestine' groups who act from the underground and use political violence as their main tool, two of our authors provide insights into recent developments and historical continuities, differentiating among two addressees of their actions. Describing 'counter-state terror' in Germany and beyond, Daniel Koehler showcases quantitative figures about how far-right violence is directed against the stability of state institutions. In contrast, Alex Carter reviews the historical evolution of right-wing terrorism and hate crime targeting civil society in the United Kingdom.

▶ Trouble Within

Considering the far right as a heterogeneous space, we find it important to deal with internal struggles over representation and recognition as a factor shaping far-right politics. Beginning with a detailed insight into anti-Muslim mobilizations in the United Kingdom, Graham Macklin evaluates the far right's chances for success given a high fragmentation and various conflicting lines within it. For the Finnish case, Oula Silvennoinen shows how nationalist groups have thrived after the demise of *The Finns Party*.[41] He describes the ways through which they exploit a situation of political crisis and how they have ended up creating a highly fragmented far-right scene. In Latvia, internal disputes within the far right are mainly due to a divide between Latvian ethno-nationalists and pro-Russian neo-fascists, as Matthew Kott explains in his chapter. Yordan Kutiyski deals with the dependency of the *Patriotic Front* on the militant fringe of the Bulgarian far right and its ambiguous behavior in different political arenas. Finally, the development of the Greek *Golden Dawn* is put into the broader Greek context by Maik Fielitz, who shines light on emerging issues of their credibility, attempts at demarcation, and criticism by other far-right groups.

Acknowledgment

We would like to express our gratitude to the critical and professional assistance of our colleagues and friends Philip Wallmeier, Janusz Biene and Lisa Bogerts. Further, the artistic work done by Deniz Beşer has enhanced this volume greatly – thank you! Last, but not least, we thank our extremely reliable and highly creative language editor, Nick Gemmell. We hope that this exchange beyond borders, disciplines and academia will provide new insights that allow for a better understanding of contemporary far-right politics as well as a critical appraisal of the conditions in which they breed. Knowing the terrains ultimately means knowing where to engage.

Annotations

1 | LGBTQ is the acronym of Lesbian, Gay, Bi-Sexual, Trans-Gender, Queer and expresses the diversity of sexuality and gender identities and/or subsumes subjects typically excluded from the heterosexual mainstream.
2 | See Chantal Mouffe (2005): The End of Politics and the Challenge of Right-Wing Populism. In: Francisco Panizza (ed.): Populism and the Mirror of Democracy. London, New York: Verso (Phronesis), pp. 50-71.
3 | We want to point out some noteworthy exceptions: Stephan Braun/Alexander Geisler/Martin Gerster (eds.) (2009): Strategien der extremen Rechten: Hintergründe - Analysen - Antworten [Strategies of the Extreme Right: Background Analysis-Responses]. Wiesbaden: VS Verlag für Sozialwissenschaften; Claudia Globisch (ed.) (2011): Die Dynamik der europäischen Rechten: Geschichte, Kontinuitäten und Wandel [The Dynamic of the European Right: History, Continuity, and Change]. Wiesbaden: VS Verlag für Sozialwissenschaften; Andrea Mammone/Emmanuel Godin/Brian Jenkins (eds.) (2012): Mapping the Extreme Right in Contemporary Europe: From Local to Transnational. London, New York: Routledge (Routledge Studies in Extremism and Democracy, No. 16); Andrea Mammone/Emmanuel Godin/Brian Jenkins (eds.) (2013):

Varieties of Right-Wing Extremism in Europe. Abingdon: Routledge (Routledge Studies in Extremism and Democracy).

4 | Manuela Caiani/Donatella Della Porta/Claudius Wagemann (2012): Mobilizing on the Extreme Right: Germany, Italy, and the United States. Oxford: Oxford University Press.

5 | Aristotle Kallis (2015): When Fascism Became Mainstream: The Challenge of Extremism in Times of Crisis. Second Lecture on Fascism. In: Fascism: Journal of Comparative Fascist Studies, 4/1, pp. 1-24.

6 | In English it means New Right, but the French name is used as an exception, as it is known internationally.

7 | The *Identitarians* (original name in French: *Les Identitaires*) are a far-right youth movement originally from France and at the same time a school of thought close to the New Right. This model of organization spread transnationally.

8 | See Manuela Caiani/Patricia Kröll (2014): The Transnationalization of the Extreme Right and the Use of the Internet. In: International Journal of Comparative and Applied Criminal Justice, 4/39, pp. 1-21; Christina Schori Liang (ed.) (2007): Europe for the Europeans: The Foreign and Security Policy of the Populist Radical Right. Aldershot, England, Burlington: Ashgate; Graham Macklin (2013): Transnational Networking on the Far Right: The Case of Britain and Germany. In: West European Politics, 36/1, pp. 176-198; Stuart A. Wright (2009): Strategic Framing of Racial-Nationalism in North America and Europe: An Analysis of a Burgeoning Transnational Network. In: Terrorism and Political Violence, 21/2, pp. 189-210.

9 | Cf. Piero Ignazi (2003): Extreme Right Parties in Western Europe. Oxford, New York: Oxford University Press; Piero Ignazi/Colette Ysmal (1992): New and Old Extreme Right Parties. In: European Journal for Political Research, 22/1, pp. 101-121.

10 | Original name in Greek: Χρυσή Αυγή. See Angélique Kourounis and Maik Fielitz in this volume.

11 | See Samuel Bouron and Natascha Strobl/Julian Bruns in this volume.

12 | The original Italian name will be used throughout the text because the original goes back to a personal name that cannot be translated. See Heiko Koch in this volume.

13 | See Mathias Schmidt, Oula Silvennoinen and Matthew Kott in this volume.

14 | Klaus von Beyme (1988): Right-Wing Extremism in Western Europe. London: Frank Cass.

15 | Piero Ignazi (1992): The Silent Counter-Revolution. In: European Journal for Political Research, 22/1, pp. 3-34. See also Stijn van Kessel on the diverse focuses of populist-radical right parties.

16 | See Holger Marcks in this volume.

17 | Jens Rydgren (2005): Is Extreme Right-Wing Populism Contagious? Explaining the Emergence of a New Party Family. In: European Journal of Political Research, 44/3, pp. 413-437 and Aristotle Kallis (2013): Far Right 'Contagion' or a Failing 'Mainstream'? How Dangerous Ideas Cross Borders and Blur Boundaries. In: Democracy and Security, 9/3, pp. 221-46.

18 | Cas Mudde (2013): Three Decades of Populist Radical Right Parties in Western Europe: So What? In: European Journal of Political Research, 52/1, pp. 1-19.
19 | William M. Downs (2002): How Effective Is the Cordon Sanitaire? Lessons from Efforts to Contain the Far Right in Belgium, France, Denmark and Norway. In: Journal für Konflikt- und Gewaltforschung, 4/1, pp. 32-51.
20 | For an overview, see Piero Ignazi (2002): The Extreme Right, pp. 21-37.
21 | Cas Mudde (2000): The Ideology of the Extreme Right. Manchester: Manchester University Press.
22 | Eckhard Jesse/Tom Thieme (eds.) (2011): Extremismus in den EU-Staaten [Extremism in EU Member States]. Wiesbaden: VS Verlag für Sozialwissenschaften.
23 | The abbreviation is used here since it is more widely known than the official name *Alliance of Young Democrats*. The original name in Hungarian is: *Fiatal Demokraták Szövetsége*.
24 | Original name in Polish: *Prawo i Sprawiedliwość*.
25 | Andrea Mammone (2009): The Eternal Return? Faux Populism and Contemporarization of Neo-Fascism across Britain, France and Italy. In: Journal of Contemporary European Studies, 17/2, pp. 171-192; Nigel Copsey (2013): 'Fascism... But with an Open Mind': Reflections on the Contemporary Far Right in (Western) Europe. In: Fascism: Journal of Comparative Fascist Studies, 2/1, pp. 1-17.
26 | Cas Mudde (1996): The War of Words Defining the Extreme Right Party Family. In: West European Politics 19/2, pp. 225-248.
27 | Roger Eatwell (2003): Ten Theories of the Extreme Right. In: Peter H. Merkl/ Leonard Weinberg (Hg.): Right-Wing Extremism in the Twenty-First Century. London, Portland: Frank Cass, p. 46.
28 | Sonia Alonso/Cristóbal Rovira Kaltwasser (2014): Spain: No Country for the Populist Radical Right? In: South European Society and Politics 20/1, pp. 21-45; Daphne Halikiopoulou/Sofia Vasilopoulou (2016): Breaching the Social Contract: Crises of Democratic Representation and Patterns of Extreme Right Party Support. In: Government & Opposition, pp. 1-25.
29 | See Mihnea Stoica in this volume.
30 | Cf. Roger Eatwell (2003): Ten Theories, pp. 55-63.
31 | See for example Kai Arzheimer/Elisabeth L. Carter (2006): Political Opportunity Structures and Right-Wing Extremist Party Success. In: European Journal Political Research 45/3, pp. 419-443.
32 | See Bert Klandermans/Nonna Mayer (2006): Extreme Right Activists in Europe: Through the Magnifying Glass. London: Routledge.
33 | See for example Michael Minkenberg (ed.): Transforming the Transformation.
34 | Original name in German: *Nationalsozialistischer Untergrund*. For further examples of 'collusion' between state institutions and far-right groups, see Liz Fekete.; for the involvement of the Turkish state and the Gülen Movement, see Lotte Laloire – both in this volume.

35 | Uwe Backes/Patrick Moreau (eds.) (2012): The Extreme Right in Europe: Current Trends and Perspectives. Göttingen: Vandenhoeck & Ruprecht (Schriften des Hannah-Arendt-Instituts für Totalitarismusforschung, No. 46).

36 | Original name in German: *Freiheitliche Partei Österreichs* (FPÖ).

37 | Original name in Romanian: *Partidul România Mare* (PRM).

38 | Full name: *All-Ukrainian Union Svoboda*; *Svoboda* translates as Freedom. Original name in Ukrainian: *Всеукраїнське об'єднання "Свобода"*.

39 | Original name in German: *Bürgerwehr FTL/360*. FTL is the abbreviation of the Saxon town Freital where this group is from.

40 | Original name in French: *Bloc Identitaire*.

41 | Also called *True Finns*, original name in Finnish: *Perussuomalaiset*.

Europe's Far Right in Flux

Liz Fekete

Since 2011, signs have been multiplying in Europe of a far-right grassroots insurgency in the making.[1] At the same time, signals of a racist insurrection have been surfacing as well, by way of arson attacks, petrol bombs, paramilitary and vigilante activities, and the stockpiling of weapons. The first major indication of the far right's capacity for mass murder came from Norway on July 22, 2011, when Anders Behring Breivik killed 77 people, mainly teenagers, whom he shot dead at the Norwegian *Labor Party*[2] youth summer camp on Oslo's Utøya Island. At his trial, Breivik described the youngsters he so cruelly murdered as 'traitors' who had embraced immigration in order to promote an 'Islamic colonization of Norway'.[3]

Breivik's actions were set against the backdrop of his 1,500-page manifesto, *2083: A European Declaration of Independence*, which was sent out to 1,003 people he considered fellows 90 minutes before he embarked on his killing spree. This should very well have alerted people of the dangerous ideological underpinnings of the defense leagues, pro-identity and anti-Islam movements that were blossoming all across Europe. These supporters of more and more wars in the 'Muslim world', which can broadly be described as 'counter-jihadism', began to emerge during the Gulf War but became more visible and vocal following the events of September 11, 2001. For a variety of reasons, the threat posed by these ultra-patriotic movements was not taken seriously enough, nor was there much reflection upon the broader political context that was nourishing the far right.

Neoliberal economic policies, emergency laws, a permanent culture of war and the securitization of migration have all inflated the cause of the far right; of course, this finds echoes of its racist politics in the prevailing rhetoric against migrants, Muslims, Roma and the indolent poor – the 'scroungers' that hold the 'strivers' back. Yet the far right is insurgent: its growth represents a challenge to the neoliberal status quo inasmuch as it sees neoliberalism as antithetical to a hierarchical, nationalist, mono-cultural society with a strong state. But who are the political actors that harbor such views? In this chapter, I provide an anatomy of the far right, from its various currents and mutations to its web of relationships, fanatical fronts, criminal subculture, provocations and violence.

ANATOMY OF THE FAR RIGHT

It is hard to delineate Europe's far right precisely. It comprises a fluid, constantly mutating and evolving scene. Differing ideological factions are loosely linked in a web of relationships, sometimes splitting off, sometimes coming together in the spaces provided by specific subcultures – such as around music and sports. Football firms[4] are now an integrated part of the far right. *Hooligans Against Salafists* (Ho.Ge.Sa)[5], for instance, which first emerged in Cologne in 2014, describe themselves as a temporary fighting alliance between rival football firms and the resistance against "the true enemies of our common homeland"[6].

These various factions include the anti-capitalist *CasaPound Italia* in Italy and the *Autonomous Nationalists*[7], which originated in Germany but are now moving both westwards and eastwards. Their long hair and black clothes stand in stark contrast to the *Free Forces*[8], whose middle-class and professional supporters in Germany are sometimes referred to as 'Tie Nazis'[9]. Easier to pinpoint are the white supremacists (*Blood & Honour, Ku Klux Klan, Stormfront, White Aryan Resistance*), the National Socialists (the most high-profile of which include the *National Democratic Party of Germany*[10] and the *Party of the Swedes*[11]), pro-identity movements (such as the *Identitarian Bloc*[12] in France), and the defense leagues (such as the notorious *English Defence League*). More complex, on account of their greater hybridity, are the identity movements amongst the non-white dispossessed, particularly in France and Belgium, where anger and a sense of persecution amongst young people from the suburbs has been manipulated by demagogic figures (such as Alain Soral, Dieudonné M'bala M'bala and Laurent Louis) and directed towards antisemitic gesture politics – epitomized in exhibiting the inverted Nazi salute, the *quenelle*.[13]

The more traditional ideological brands on sale in the modern far-right marketplace include Strasserism along with anti-capitalist and anti-Marxist Third Positionism, with working-class appeal, while a modernized variation can be found in *CasaPound Italia*, the 'fascists of the third millennium'[14]. Then, of course, there is 'counter-jihadism', which is best understood as a spectrum with street fighting forces at one end and cultural conservatives and neoconservative writers at the other. Riding all of these tendencies and bringing the mutations together over specific causes are the nebulous and fanatical fronts that spring up from time to time, seemingly spontaneously, as vessels for discontent.

Examples abound of the activities that these fanatical fronts undertake, from the summer 2013 protests of the so-called 'decent citizens' against the 'inadaptable citizens' (i.e., Roma), which swept through Bohemia in the Czech

Republic[15], to *French Spring*[16], a homophobic network of Catholic fundamentalists and the far-right activists which brought 150,000 people to the streets of Paris in protest against the proposed same-sex marriage law. The latter was the largest far-right demonstration in France in thirty years. More recently, the *Patriotic Europeans Against the Islamization of the Occident* (PEGIDA)[17] swept onto the scene, seemingly out of nowhere. Racist mobilizations from below, swelling up on a wave of anger, fear and machismo at the grassroots are manipulated by the far right, as fascism flows from the same springs as racial hatred and social anomie.

FROM COMMUNITY POLITICS ...

Often starting out as nebulous virtual protests on Facebook centered around a specific local social tension (such as the housing of refugees or Roma, or a planning application for a mosque), they are elevated into national causes via social media. So-called 'citizens initiatives' are organized, uniting the various fascist mutations with the so-called 'decent, ordinary citizens' in a frenzy of aggression expressed by way of angry demonstrations in minority neighborhoods. The violence has been well documented in many short films on YouTube, such as *Captive Audience* (an account of the anti-Roma mobilizations in the Czech Republic).[18] Much is made of the 'ordinariness' of the people who attend PEGIDA demonstrations; but this ordinariness does not consider that neo-Nazis are taken to be 'ordinary' in many parts of eastern Germany.

A closer examination of its program and activities shows that Islam merely serves as a convenient code word for PEGIDA; its anti-Islam agenda, as Anthony Fano Fernadez so rightly pointed out, is an act of "sly, tactical opportunism"[19]. PEGIDA is a classic far-right anti-immigration movement. Throughout 2013 and 2014, there were 'citizens' initiatives' against refugees in Saxony, with protests outside of asylum reception centers in towns such as Chemnitz and Schneeberg in the Ore mountains and Borna near Leipzig. PEGIDA's supporters want to keep this part of eastern Germany white and free of immigrants. They are particularly angry that the federal government has been dispersing asylum-seekers from Syria to the region, and have sought to force a reversal of this stance.

... TO CRIMINALITY AND PARAMILITARISM

The far right may consist of various strands, but it has a common rendezvous point in criminality. Today's far-right scene offers apprenticeships in pimping and extortion, money laundering, drugs and arms running, human smuggling, vigilantism and armed combat.[20] Major trials involving far-right criminal conspiracies have either recently taken place or are ongoing in many countries: *National Socialist Underground* (Germany)[21], *Anti-System Front* (Spain)[22], *Objekt 21* (Austria)[23], *New Order* (Italy)[24], and Roma serial murders by neo-Nazis who formed their own private militia (Hungary)[25]. Closer investigation reveals either direct or indirect collusion in each of them between neo-Nazis, the police, the military, the intelligence services or a mixture of these elements. The year 2015 saw 69 members of the Greek *Golden Dawn* (XA)[26] (including 18 Members of Parliament) brought to trial on charges of forming a criminal organization, weapons procurement and soliciting murder. This includes the trial of the XA supporter who murdered Pavlos Fyssas[27] and the trial of three far-right skinheads for the killing of the French 18-year-old anti-fascist Clement Méric in Paris in June 2013[28]. The three defendants are allegedly linked to the groups *Third Way*[29] and the *Young Revolutionary Nationalists*[30], which were both banned immediately after Méric's murder on the grounds that they constituted a private militia and operated paramilitary training camps.

The far right has also taken it upon itself to impose its law, namely vigilante justice, with its own private militia and paramilitary squads. In Greece, prior to the provisional arrest of its Members of Parliament in 2013, black-clad XA supporters armed with clubs were in the habit of sweeping through migrant areas on motorbikes, beating anyone in sight. This took place under the watchful eye of the Hellenic Police, who were involved in their own sweep against migrants between August 2012 and February 2013. The police undertook a racial profiling exercise called *Operation Xenios Zeus*, which led to nearly 85,000 suspected foreigners being forcibly taken into custody to verify their immigration status; it was then found that 94 percent had a legal right to remain in Greece.[31] The court in the trial of the XA members will show video evidence of party members dressed in paramilitary uniforms carrying out weapons training, their faces covered by motorcycle helmets.

To sum up: examining this record, it is important to remember that far-right groups have not emerged in a vacuum, nor are they entirely disconnected from the more respectable right and anti-immigration parties now represented in the parliaments and municipalities of every European country. It is important to acknowledge that far-right violence grows when state institutions fail. A pattern of collusion, direct or indirect, between the military, the police and the intelligence services (or a combination of all three) with the far right has not only been detected in Greece, but all over Europe as well. Fascism does not simply hatch its eggs on the margins of society: it breeds within existing authoritarian structures, in those spaces most shielded from public scrutiny, such as the police and intelligence services, which prove to be the perfect incubators.

Annotations

1 | This text is an edited and updated version of the original "Neoliberalism and Popular Racism: The Shifting Shape of the European Right". In: Leo Panitch/Greg Albo (eds.) (2016): The Politics of the Right: Socialist Register, Vol. 52. London: Merlin Press, pp. 1–23. We are grateful to Merlin Press for permitting us to reuse the material.
2 | Original name in Norwegian: *Arbeiderpartiet*.
3 | Sindre Bangstad (2014): Anders Breivik and the Rise of Islamophobia. London: Zed Books.
4 | Football firms are organized hooligan groups of a specific football club.
5 | Original name in German: *Hooligans gegen Salafisten*.
6 | Olaf Sundermeyer (2014): Schrei nach Aufmerksamkeit [Cry for Attention]. In: Deutschlandradio, September 29, (http://www.deutschlandfunk.de/hooligans-gegen-sa lafisten-schrei-nach-aufmerksamkeit.890.de.html?dram:article_id=298959), accessed July 15, 2015.
7 | Original name in German: *Autonome Nationalisten*.
8 | Original name in German: *Freie Kräfte*. These are collectives of loosely organized, party-remote neo-Nazi groups with a strong focus on direct action and militant habitus. Among them are the '*Kameradschaften*' which in English means 'comradeships'.
9 | Original name in German: *Krawattennazis*.
10 | Original name in German: *Nationaldemokratische Partei Deutschlands (NPD)*.
11 | Original name in Swedish: *Svenskarnas Parti (SVP)*.
12 | Original name in French: *Bloc Identitaire*.
13 | Alain Soral founded the movement party *Reconciliation in France and in Belgium* (Original name in French: *Reconciliation Nationale*). Laurent Louis heads the party *Belgians, Rise up!* (original name in French: *Debout Les Belges*). Soral, once a member of the *French Communist Party* (original name in French: *Parti Communiste Français*), joined the *Front National*, which he left in 2009. Jean-Marie Le Pen is the godfather of Dieudonné's son.
14 | See Heiko Koch and Caterina Froio in this volume.
15 | See Liz Fekete (2013): It's like a War. In: IRR News, July 25, (http://www.irr.org.uk/news/its-like-a-war/), accessed July 7, 2016.
16 | Original name in French: *Printemps Français*.
17 | Original name in German: *Patriotische Europäer gegen die Islamisierung des Abendlandes*.
18 | Barbora Cernusakova/Philip Lowman (2013): Captive Audience: Europe Roma International, December 21, (https://youtu.be/ep8PwvBujKo), accessed July 7, 2016.
19 | Anthony Fano Fernadez (2015): Germany's New Far Right. In: Jacobin, February, (https://www.jacobinmag.com/2015/02/germany-far-right-pegida/), accessed July 17, 2016.

20 | For example, Scandinavian neo-Nazis are fighting in the Ukraine, see Dina Newman (2014): Ukraine Conflict: "White Power" Warrior from Sweden. In: BBC News, July 16, (http://www.bbc.co.uk/news/world-europe-28329329), accessed July 7, 2016.
21 | Original name in German: *Nationalsozialistischer Untergrund*.
22 | Original name in Spanish: *Frente Anti-Sistema*.
23 | See BBC News (2013): Austria Court Jails Seven Members of Neo-Nazi Group. In: BBC News, November 5, (http://www.bbc.co.uk/news/world-europe-24819883), accessed July 7, 2016.
24 | Original name in Italian: *Ordine Nuovo*.
25 | See blog post by Eszter Hajdu (2016): Judgment in Hungary: A filmmaker Reflects, April 13, (http://www.sicherheitspolitik-blog.de/2016/04/13/judgment-in-hungary-a-filmmaker-reflects/), accessed August 3, 2016.
26 | Original name in Greek: *Χρυσή Αυγή*.
27 | See Helena Smith (2013): Greek Golden Dawn Member Arrested over Murder of Leftwing Hip-Hop Artist. In: The Guardian, September 18, (https://www.theguardian.com/world/2013/sep/18/greece-murder-golden-dawn), accessed July 7, 2016.
28 | See Angelique Chrisafis (2013): Eight Held Over Killing of Teenage Anti-Fascist Campaigner. In: The Guardian, June 7, (https://www.theguardian.com/world/2013/jun/07/eight-held-skinheads-france-death), accessed July 7, 2016.
29 | Original name in French: *Troisième Voie*.
30 | Original name in French: *Jeunesses Nationalistes Révolutionnaires*.
31 | Human Rights Watch (2013): Unwelcome Guests. Greek Police Abuses of Migrants in Athens. New York: Human Rights Watch, p. 16.

In Coat and Tie: Demonstration by the German far-right political party *Alternative for Germany* (AfD) in Hamburg on October 31, 2015. (Original photograph taken by *Wut auf der Straße*, edited by Deniz Beşer, 2016).

... At The Ballot Box

No One-Trick Ponies
The Multifaceted Appeal of the Populist Radical Right

Stijn van Kessel

The present environment for far-right parties in Europe is favorable. Both the refugee crisis as well as well as the recent terrorist attacks across Europe and beyond have ostensibly further fueled xenophobic and anti-Islam sentiments among European publics; it has arguably been on this basis that populist radical right (PRR) parties have built their support. Recent elections in Europe have indeed seen gains for parties with an outspoken xenophobic message: the success in March 2016 for the *Alternative for Germany* (AfD)[1] in the German regional elections and two far-right parties *Slovak National Party* (SNS)[2] and *People's Party Our Slovakia* (L'SNS)[3] in the Slovak national elections being cases in point. Moreover, opinion polls in countries such as France, Austria and the Netherlands show equal promise for PRR parties. Though not all European countries have witnessed the successful mobilization of the PRR, it is fair to conclude that this party family is fairing very well. Nevertheless, it would be too premature to conclude that PRR parties have only thrived on the recent salience of the immigration issue.

THE POPULIST RADICAL RIGHT'S CULTURAL AGENDA

Immigration certainly entails an important issue for PRR parties, which, according to Cas Mudde, share an ideological core of nativism, authoritarianism and populism.[4] Besides its belief in a strictly ordered society with clear norms and lines of authority, and its populist anti-establishment criticism – which puts forth a positive valorization of the ('ordinary') people and a negative portrayal of the 'elites' – the PRR's most defining characteristic is nativism. Mudde defines this concept as

"an ideology, which holds that states should be inhabited exclusively by members of the native group ('the nation') and that non-native elements (persons and ideas) are fundamentally threatening to the homogeneous nation-state"[5].

Nativism naturally correlates with hostility towards immigrants, who are inherently non-natives. While anti-immigration rhetoric was mainly voiced by PRR parties in the western part of the continent in the past, the recent refugee crisis has also made immigration a more significant issue in Central and Eastern European countries. Previously, relatively few ('non-Western') immigrants chose to settle in post-communist countries, and PRR parties in this part of Europe mainly targeted minority populations, such as the Roma. More recently, however, immigration has become an electoral issue in the post-communist context – with hostile language not only being voiced by the PRR, but also by dominant 'mainstream' party figureheads, such as Jarosław Kaczyński in Poland[6], Prime Ministers Victor Orbán in Hungary[7] and Robert Fico in Slovakia[8].

The 'supply' of anti-immigration positions among political actors is meeting 'demand' from citizens across Europe. Public opposition to immigration and related anxieties about the decay of national culture – not least due to the alleged 'Islamization' of European societies – form the basis of PRR party support. Scholarly contributions have shown that PRR supporters are primarily motivated by the stances that parties take on 'cultural' issues, not least immigration and multiculturalism.[9] Socio-economic issues such as welfare redistribution and market regulation, it has been argued, are secondary concerns on PRR party programs, as they are to their voters. What is more, PRR parties ostensibly have little to gain from placing more emphasis on socio-economic issues, as their electorates typically constitute a coalition between less-educated 'blue-collar' workers and petit bourgeois entrepreneurs, two groups with contrasting economic interests and attitudes.[10] As such, analysts have suggested that it is sensible for these parties to devote little attention to, and even 'blur' their positions on, socio-economic matters.[11]

Beyond Immigration: Europe and Welfare

It would be inaccurate, however, to portray PRR parties as single-issue 'anti-immigration' parties. For one, most are also characterized by their opposition to European integration. This position is also related to the PRR's nativism: European integration is associated with a loss of national identity and sovereignty. The European Union (EU) is generally portrayed as an undemocratic 'super state' that threatens the native community and facilitates unwanted immigration.[12] In addition, the PRR formulates its populist arguments against the EU: European integration is considered an elitist project with little regard for the 'popular will', while the EU's decision-making procedures are complex and opaque.[13] The recent Euro crisis has provided PRR parties with further ammunition against 'Europe'. Various PRR parties in Northern Europe, such as the AfD, the *True Finns*[14] and the Dutch *Party for Freedom*[15], for instance, have voiced opposition to the bailouts for troubled Eurozone members and the pooling of more sovereignty at the European level as a response to the crisis. While Euroskepticism is not the exclusive prerogative of the PRR party family (the radical left, for one, laments the EU's neoliberal character) and though degrees of opposition vary across individual cases, the anti-EU position is a defining characteristic of contemporary PRR parties.[16]

Moreover, even though the prevailing consensus states that PRR parties are mainly characterized by their cultural agenda, there is an increasing body of scholarly research which shows that (Western European) PRR parties are converging around what has been called a 'welfare chauvinist' position.[17] This essentially entails support of economic redistribution and the preservation of welfare state entitlements, whereby non-natives (most notably, immigrants) are excluded from receiving welfare or only receive limited access to it. This implies that the PRR is not necessarily 'right-wing' in terms of socio-economic issues; indeed, PRR parties may support traditionally 'leftist' causes such as safeguarding pensions and workers' rights. The conception of welfare held by PRR parties is, however, hardly universal, and excluding non-natives from it – who are often portrayed as 'underserving scroungers' – is typically argued to be a precondition for the survival of the welfare state.

The identification of welfare chauvinist appeals among PRR parties represents a departure from a few influential scholarly accounts from the 1990s. Notably, Herbert Kitschelt and Anthony McGann initially spoke of an ideological "winning formula" for the radical right in Western Europe, which entailed a combination of neoliberalism with authoritarianism and xenophobia.[18] It is still something of a moot point whether such early accounts were off the mark as far as the socio-economic program of the radical right is concerned, or whether the adoption of more 'leftist' welfare protection positions by PRR parties is a relatively recent trend. For at least a number of cases, such as the French *Front National*[19], the latter interpretation appears valid.[20] It is, in any case, worth noting that this debate primarily centers on the western part of the continent, as many PRR parties in post-communist countries were geared towards defending the social rights of the 'transition losers' from the outset: citizens who did not benefit from the transition to the free-market economy.[21]

WHERE CULTURE MEETS ECONOMY

Whether taken as a new phenomenon or not, does the PRR's welfare chauvinist appeal signify that the socio-economic agenda of this family of parties is (becoming) more relevant than previously assumed? On the one hand, one could argue that the economic and welfare policies promoted by the PRR are primarily informed by their cultural agenda. Ostensibly, the most important aim for these parties is to protect the natives, and the economic policies they advocate can also be seen in this light. On the other hand, however, it seems that current scholarship is too preoccupied with the analytical distinction between the cultural and economic dimensions of political competition. It is difficult, and arguably misguided, to interpret the welfare chauvinism of the PRR in *either* economic *or* cultural terms; economic interest and identity are not as easily distinguishable as scholars often suggest. The desired exclusion of immigrants from entitlements may be based on identity, but welfare redistribution inherently remains an economic issue as well. In the same way, it would be too simplistic to attribute the success of PRR parties only to fear among their electorates about the loss of culture and identity, or anxieties about Islamic extremism. Citizens do not necessarily perceive cultural and material threats as clearly distinct from one another, and resistance to immigration is partly borne out of fears of economic competition and welfare deprivation. In fact, the 'exclusive solidarity' agenda[22] promoted by the PRR is likely to be electorally potent precisely because it taps into an amalgamation of cultural and economic concerns found among a significant share of the electorate.

Conclusion

In light of current events, it is clear that immigration is now primarily framed as a cultural and security issue. This no doubt plays into the hands of the PRR, as this is how such parties prefer to address the topic. This does not mean, however, that support for PRR parties will automatically drop when the salience of other issues rises, or when immigration is associated more with economic bread-and-butter issues. Ultimately, the PRR's agenda is about more than cultural anxieties alone.[23]

Annotations

1 | Original name in German: *Alternative für Deutschland*.
2 | Original name in Slovakian: *Slovenská Národná Strana*.
3 | Original name in Slovakian: *Ľudová Strana Naše Slovensko*, also abbreviated as L'S NS or LS-NS.
4 | Cas Mudde (2007): Populist Radical Right Parties in Europe. Cambridge: Cambridge University Press.
5 | Ibid., p. 22.
6 | Reuters (2015): Polish Opposition Warns Refugees Could Spread Infectious Diseases, October 15, (http://www.reuters.com/article/us-europe-migrants-poland-idUSKCN0S918B20151015), accessed June 22, 2016.

7 | Georgi Gotev (2015): Orbán Slams EU Migration Policies Ahead of Juncker's Mini-Summit. In: Euractiv, October 22, (https://www.euractiv.com/section/justice-home-affairs/news/orban-slams-eu-migration-policies-ahead-of-juncker-s-mini-summit/), accessed June 22, 2016.
8 | Euractiv.com (2016): Fico: EU's Migration Policy Is 'Ritual Suicide', January 26, (http://www.euractiv.com/section/central-europe/news/fico-eu-s-migration-policy-is-ritual-suicide/), accessed June 22, 2016.
9 | See e. g. Elisabeth Ivarsflaten (2008): What Unites the Populist Right in Western Europe? Reexamining Grievance Mobilization Models in Seven Successful Cases. In: Comparative Political Studies, 41/1, pp. 3-23; Daniel Oesch (2008): Explaining Workers' Support for Right-Wing Populist Parties in Western Europe: Evidence from Austria, Belgium, France, Norway and Switzerland. In: International Political Science Review, 29/3, pp. 349-373.
10 | Elisabeth Ivarsflaten (2005): The Vulnerable Populist Right Parties: No Economic Realignment Fuelling Their Electoral Success. In: European Journal of Political Research, 44/3, pp. 465-492.
11 | Jan Rovny (2013): Where Do Radical Right Parties Stand? Position Blurring in Multidimensional Competition. In: European Political Science Review, 5/1, pp. 1-26.
12 | See e. g. Cas Mudde (2007): Populist Radical Right Parties, p. 168; Liesbet Hooghe/Gary Marks/Carole Wilson (2002): Does Left/Right Structure Party Positions on European Integration? In: Comparative Political Studies, 35/8, pp. 965-89; Catherine de Vries/Erica Edwards (2009): Taking Europe to Its Extremes: Extremist Parties and Public Euroscepticism. In: Party Politics, 15/1, pp. 5-28.
13 | Paul Taggart (2004): Populism and Representative Politics in Contemporary Europe. In: Journal of Political Ideologies, 9/3, pp. 269-288; Stijn van Kessel (2015): Populist Parties in Europe: Agents of Discontent? Basingstoke: Palgrave Macmillan.
14 | Also called *Finns Party*, original name in Finnish: *Perussuomalaiset*.
15 | Original name in Dutch: *Partij voor de Vrijheid*.
16 | See e. g. Margarita Gómez-Reino/Iván Llamazares (2013): The Populist Radical Right and European Integration: A Comparative Analysis of Party-Voter Links. In: West European Politics, 36/4, pp. 789-816.
17 | Jørgen Andersen/Tor Bjørklund (1990): Structural Changes and New Cleavages: The Progress Parties in Denmark and Norway. In: Acta Sociologica, 33/2, pp. 195-217.
18 | Herbert Kitschelt/Anthony McGann (1995): The Radical Right in Western Europe. Ann Arbor: University of Michigan Press; see also Hans-Georg Betz (1994): Radical Right-Wing Populism in Western Europe. New York: St. Martin's Press.
19 | The English translation is *National Front*. However, to avoid confusion with groups or parties from other countries carrying the same name, the original name in French is used in this text.
20 | Gilles Ivaldi (2015): Towards the Median Economic Crisis Voter? The New Leftist Economic Agenda of the Front National in France. In: French Politics, 13/4, pp. 346-369.

21 | Andrea Pirro (2014): Populist Radical Right Parties in Central and Eastern Europe: The Different Context and Issues of the Prophets of the Patria. In: Government & Opposition, 49/4, pp. 600-629.

22 | Zoe Lefkofridi/Elie Michel (2014): Exclusive Solidarity? Radical Right Parties and the Welfare State, EUI RSCAS Working Paper, EUI RSCAS 120.

23 | The author would like to thank Koen Abts and Emmanuel Dalle Mulle for their useful feedback; some ideas conveyed in this chapter are borne out of a joint research project on the socio-economic agenda of the populist radical right.

The Far Right in Austria
Small on the Streets, Big in Parliament

Bernhard Weidinger

Since around 1990, the Austrian far right[1] has been characterized by the strength of the *Austrian Freedom Party* (FPÖ)[2] and the relative weakness of extra-parliamentarian far-right activism. Far from a mere coincidence, these two features are closely linked: the FPÖ's electoral successes have brought far-right causes and talking points onto the political center stage at a national level, granted them ample media coverage, and made street militancy increasingly unnecessary. As such, the Austrian far-right spectrum could – until recently at least – be described as a photographic negative of the situation in Germany: successful party politics, weak bottom-up mobilizations, and a comparatively low incidence of street violence. Currently, however, long-held hopes among German right-wingers of a party both in the mold and strength of the FPÖ are apparently being fulfilled by the emergence of the *Alternative for Germany* (AfD)[3]. Conversely, legal as well as illegal forms of street activism have been on the rise in Austria in recent years, particularly since the beginning of the asylum crisis in Europe. Numerous violent incidents were reported in 2015, including a minimum of 25 attacks on housing facilities for asylum-seekers[4]. The number of criminal offences with a right-wing extremist background – the ones which have been registered by the Austrian security authorities – sharply increased by 54.1 percent from 2014 to 2015[5]. The following pages provide an overview of key far-right protagonists in Austria and depict current noteworthy developments.

THE FREEDOMITES:
THE AUSTRIAN FAR RIGHT'S CENTER OF GRAVITY

The FPÖ won 20.5 percent of the vote in the last national parliamentary elections in 2013 – a moderate increase from their 2008 results, but still well below the 26.9 percent obtained under the leadership of Jörg Haider in 1999. Thirteen years prior to his biggest victory on the national stage, Haider had taken over a party which had never before attained double-digits in elections to the Austrian Federal Parliament *(Nationalrat)*. In the following years, he skillfully harnessed nativist resentment and dissatisfaction with the 'Grand Coalition' comprised of the *Social Democratic Party of Austria* (SPÖ)[6] and the conservative *Austrian People's Party* (ÖVP)[7], advancing it to new levels. In 2000, the party entered the federal government in a coalition with the ÖVP. Once polling and regional election results started plummeting, Haider broke away from the FPÖ in 2005 to found the *Alliance for the Future of Austria* (BZÖ)[8], which took over all formerly *Freedomite* government positions and a large majority of the parliamentary faction.[9] Since Haider's death in a car accident in 2009, the BZÖ has rapidly waned, and is now all but defunct. The FPÖ, on the other hand, underwent an impressive recovery, winning election after election, and has been leading national polls for years now. The 35.1 percent achieved by its candidate (and federal co-chairman) Norbert Hofer in the first round of the presidential elections in 2016 marks the best result that the FPÖ has ever accomplished in nationwide elections. The party also cleared the 30 percent threshold in the two most recent regional elections (Vienna and Upper Austria) in the fall of 2015.

The key question remaining is whether or not the *Freedomites* will be able to find a partner willing to assume the junior role in a coalition government. Here, the ÖVP again appears as the most likely, if not the only candidate. While the SPÖ has so far ruled out any coalitions with the FPÖ at the national level, this commitment seems to be crumbling, particularly since the SPÖ in the eastern region of Burgenland decided to form a coalition with the *Freedomites* in June 2016. The remains of what never managed to be a French or Belgian-style anti-far-right firewall have been rapidly eroding, instead relying on a policy alignment between the far-right fringe and the political center, which has persisted for many years. Even as an opposition party, the FPÖ has managed to exert considerable influence on governmental policies since the Haider era. Just like during the 1990s, social democrats and conservatives are currently trying to slow the momentum of the *Freedomites* by shifting their own policies rightwards, particularly those concerning migration issues. This strategy appears to be failing now, as it did before, insofar as it effectively legitimizes far-right stances rather than weakening their party-political representatives.

Beyond its electoral victories, over the course of its rapid ascent under Haider, the FPÖ has managed to integrate large parts of the far right in Austria. It acts as an amplifier for far-right talking points and demands, shares its recruiting pool (repeatedly boasting overlaps in personnel) with extra-parliamentary far-right groups, including neo-Nazis, and, rather unsurprisingly, is endorsed by those groups on a regular basis. As of late, the party has, however, demonstrated an increased willingness to rid itself of representatives who hurt its governmental aspirations with overly explicit hate speech or the display of neo-Nazi inclinations.

PAN-GERMAN STUDENT FRATERNITIES: THE AUSTRIAN FREEDOM PARTY'S CORE

One interesting peculiarity of Austrian far-right politics worth mentioning is the central role played by student fraternities (and, to a much lesser extent, sororities[10]). As an important part of the still-existent German-nationalist camp in Austria – which also includes a number of sports, arts and folk culture groups – these organizations have been a notorious hotbed for far-right activists since the 19th century. The sororities in particular, as the most political fraternity type in Austria, have been the primary recruitment base for high-ranking *Freedomite* officeholders since the founding of the FPÖ in 1956; this status did, however, diminish somewhat in the second half of the Haider era (1986 through 1999) and during the subsequent participation of the FPÖ in federal government (2000 through 2005). Under Chairman Heinz-Christian Strache, a member of one of the *Burschenschaften* himself, the party has again been leaning heavily on fraternity members. Unlike Haider, Strache has remained loyal to them even as election victories kept coming and the propensity towards a broader, vote-maximizing approach to personnel and policy decisions grew stronger. As of June 2016, at least 17 of 38 *Freedomite* Members of Parliament and a majority of the federal party board (19 of 35) are fraternity/sorority members. On a programmatic level, fraternity influence has contributed decisively to maintaining the German-nationalist and antisemitic tradition of thought within the FPÖ. The emergence of anti-Muslim racism as a central *Freedomite* topic and tool for agitation since around 2005[11] has pushed antisemitism to the background, though, as Peham argues[12], this has complemented rather than replaced it. This holds true despite the tactical courting of Israel that some party strategists have endorsed, which large segments of the party base still frown upon.[13]

THE FAR-RIGHT MEDIA SCENE: IN THE STATE OF TRANSFORMATION

The privileged position that fraternities assume in relation to the FPÖ has so far spared them from sharing the political irrelevance of other extra-parliamentary far-right groups and traditional print publications, such as *Phoenix* and *fakten*, which almost exclusively preach to the choir, so to speak. *Info-DIREKT*, launched just one year ago, might be able to appeal to a larger audience due to its timely layout and transmedia (print and online) approach. Both in content and style, it resembles the German *COMPACT* magazine: it has a strong penchant for conspiracy myths and left/right transgressions in its rhetoric and the topics it brings forth, and it is fervently anti-American and pro-Putin to such an extent that one wonders whether financial aid from Russia may be at play. In general, the Austrian far right, including the FPÖ, has abandoned its traditional Russophobia in recent years, idolizing Vladimir Putin as a strong leader with a clear vision and a value system compatible with the European far right.

The Internet in general, and social media in particular, have emerged as key propaganda tools for the far right all over the world, with Austria being no exception. The FPÖ, which chronically complains about alleged media misrepresentation – particularly by public service broadcaster ORF – entertains a highly popular YouTube channel, and Strache leads all other Austrian politicians in the number of Facebook fans by a wide margin. Still, the importance of the (social) web is arguably even more crucial for smaller groups due to the potentially large impact it affords at little to no cost, combined with the difficulties that legal authorities often encounter in tracing online hate speech and neo-Nazi activities. Facebook groups can rapidly reach broad audiences, though this often proves to be a Potemkin village when trying to transfer online resentment to the streets. The *Patriotic Europeans Against the Islamization of the Occident* (PEGIDA)[14], for instance, acquired a large amount of Facebook likes (and media coverage based on it) in Austria in no time at all, but they still could not manage to mobilize more than a couple of hundred people for a demonstration. Hate speech in social media, both by groups and individuals, is also an epidemic in Austria that propelled the reform of anti-incitement legislation into force in January 2016. Along with the (NS-)Prohibition Act of 1947, the respective penal code paragraph 283 for 'sedition' (*Verhetzung*) is the most important legal instrument for combating (certain) far-right activities in Austria.

THE IDENTITARIAN MOVEMENT: FASCISM'S FRESH FACE?

Finally, the *Identitarian Movement*[15], an offshoot of the French *Identitarian Bloc*[16], deserve attention, both for their media exposure and for their (potential) appeal to Austrian youths. While presenting themselves as New Right, or 'neither right nor left'[17], they are actually quite classically far-right both in their theoretical references (Ernst Jünger, Julius Evola and other masterminds of fascism) and their demands (sealed-off borders, large-scale deportations, ethnic homogeneity). What sets them apart from the traditional Austrian far right is their relatively unambiguous rejection of classical Nazism (individual biographical episodes with neo-Nazism notwithstanding), their willingness to cooperate with, among others, Slovenian and Italian neo-fascists, in spite of historical border issues, a modernized rhetoric ('pro-identity' instead of anti-foreigner), a fresh style, and competence in using online tools.[18]

The asylum crisis has fueled the already rampant popular discontent over the 'Grand Coalition' administration even further and has provided a boost for

Identitarians as well as for the far right as a whole. Not least an effect of mobilizations by the former, Austria has experienced a surge in far-right demonstrations since 2015, including a number of events in the countryside that reflect intentions to establish the *Identitarian Movement* beyond Austria's university cities. As the low turnout for these demonstrations suggests, the *Identitarians'* social media coverage of their own activities and the excessively alarmist coverage by mainstream media inflate the group's actual strength.

The FPÖ is sympathetic to them, presenting their activities as evidence of popular dissatisfaction with the federal government as well as honoring their efforts to politicize and activate young people who will, in all likelihood, vote *Freedomite*. At the same time, it is the FPÖ and its strength that places a low ceiling on the *Identitarian* aspirations. "In Austria, the FPÖ is [...] the real PEGIDA", Strache claimed in a 2015 interview[19]. Moreover, they are arguably also the 'real *Identitarians*'[20].

ANNOTATIONS

1 | In line with the editors' practice, *far right* is understood here as an umbrella term for the political spectrum ranging from 'populist radical right parties' (see Stijn van Kessel in this volume) that operate within the realms of democratic institutions and procedures to openly fascist fringe groups. Ideologically, this spectrum, in my understanding, centers around three key features: anti-egalitarianism (most commonly as racism, including the latter's 'ethno-pluralist' modernization, antisemitism and sexism), authoritarianism and nativism.

2 | Original name in German: *Freiheitliche Partei Österreichs* (FPÖ). More precisely translated as *Freedomite Party of Austria*. Apart from mirroring the German name more accurately, the term *Freedomite* ("freiheitlich") accentuates the blend of liberal and nationalist traditions of thought that is characteristic of the FPÖ and that, among other things, distinguishes it from liberal parties in other European countries. In contrast to liberalism, *Freedomite* ideology emphasizes the collective dimension of freedom (the freedom of a people in an ethnic sense) at the expense of individual rights and freedoms.

3 | Original name in German: *Alternative für Deutschland*.

4 | Albert Steinhauser/Harald Walser (2016): Rechtsextremismusbericht 2016 [Report on Right-Wing Extremism]. Vienna: The Greens – Parliamentary Group, pp. 22-25, (https://www.gruene.at/themen/demokratie-verfassung/rechtsextremismus-bericht-2016-straftaten-verdoppelt/rechtsextremismusbericht-2016-1.pdf), accessed June 17, 2016.

5 | Federal Ministry of the Interior (2016): Verfassungsschutzbericht 2015 [Report of the Federal Office for the Protection of the Constitution 2015], (http://www.bmi.gv.at/cms/BMI_Verfassungsschutz/Verfassungsschutzbericht_2015.pdf), accessed June 17, 2016, p. 75.

6 | Original name in German: *Sozialdemokratische Partei Österreichs*.
7 | Original name in German: *Österreichische Volkspartei*.
8 | Original name in German: *Bündnis Zukunft Österreich*.
9 | For more detail on the FPÖ's rise and fall between 1986 and 2006, see Kurt Richard Luther (2008): Electoral Strategies and Performance of Austrian Right-Wing Populism, 1986–2006. In: Gunter Bischof/Fritz Plasser (eds.): The Changing Austrian Voter. New Brunswick: Transaction, pp. 104–122.
10 | The German term is *Burschenschaften*. Bernhard Weidinger (2015): Im Nationalen Abwehrkampf der Grenzlanddeutschen: Akademische Burschenschaften und Politik in Österreich nach 1945 [In the National Defense Struggle of the Borderland Germans: Academic Student Fraterniteis and Politics in Austria after 1945]. Vienna: Böhlau.
11 | Michał Krzyżanowski (2013): From Anti-Immigration and Nationalist Revisionism to Islamophobia: Continuities and Shifts in Recent Discourses and Patterns of Political Communication of the Freedom Party of Austria (FPÖ). In: Ruth Wodak/Majid Khosravinik/Brigitte Mral (eds.): Right-Wing Populism in Europe: Politics and Discourse. London: Bloomsbury, pp. 135–148.
12 | Andreas Peham (2010): Die zwei Seiten des Gemeinschaftsdünkels: Zum Antisemitischen Gehalt Freiheitlicher Identitätspolitik im Wandel [The Two Sides of Collective Arrogance: the Antisemitic Dimension of Libertarian Identity Politics in a State of Flux]. In: Österreichische Zeitschrift für Politikwissenschaft, 39/4, pp. 467–481.
13 | Cf. Julia Edthofer (2016): Debates on Islamized Antisemitism in Austria in the Wake of the Israel-Gaza Conflict 2014, Kantor Center Position Papers, (http://kantorcenter.tau.ac.il/sites/default/files/PP%20Austria%20160120b_0.pdf), accessed June 17, 2016.
14 | Original name in German: *Patriotische Europäer gegen die Islamisierung Europas*.
15 | Original name in German: *Identitäre Bewegung Österreich*. The terms *Identitariam Movement* and *Identitarians* are used interchangeably in this text.
16 | Original name in French: *Bloc Identitaire*. See also Samuel Bouron in this volume.
17 | See Tamir Bar-On in this volume.
18 | For a more extensive characterization of the *Identitarian* franchise's Austrian branch, see DÖW (2016): Identitäre Bewegung Österreich (IBÖ) [Identitarian Movement in Austria (IBÖ)], (http://www.doew.at/erkennen/rechtsextremismus/rechtsextreme-organisationen/identitaere-bewegung-oesterreich-iboe), accessed June 17, 2016.
19 | News.at (2015): FPÖ-Strache: In Österreich sind wir die wahre PEGIDA [In Austria We are the Real PEGIDA], January 15, (http://www.news.at/a/fpoe-strache-wahre-pegida), accessed June 17, 2016.
20 | The author would like to thank Karin Kuchler for her meticulous proof-reading and helpful suggestions.

The Turning Fortunes of Romania's Far Right
The Rise and Fall of Greater Romania Party

Mihnea-Simion Stoica

Since the fall of the communist regime, Romania's political system has undergone a series of dramatic changes from one electoral cycle to the next – along with its fellow countries in Eastern Europe. This began with what was considered to be the inflation of political parties[1] at the beginning of the 1990s, leading up to the approximation of a two-party system today – comprised of the *Social-Democratic Party* (PSD)[2] on the left and the *National Liberal Party* (PNL)[3] on the right. However, the fog surrounding the ideological identities of virtually all Romanian political parties has only thickened over time, leaving the party system in a state of flux and creating the idea that there are not any significant differences among the major political players.[4]

As was the case in many other countries, this situation has generated (at least partial) success for a radical anti-establishment discourse. However, unlike other European states, the far right in Romania did not benefit from the financial crisis. Throughout the entire post-communist period, the *Greater Romania Party* (PRM)[5] – founded and led with an iron fist by Corneliu Vadim Tudor, its late leader who famously declared that "the party is me"[6] – produced most of the ethno-nationalist rhetoric on the Romanian political scene. Radical stances on many issues, including those related to the Hungarian ethnic minority, shaped this highly controversial figure. He repeatedly declared that Transylvania is being "forcefully magyarized"[7] by the ethnic Hungarians who live there and reportedly said that Romania could only be led with a machine gun, praising the idea of public executions in stadiums.[8] He at times claimed his party to be ideologically rooted in the left, having declared his admiration for the former Romanian communist dictator Nicolae Ceaușescu. It therefore comes as no surprise that the media and his political opponents labeled him a populist, extremist, xenophobic, authoritarian and, above all, a threat to Romania's democracy.[9]

In explaining the evolution of the Romania's post-communist far right – invariably related to the development of PRM – there are four important moments in the country's recent history that deserve closer examination: the presidential elections of 2000, the electoral results of the 2008 general elections, the European Parliament elections of 2009, and, finally, post-2014 political realities. They represent more than just electoral victories or failures for Romania's far right: they are instances of a tumultuous evolution of the electorate that began with the romanticism of the years immediately after the fall of communism and continue until today in the form of rough electoral pragmatism.

A CLOSE CALL: THE PRESIDENTIAL ELECTIONS OF 2000

The creation of PRM is surrounded by many conspiracy myths, some of which revolve around the idea that the party was artificially created by establishment politicians who were unable to make use of strong nationalist rhetoric within their own parties. However, few had realized that PRM would develop into more than simply an insignificant political force at the fringes of the Romanian political spectrum. The rising popularity of PRM's young and charismatic leader as a major anti-establishment figure radically differentiated the party from all others, which were mostly led by older politicians. His rhetoric mainly blasted corruption, which was (and still is) perceived by the Romanian electorate as one of the major hindrances to the country's development.[10] The radical style of this new politician became a source of pride for his supporters. Asked why he voted for Vadim Tudor, one of his young supporters put it bluntly: "I appreciate his extremism"[11]. Acting as a whistleblower proved to be quite an effective strategy for the leader of PRM, who was voted in because he apparently "got the nerve" to pick on the establishment and since he was the promoter of "an aggressive political style"[12]. The unprecedented, and quite unexpected, support for Vadim Tudor managed to give him a boost in the second round of the 2000 presidential elections – which he eventually lost due to the *cordon sanitaire*[13] created by all other parties that declared their support for his counter-candidate, social-democrat Ion Iliescu. Even so, PRM gathered enough votes to become the second-largest party in the Romanian Parliament, with just over 20 percent of the seats.

THE FADING FORTUNES OF THE GREATER ROMANIA PARTY

The outbreak of the global financial crisis around 2008 served as a breath of fresh air for most far-right parties in Europe. The PRM was expected to experience a fate similar to that of the *Front National*[14] in France, the *Party for Freedom*[15] in the Netherlands, the *Austrian Freedom Party*[16], and the like, all of which regained the popular support they had consistently been losing in the previous years. However, this was not the case in Romania. The 2008 parliamentary elections brought about a political reality that would have been unconceivable not long ago: PRM did not manage to win even one constituency nation-wide. Vadim Tudor accused the elections of being a fraud[17], as the complete defeat of his party was a bitter reality he would have never expected and – as would become apparent later on – did not know how to manage. The former champion of anti-establishment discourse seemed to have been abandoned by his former staunch supporters, who now turned to politicians who they considered to represent more credible voices on the Romanian political scene, with similarly strong anti-corruption messages, less xenophobia and, most importantly, with higher chances of winning an election. Having lost so many elections since its creation, PRM seemed to have fallen victim to the inexorable laws of political Darwinism. Other explanations for the fading fortunes of PRM were related to the softening rhetoric of Vadim Tudor, who, after the 2000 elections, publicly declared that he would end his opposition to Romania joining NATO and the European Union (EU), and also admitting he was wrong in denying the Holocaust. This, together with his (eventually failed) attempt to affiliate PRM to the *European People's Party*[18] took his image too close to the 'establishment', thus making his messages appear unauthentic.[19]

BACK IN THE GAME: THE GREATER ROMANIA PARTY GOES BRUSSELS

The 2009 elections for the European Parliament (EP) represented a moment of unexpected comeback for PRM, which had steadily been losing members – and, as a consequence, financial support ever since its (what seemed to be) total defeat in 2008. Shortly prior to the EU elections, Vadim Tudor had even declared that he would sell his car and a number of valuable books from his private library to gather enough money to campaign, showing that it had become quite difficult for PRM to make ends meet. The major event that helped revitalize the party was not determined by PRM's communication strategies but by what happened to its political competitor. George Becali, leader of the *New Generation Party – Christian-Democrat* (PNG-CD)[20], a smaller populist party, had been placed under arrest just a few days before the electoral campaign.[21] Despite the fact that Becali's popularity was surging on account of his arrest (labeled an 'abusive measure' against him by the state), polls showed that his party was not strong enough to reach the five percent needed to enter the EP, similar to the situation faced by PRM, which was also just below the threshold. Understanding the political opportunity of adding numbers and the chance to gain extensive media coverage due to Becali's arrest, Vadim Tudor included his competitor's name on PRM's list for the EU elections, thus forging an indirect alliance with PNG-CD and redirecting the sympathy for Becali towards his own party. This is how PRM turned from a non-player on the Romanian political arena to regaining public attention, gathering ten percent of the popular vote and sending three Members of Parliament to Brussels, among them Vadim Tudor and George Becali.[22]

WHAT'S LEFT OF ROMANIA'S FAR RIGHT?

Since 2014, PRM has developed the characteristics of a politically deceased organization. Today, in 2016, nothing any longer resembles the (quite) successful party that it used to be in the 1990s and the 2000s. The party's extremely weak – or, rather, lacking – local/grassroots organizations have dramatically decreased its visibility. Even in urban constituencies such as Cluj-Napoca, where the party's leading figure, Gheorghe Funar, won three mayor elections in a row until 2004, PRM is now completely absent from political debates. After failing to win any seats in the 2012 national elections or in the 2014 elections for the EP, and especially after its leader passed away of in September 2015, PRM seems to have vanished from the political arena. This can, however, have various consequences.

On the one hand, this relates to developments on the far right. Several smaller parties are now trying to fill the void left by PRM's demise. Their rhetoric is more violent than that of PRM, though they have been incapable of gathering a minimum amount of political support so far. Implications related to the populist discourse are also present. Based on the principle of 'communicating vessels', this strategy did not disappear with PRM, but has diffused to the larger mainstream parties, which sometimes are glad to make use of it. Perhaps one last important aspect relates to how much the Hungarian party *Democratic Union of Hungarians in Romania* (UDMR)[23] will be affected by the disappearance of PRM. Having lost its main political enemy, is this small ethnic party going to be faced with 'aimless activity'? Despite various opinions, there are no serious reasons to believe that the faithful ethnic Hungarian electorate will severely defect. Moreover, and among many other factors, a law reversing the national electoral system from a 'first-past-the-post' system to proportional representation may also help UDMR remain in the national political arena, although with marginal influence. At a local level, however, its political influence will remain untouched by the disappearance of PRM.

The beginning of the 2010s saw the dismantling of what one might call the 'party-organized' Romanian far right. While the social phenomena in which its evolution was embedded have disappeared, the primary infrastructure which serves various forms of manifestation – this time perhaps outside of the logic of party politics – has remained in place; given the 'refugee crisis', it may have even, unfortunately, evolved. It remains to be seen how long it will take for a new political movement to emerge in Romania that successfully picks up the issues of the far right.

Annotations

1 | Ion Bucur (2014): Anul 1990: Partide, ideologii și mobilizare politică, [Year 1990: Parties, Ideologies and Political Mobilisation]. Bucharest: Editura Institutului Revoluției Române din Decembrie 1989, p. 44.
2 | Original name in Romanian: *Partidul Social-Democrat*.
3 | Original name in Romanian: *Partidul Național Liberal*.
4 | Mihnea Stoica (2015): Romania's Party System Remains in Flux ahead of Next Year's Local and Parliamentary Elections, August 6, (http://blogs.lse.ac.uk/europpblog/2015/08/06/romanias-party-system-remains-in-flux-ahead-of-next-years-local-and-parliamentary-elections/), accessed June 10, 2016.
5 | Original name in Romanian: *Partidul România Mare*.
6 | Marian Sultănoiu (2013): CV Tudor exclus din PRM: Funar, noul președinte al partidului. Vadim: "PRM sunt eu" [CV Tudor Ousted From PRM. Funar, the New President of the Party. Vadim: "PRM Is Me!"], July 27, (http://www.gandul.info/politica/cv-tudor-exclus-din-prm-funar-noul-presedinte-al-partidului-vadim-prm-sunt-eu-11165162), accessed June 10, 2016.
7 | Realitatea TV (2010): Lupta pentru Autonomie [Fight for Autonomy], (https://www.youtube.com/watch?v=7UUHRyHDY6g), accessed June 10, 2016.
8 | Romania Insider (2015): Corneliu Vadim Tudor: Romania's Most Influential Extremist Politician Dies at Age 65. In: Romania Insider, September 14, (http://www.romania-insider.com/corneliu-vadim-tudor-romanias-most-influential-extremist-politician-dies-at-age-65/155494/), accessed June 11, 2016.
9 | Radio Free Europe (2010): Corneliu Vadim Tudor sau despre dimensiunea unui eșec al democrației românești [Corneliu Vadim Tudor or about the Dimension of a failure of Romanian democracy], (http://www.europalibera.org/a/2232501.html), accessed June 11, 2016.
10 | IRES (2015): Barometrul încrederii în instituții. Partea Întâi: Justiția [The Barometer of Trust in Institutions: First Part: Justice], (http://www.ires.com.ro/articol/295/barometrul-increderii--n-institutii---partea-întai-:-justiția), accessed June 11, 2016.
11 | PRO TV (2009): România Decide 2000 [Romania Decides 2000], (https://www.youtube.com/watch?v=63YOWVjDzRU&t=4m35s), accessed June 11, 2016.
12 | Ibid.
13 | For an explanation of the term see Maik Fielitz/Lotte Laloire in this volume; Radu Cinpoes (2015): Righting it up: An Interplay-Based Model for Analyzing Extreme Right Dynamics in Romania. In: Michael Minkenberg (ed.): Transforming the Transformation?

The East European Radical Right in the Political Process. London: Routledge (Routledge Studies in Extremism and Democracy), p. 288.

14 | To avoid confusion with groups from other countries that carry the name *National Front*, the original is used throughout the text.

15 | Original name in Dutch: *Partij voor de Vrijheid*.

16 | Original name in German: *Freiheitliche Partei Österreichs*.

17 | Antena 3 (2008): Vadim Tudor: Exit poll-urile mint: PRM va intra in Parlament [Exit-Polls Are Lying: PRM Will Make It into the Parliament], (http://www.antena3.ro/politica/vadim-tudor-exit-poll-urile-mint-prm-va-intra-in-parlament-59117.html), accessed June 12, 2016.

18 | Original name in Romanian: *Partidul Popularilor Europeni*.

19 | Andrei Tiut (2006): Strategiile PRM de maximizare a capitalului electoral (1996–2005). [The Strategies of PRM to Maximise Its Electoral Capital (1996–2005)]. In: Sfera Politicii, 14/120-121-122, pp. 95–98.

20 | Original name in Romanian: *Partidul Noua Generație – Creștin-Democrat*.

21 | Mediafax (2009): Gigi Becali Arestat pentru 29 de Zile. Video [Gigi Becali Arrested for 29 Days. Video], (http://www.mediafax.ro/social/gigi-becali-arestat-pentru-29-de-zile-video-4137166), accessed June 13, 2016.

22 | The important score of PRM was also determined by low electoral turnout for the European Parliament elections in Romania (less than 30 percent in 2009) – as has been the case all over Europe.

23 | Original name in Romanian: *Uniunea Democrată Maghiară din România*.

Svoboda and the Restructuring of Ukrainian Nationalism

Mathias Schmidt

Just to point it out from the beginning: writing about far-right tendencies in Ukraine is nowadays akin to walking a high wire. That is to say, the debate is embedded in a much broader context: ever since the events at *Maidan* (the main square of Ukraine's capital Kiev), in 2014, along with the subsequent regime-change, pro-Russian media have repeatedly accused the West of misconceiving the character of the 'fascist junta in Kiev', while some publications tend to downplay the actual threat of right-wing activities in Ukraine. As such, one is quickly accused of either protecting 'the fascist Ukrainians' or 'the imperialist Russians'. The task remaining at this point is to sort the opinions from the facts.

The most significant force in the parliamentarian far right is *Svoboda*[1]. Some observers believe that its involvement in the transitional government following the protests at *Maidan* was evidence of Ukraine's shift to the right. Meanwhile, however, this party does not even possess a faction in parliament. What are the dynamics that have brought this about? Could the threat from the right be at an end?

UKRAINIAN INDEPENDENCE: NOT TO BE TAKEN FOR GRANTED

When the Soviet Union collapsed and Ukraine once again set sail towards its own statehood, new opportunities emerged for radical nationalists. In contrast to the 'free' eastern bloc states, such as Ceausescu's Romania – where nationalism already ended in anti-Hungarian aggression – Ukraine, as a former 'autonomous' Soviet republic, found itself at the very beginning of sovereign nation-building. Moscow's policies towards these nations was generally expressed in the only mandated form of folklore that sought to evoke brotherhood and unity among the socialist sister nations.[2] Radical Ukrainian nationalists were prosecuted as counter-revolutionary elements and did not possess any political influence in official politics.

The matter of Ukraine's national autonomy stands out among the crowd of other nations within the former Union. Whereas it is generally accepted that the Baltic States have made use of sovereign historiography and have derived demands for political independence from it, Ukraine is faced with the argument that its autonomy is an operational accident of history. The Russian perspective considers Ukrainians to be 'Little Russians' who share a common eastern-Slavic, Christian-orthodox destiny along with their Belorussian and 'Great Russian' neighbors. Ukraine's nationalists contradict this representation and face a double-task: on the one hand, they fight to establish the primacy of the nation above the primacy of the individual in domestic politics. On the other hand, they struggle for outright recognition of their national autonomy in international politics.

STRUGGLING FOR THE NATION

During the 1990s, several radical nationalist parties addressed that specific task. Operating through shifting coalitions, they acted mostly below the radar of public perception. Besides the *Ukrainian National Assembly* (UNA)[3] and the *Congress of Ukrainian Nationalist* (KUN)[4], the *Social-National Party of Ukraine* (SNPU)[5] has to be considered in this context. The SNPU was founded in Lviv in 1991 by a group including today's party leader Oleh Tyahnybok; it advanced from the margins to being the most influential radical nationalist organization in Ukraine. Especially at the beginning, the party did not shy away from publicly flirting with National Socialist symbols and language – which distinguished it from its ideological competitors, the UNA and KUN.

Semantically, the party's 'social'-nationalism insinuates National Socialism, though there are differences in the emphasis of the political ideas. The SNPU can be classified as neo-fascist in the broader sense, as right-wing radical in either case, but not explicitly as National Socialist. Even though antisemitism and biological racism make their way into statements by party officials, other topics such as national identity, anti-liberalism and Russophobia are far more important. The categorization of the party varies correspondingly: Andreas Umland and Anton Shekhovtsov label SNPU's party platform as "open revolutionary ultra-nationalism"[6], whereas the World Jewish Congress classifies it as "neo-Nazi"[7].

SUCCESS IN THE NAME OF FREEDOM

After the SNPU only managed to win 0.16 percent of votes in 1998 and abstained from competing in the elections of 2002, the organization restructured itself and adopted the name *All-Ukrainian Union Svoboda*. As a result, significant successes have been achieved at the regional level. For instance,

Svoboda won nearly 35 percent of votes in regional elections in the province Ternopil. It is, however, doubtful whether this breakthrough can be considered a direct consequence of the restructuring. Low turnout and limited commitment by other opposing parties during the election may be relevant factors as well. Moreover, some observers suspected that the state-run media showed preferential treatment towards *Svoboda*, which split the opposition further.[8]

Since these elections, *Svoboda* managed to gain more influence in regional parliaments, claiming its demand to be a heavyweight among organized Ukrainian nationalists. When the revolt of *Maidan* erupted in 2014, Oleh Tyahnybok confidently presented himself as a member of the 'troika', as the heads of the three oppositional parties – *All-Ukrainian Union Fatherland*[9], *Ukrainian Democratic Alliance for Reform*[10] and *Svoboda* – were called. Even though the presence of far-right groups was not welcomed by all participants, this could not be avoided and the group was eventually approved. After president Yanukovych fled and the regime collapsed, a transitional government was created in which *Svoboda* held three ministries. At this point, the party was at the peak of its career and also stirred sensation abroad. For Russian observers, a 'fascist junta' had successfully instigated a coup d'état, actively threatening the lives of Russians in Ukraine.

AN ABRUPT END? APPROACHES TO AN EXPLANATION

The triumph of *Svoboda* only lasted briefly: during the elections in October 2014, the party failed to overcome the 5 percent threshold, and was thus unable to form a parliamentary group or hold on to any of its ministries. In May of the same year, Tyahnybok already had to accept the party's weak results of 1.1 percent in the early elections for presidential office. In spite of grave fears in foreign countries, no explicit radical right-wing party was able to establish itself in the national parliament. How did this happen?

Regarding the ideological component, *Svoboda*'s party program operates with elements of different right-wing, anti-liberal schools of political thought. The main source of ideological inspiration is the *Organization of Ukrainian Nationalists* (OUN)[11] – the inter-war union of Ukrainian nationalist military personnel and intellectuals[12] –, with which *Svoboda* situates itself and its ideas as part of the history of European political thought. This does not automatically include sympathy for the political West, but strict dissociation from everything considered to be Soviet. And this delineation is accompanied by a different historical truth.

Broadly speaking, in Ukraine two historic narratives compete: a soviet narrative prevails in the eastern parts, which considers the 'Great Patriotic War' to be the central historical event that unified the identity of a multi-ethnic

Soviet state. In this myth, Soviet society merged into an inseparable socialist bulwark in the constant struggle against fascism.

In western Ukraine, the OUN and its military arm, the *Ukrainian Insurgent Army* (UPA)[13], fought for Ukrainian independence in the Second World War. Here, history faces more complex interpretations: opinions especially differ on the subject of Stepan Bandera. As leader of the radical faction of the OUN, under Bandera's command, pogroms were committed against Jews and communists. During the Second World War, he cooperated in constantly changing alliances, even with the National Socialists. Though they were not in favor of Ukrainian independence, they exploited the Ukrainian nationalists to their own ends. Bandera was ultimately deported as 'prisoner of honor' to the concentration camp at Sachsenhausen; he eventually died in German exile in 1959. Bandera is classified as war criminal in Germany, Russia, Poland and Israel, whereas, in parts of Ukraine, he is considered to be a national hero.

In this 'western-Ukrainian' narrative, both *Svoboda* and Russia claim numerous historical arguments to either prove the legitimacy of territorial demands or their own moralistic superiority. Voting for *Svoboda* for ideological reasons is hardly conceivable for an 'East Ukrainian': otherwise, such a person would have to abrogate core assumptions of the construction of political reality. As such, it is also unlikely that *Svoboda* will ever surpass a certain amount of votes in national elections.

Andreas Umland establishes a series of 'non-ideological motivations' among the electorate that voted for *Svoboda* during and directly after *Maidan*. Consequently, *Svoboda's* outstanding results were made possible by strategic voters who wished for "possible hard opposition against the government"[14]. Another non-ideological reason for voting *Svoboda* was to enable the entry of a third opposition party into parliament – though *Svoboda* would lose this type of voter afterward. Moreover, one can assume that some of these voters feared the negative repercussion on Ukraine's reputation abroad. Last, but not least, *Svoboda's* participation in the transitional government became the main target of Russia's strong rhetoric against Ukraine.

Another reason for the decline in influence lies in the newly formed competition within the right-wing scene. Votes from the radical nationalists are split among different parliamentarian organizations, which reproach *Svoboda* as being too merciful with regard to fighting in the east of the country. Connected to this issue is the general matter as to the value of parliamentarian representation within the Ukrainian right. Through the use of militias, platoons of 'volunteers' and privately financed combat groups, the nationalists discovered a new, more successful form of mobilization. 'Successes' by paramilitary groups on the streets serve as a boost to the traditionally low level of confidence in political parties. A hybrid concept can be found in the structure of the infamous *Right Sector*[15]: as a party, it has a Member of Parliament at its disposal and, as a combat group, it is involved in fights with separatists and Ukrainian security forces. These double structures may be a model for success for the sphere of right-wingers, which predominantly address young, action-orientated men.

Prospects

What remains of *Svoboda*? The party is still active and one cannot rule out a comeback in the notoriously changing composition of the Supreme Council of Ukraine (*Verkhovna Rada*)[16]. It is difficult to accurately estimate *Svoboda's* influence on parties within the political mainstream – the policies adopted by these parties are very generic. Their parliamentarian faction comprises political deputies of competing entrepreneurs rather than policy-orientated parties with staunch supporters. As an ideological party, *Svoboda* has not had any difficulties exhibiting a clear profile for the next elections. The partial appropriation of anti-Russian and nationalistic speech among the functionaries of other parties can be considered the result of *Svoboda's* presence. All in all, one can observe a rather pragmatic approach to civil society and the Ukrainian state through *Svoboda* and its ideology. As long as certain political actors expect to gain personal advantage, the party will receive support and collaboration, before being exploited and eventually abandoned. This approach to radical nationalists is not, of course, what one sees in the hostile relations between Ukrainian authorities and the *Right Sector*.

The course that the central government adopts towards the armed conflict in eastern Ukraine will determine the influence of Ukrainian nationalists considerably. As long as this question remains, other more conventional issues taken on by European right-wingers, such as the migrant crisis, will receive little attention. It is possible that other right-wing parties will adopt this matter more skillfully at some point in the future. This also illustrates that the threat from the political right cannot solely be linked to the success of any specific organization. Despite the presence of a strong, radical, right-wing faction within parliament, a preference for authoritarian ideas persists in the minds of many people – and this is what constitutes the real threat.

Annotations

1 | Full name: *All-Ukrainian Union Svoboda*; Svoboda translates as Freedom. Original name in Ukrainian: Всеукраїнське об'єднання Свобода.
2 | See Uwe Halbach (1992): Das sowjetische Vielvölkerimperium: Nationalitätenpolitik und nationale Frage [The Soviet Multi-Ethnic Empire: Politics of Nationality and the National Question]. Mannheim: B. I.-Taschenbuch, p. 32.

3 | Original name in Ukrainian: *Українська національна асамблея* (УНА).
4 | Original name in Ukrainian: *Конгрес українських націоналістів* (КУН).
5 | Original name in Ukrainian: *Соціал-національна партія України* (СНПУ).
6 | Anton Shekhovtsov/Andreas Umland (2012a): Die Entstehung des ukrainophonen parteiförmigen Rechtsextremismus in der Ukraine der 1990er [The Creation of Ukrainophone Party-based Right-wing Extremism in Ukraine in 1990s]. In: Ukraine-Analysen, No. 105, p. 15.
7 | Sam Sokol (2013): Ukrainian Jews Split on Dangers of Protest Movement. In: The Jerusalem Post, April 12, (http://www.jpost.com/Jewish-World/Jewish-Features/Ukrainian-Jews-split-on-dangers-of-protest-movement-333907), accessed April 14, 2016.
8 | See Anton Shekhovtsov/Andreas Umland (2012b): Der verspätete Aufstieg des ukrainophonen Rechtsradikalismus in der postsowjetischen Ukraine – Teil II [The Delayed Rise of Ukrainophone Right-Wing Radicalism in Post-Soviet Ukraine – Part II]. In: Ost-West: Europäische Perspektiven, No. 3, p. 209; Tadeusz A. Olszanski (2011): Svoboda Party: The New Phenomenon on the Ukrainian Right-Wing Scene. In: OSW Commentary, No. 56, p. 5.
9 | Original name in Ukrainian: *Всеукраїнське об'єднання "Батьківщина"*, also called *Batkivschina*.
10 | Original name in Ukrainian: *Український демократичний альянс за реформи* (УДАР).
11 | Original name in Ukrainian: *Організація українських націоналістів* (ОУН).
12 | Anton Shekhovtsov (2011): The Creeping Resurgence of the Ukrainian Radical Right? The Case of the Freedom Party. In: Europe-Asia Studies, 63/2, pp. 207-210.
13 | Original name in Ukrainian: *Українська Повстанська Армія* (УПА).
14 | Umland Andreas (2012): Nichtideologische Motivationen der Swoboda-Wähler: Hypothesen zum Elektorat der ukrainischen radikalen Nationalisten bei den Parlamentswahlen vom Oktober 2012 [Non-Ideological Motivations of Svoboda-Voters: Hypotheses to the Electorat of Ukrainian Radical Nationalists at the Parliamentary Election in October 2012]. In: Ukraine-Analysen, No. 109, p. 8.
15 | Original name in Ukrainian: *Правий сектор*.
16 | Verkhovna Rada is the unicameral national parliament of Ukraine. Original name in Ukrainian: *Верховна Рада України*.

Troubled Memory: Polish neo-fascists taking over the memorial day events for the Warsaw Uprising. August 1, 1944 was the first day of Polish resistance against the German National Socialist aggressors. (Original photograph taken by Karol Grygoruk on August 1, 2015, edited by Deniz Beşer, 2016).

... On The Street

Don't Call Me Right!
The Strategy of Normalization in German Right-Wing Extremism

Holger Marcks

When it comes to change in social environments, a parable by the philosopher Charles Handy readily comes to mind: If you drop a frog in boiling water, it jumps out immediately; but placed in cold water slowly heating up, it acclimates itself and falls to sleep, unaware of being boiled alive.[1] The parable reminds us of the perceptional relativity of change: within communities, creeping developments cause habituation, while abrupt breaks arouse shock. In terms of social movements, this truism becomes apparent in two ways. On the one hand, an erupting crisis can destabilize a social order and create the space necessary for dissident actors to gain momentum – who would otherwise fail to mobilize outside the scenario of an anxious community gasping for a new guarantor of order. On the other hand, the rise of a dissident actor with unconventional methods may operate as a shock that triggers withdrawal reflexes within the broader society, while dissidents with relatively habitual sentiments may find resonance among communities disappointed with the prevailing order.

Does this perspective have the potential to explain the rise of far-right movements in Europe? Let us examine it through the example of Germany, where far-right actors have experienced a remarkable gain in political acceptance since 2014 – on the streets, in the voting booths and on talk shows. In this case, one could argue that their success in terms of protest and electoral mobilization, along with their disproportionately high presence in the media, rests on communication policies that effect the normalization of far-right positions previously in disrepute within public discourse. Through this creeping habituation in society, these movements gain momentum in crisis situations, successfully portraying themselves as a legitimate agent of the 'anxious citizens' disappointed with the government. To test this argument, a finger exercise in frame analysis seems appropriate, a tool common in studies on social movements to explain why certain ideas in particular contexts are capable of mobilizing audiences – while not in others.

How Normalization Works:
Strategic Framing and the Diffusion of Far-Right Ideas

"The far-right position of yesterday is the political centre of today"[2]. This process – here referred to the swing to the right (*Rechtsruck*) that struck Germany in the 1990s – has been subject to various studies on extremism. It can be grasped, for instance, as an interrelationship between the "contagion" of a political center by the far right and a "failing mainstream" that does not perceive of far-right positions as a threat.[3] This accords with sociological perspectives highlighting how ethnicizing discourses – a major feature of far-right politics – gain 'symbolic power' and enable the diffusion of specific publics into the general public.[4] Again, the interrelationship is clear: by activating and amplifying ethnic boundaries between an 'imagined community' and an alienated 'other', socio-political boundaries are becoming blurred in public perception. Undoubtedly, this dialectic of exclusion and inclusion is the path to normalization that far-right politics generally follow. 'Ethnic mobilization' – the symbolic empowerment of a collective identity to be protected against a dehumanized alterity threatening its homogeneity – has always been the engine of success for the far right.

Of course, ethnic mobilization does not materialize overnight: if far-right actors want to be successful, their specific discourses require a certain degree of resonance with ideas circulating within the public discourse; and often it is a crisis which opens the door for a (electoral) breakthrough. For instance, far-right ideas may have penetrated the political center but are overlaid by conventional electoral behavior. In a crisis, in which trust in established parties is exhausted, this 'extremism of the center' can become manifest through election successes for far right actors. While the crisis itself is mostly beyond their influence, they can, at least, bring themselves into a better position by increasingly diffusing their ideas into the public discourse. This indicates another interrelationship: moments of crisis can impact even minor actors of the far right, granted that they resonate with a set of rightist ideas already normalized within the public discourse – and, at once, they can enable this resonance through strategic actions that lead their ideas to become normalized in society.

It therefore stands to reason that the strategic rationality of far-right actors is also guided by considerations as to how to effect normalization. One possible way to grasp this is to analyze their 'frames': the schemata of how they construct social reality and shape the perception of their environment. Framing activities can be *strategic*, insofar as actors intend "to telegraph meaning and to focus audience attention on [...] aspects of a topic in order to gain favorable response".[5] However, strategic framing is not arbitrarily malleable for actors; after all, they hold a set of core beliefs – as diagnoses and prognoses of what is wrong in the world and how it has to be changed – and try to act in accordance with them.[6]

Moreover, this framing is also bound to normative constraints, as frames must resonate with prevailing beliefs in order to be attractive.[7] With that, a challenge is issued to far-right actors, namely, in order to create legitimacy and reliability, they must align with habitual sentiments without contradicting their core beliefs. We will see now how far-right actors in Germany have managed to build this congruence, which is the 'key to acceptance'.[8]

'PETRY'-FYING SOCIETY: THE 'ANXIOUS CITIZEN' AS A BITTER ARSONIST

After different far-right parties – such as the *National Democratic Party of Germany* (NPD)[9], the *Pro Germany Citizens' Movement*[10] or *The Right*[11] – failed to attract the broader masses, the *Alternative for Germany* (AfD)[12] has recently been able to achieve remarkable success in communal and regional elections,[13] accompanied by a notable uptick in the general polls.[14] These successes were preceded by much-noticed and persisting xenophobic mass mobilizations, mostly associated with the *Patriotic Europeans Against the Islamization of the Occident* (PEGIDA)[15], accompanied by an endemic wave of attacks on refugee shelters.[16] Both strands can be seen as the political and social arms of a new far-right movement. Not only do PEGIDA protesters identify with AfD's policies,[17] party leaders also declare their sympathy with the protesters. Indications of the movement's extremist character are numerous: the protests and attacks perpetuate the *No to Asylum Shelter*[18] campaign, for which the neo-fascist NPD was a leading force; many protest organizers, such as leading figure of PEGIDA Lutz Bachmann, are well-known for their neo-fascist background; moderate positions have been squeezed out of the AfD, while firmly extremist individuals are greatly attracted by the party;[19] and in areas where the AfD did not run in communal elections, its potential voters turned to NPD.[20]

Nevertheless, politicians and the media are zealous not to force the movement too far into the extremist corner, often speaking of 'anxious citizens' whose grievances should be taken seriously. It would be plausible to state that this already reflects an outcome of the far-right actors' normalization strategy. Indeed, the movement likes to present itself as being carried by the 'normal' people disappointed with the government. Its adherents often refuse to be called a neo-Nazi, xenophobe or even rightist. And when they recognize their right-wing proclivities, these are framed as being 'normal' as well: they simply fill the conservative gap which has been created through the alleged shift to the left by the *Christian Democratic Union* (CDU)[21]. AfD and PEGIDA, according to the narrative, merely represent the will of the people ("We are the people!"[22]) which has been ignored by the state. However, even if the movement is successful in mobilizing, it is far from attaining a majority and representing 'the people'.

In general polls, AfD consistently garners less than 15 percent, and even the notorious protests by PEGIDA have only been able to gain a real foothold in a few regions, being outdone by much bigger counter-protests in most parts of Germany.

In this sense, the claim by far-right actors that they represent the popular masses is obviously presumptuous. Nevertheless, the narrative of being 'normal' citizens gets reproduced in public discourse, which suggests that congruence building may successfully overcome this contradiction. Here, efforts at 'frame amplification' seem to be critical: by emphasizing and petrifying an ethnicized issue that touches popular sentiments – such as the so-called 'refugee crisis' – other political positions, which are by no means popular,[23] take a backseat. In addition, certain constructs help to mend the contradiction. Here, the narrative of a 'liars' press' *('Lügenpresse')* comes to mind: by diagnosing the media as manipulating the populace, a kind of context of delusion *(Verblendungszusammenhang)* is imagined which prevents people from realizing their objective interests. Beneficially, this framing allows far-right actors, such as AfD leader Frauke Petry,[24] to present themselves as being both victimized and ordinary at the same time. As a result, they are often perceived of as 'anxious citizens', not as bitter arsonists that have difficulty accepting democratic decisions.

MISSING THE FOREST:
REMARKS ON THE COMPLEXITY OF NORMALIZATION

This text has thus far highlighted just one small aspect of far right normalization, namely how actors strategically frame themselves as 'normal' in order to gain acceptance from broader audiences. Of course, the full complexity of this matter is even greater. For instance, it remains unclear how this relates to the fact that many adherents of the movement exhibit a firmly anti-mainstream attitude and bitterly lament the alleged dominance of leftist 'taboos' in society.[25] Moreover, it is unclear in which cases framing is actually strategic or just an authentic expression of a subject's cognition – a distinction which is, in general, hard to make. After all, far-right actors attempt to influence their environment systematically; in so doing, they purposefully spread misleading information (as AfD cadre Björn Höcke even admits[26]) and exaggerate interpretations (as Petry's instruction for the party's public relations demonstrate[27]).[28] While the strategic intention is not clear to the receiver of the information, he/she may nevertheless start to repeat such persuasive falsehoods,[29] thus becoming part of the strategic project.

Additionally, far-right normalization is not just about a formerly minor actor gaining acceptance, but also, and even more so, about far-right ideas being adapted by mainstream actors. The mechanism behind this process has much to do with party competition; which is to say, party actors concerned about a possible loss of voters switching to a rising far-right party may borrow from some of the content propagated by the latter. This was exemplified in the early 1990s, when the government integrated considerable parts of party program of *The Republicans* (REP)[30] into the *Asylum Compromise* (*Asylkompromiss*), a law limiting the right to asylum.[31] This can be witnessed in other countries today: the conservative *Fidesz*[32] in Hungary, for instance, took over many programmatic aspects of the neo-fascist *Jobbik*[33] for its governmental policies this past year.[34] Recently in Germany, various party actors have tried to internalize positions of the rising far-right movement. This is not just reserved for center-right parties such as the *Christian Social Union* (CSU)[35], it is also observable in the ranks of *The Left*[36]. Such moves are often justified with the intention of taking the wind out of the extremists' sails. However, the benefit of this is questionable when the political center itself is becoming more extremist.

Finally, the role of the media must be addressed. Even if far-right actors lament being victimized by it, there is no doubt that they profit enormously from its coverage. After all, one could argue that the broad reporting about early PEGIDA manifestations (initially not well-attended) gave the group a boost. Likewise, AfD has a disproportionately high presence in the media. And since its representatives are solely invited to talk shows to speak about ethnicized issues, this may perfectly suit the party's book of frame amplification. Further, the question arises as to whether the media itself is a field of far-right resonance. This is indicated by the case of the sexual assaults in Cologne on New Year's Eve 2015, which not only enjoyed intensive coverage of the incidents but also granted 'criticisms' of asylum and criminal foreigners a great deal of space in the media. In contrast, organized mobs of rioting neo-Nazis or the endemic encroachments against refugees tend to fall into oblivion.[37] One could read this as effort to take the 'anxious citizens' seriously and prevent further radicalization. It could also be a hint that far-right ideas are more normalized in public discourse than they appear. It is indeed hard to perceive when the water is slowly heating up.

Annotations

1 | See Maxim Jean-Louis (1991): Charles Handy: The Future of Work in a Changing World (Interview). In: Aurora, Fall, (http://aurora.icaap.org/index.php/aurora/article/view/52/65), accessed July 4, 2016.
2 | Dieter Rudolf Knoell (1992): Lehrmeister Hondrich als Volks-Schüler: Die (Bürger-) Kriegssoziologie als Fortsetzung der Politik des gesunden Volksempfindens mit nur zum Teil anderen Mitteln [Master Hondrich as Elementary School Child: The Sociology of (Civil) War as a Continuation of the Politics of a Healthy Public Feeling with Only Partly

Different Means]. In: Hans-Martin Lohmann (ed.): Extremismus der Mitte: Vom rechten Verständnis deutscher Nation. Frankfurt am Main: Fischer, p. 152.
3 | See Aristotle Kallis (2013): Far Right 'Contagion' or a Failing 'Mainstream'? How Dangerous Ideas Cross Borders and Blur Boundaries. In: Democracy and Security 9/3, pp. 221-46.
4 | See Klaus Eder/Valentin Rauer/Oliver Schmidtke (2004): Die Einhegung des Anderen: Türkische, Polnische und Russlanddeutsche Einwanderer in Deutschland [The Containment of the Other: Turkish, Polish and Russian German Immigrants in Germany]. Wiesbaden: VS-Verlag für Sozialwissenschaften, esp. pp. 32-40.
5 | Kirk Hallahan (2008): Strategic Framing. In: Wolfgang Donsbach (ed.), International Encyclopedia of Communication, Vol. 10. Malden: Blackwell, p. 4855.
6 | See Mayer N. Zald (2000): Ideologically Structured Action: An Enlarged Agenda for Social Movement Research. In: Mobilization, 5/1, pp. 1-16; Jochen Mayerl (2009): Kognitive Grundlagen sozialen Verhaltens: Framing, Einstellungen und Rationalität [Cognitive Bases of Social Behaviour: Framing, Attitudes, and Rationality]. Wiesbaden: VS-Verlag für Sozialwissenschaften, p. 154.
7 | See Thomas Kern (2008): Soziale Bewegungen: Ursachen, Wirkungen, Mechanismen [Social Movements: Causes, Effects, Mechanisms]. Wiesbaden: VS-Verlag für Sozialwissenschaften, p. 151.
8 | Amitav Acharya (2004): How Ideas Spread: Whose Norms Matter? Norm Localization and Institutional Change in Asian Regionalism. In: International Organization, 58/2, p. 239.
9 | Original name in German: *Nationaldemokratische Partei Deutschlands*.
10 | Original name in German: *Bürgerbewegung Pro Deutschland*, also known by the short form *Pro Deutschland*.
11 | Original name in German: *Die Rechte*.
12 | Original name in German: *Alternative für Deutschland*.
13 | See results of the communal elections in Hessen on 6 March 2016 (http://www.statistik-hessen.de/k2016/html/EK1.htm), accessed July 4, 2016; or regional elections in Baden-Wuerttemberg, Rhineland-Palatinate and Saxony-Anhalt: (http://wahl.tagesschau.de/wahlen/2016-03-13-LT-DE-BW/), accessed July 4, 2016.
14 | Development traceable on: (http://www.wahlrecht.de/umfragen/dimap.htm#fn-afd), accessed July 4, 2016.
15 | Original name in German: *Patriotische Europäer gegen die Islamisierung des Abendlandes*.
16 | Cf. Jörg Diehl (2016): Gewaltwelle: BKA zählt mehr als tausend Attacken auf Flüchtlingsheime [Wave of Violence: BKA Counts More than Thousand Attacks on Refugee Hostels]. In: Spiegel Online, January 28, (http://www.spiegel.de/politik/deutschland/fluechtlingsheime-bundeskriminalamt-zaehlt-mehr-als-1000-attacken-a-1074448.html), accessed July 4, 2016.
17 | See Stefan Locke (2016): Studie aus Dresden: "AfD und Pegida sind dasselbe" [Study from Dresden: "AfD and Pegida Are the Same"]. In: Frankfurter Allgemeine

Zeitung, February 25, (http://www.faz.net/aktuell/politik/fluechtlingskrise/studie-aus-dresden-pegida-und-afd-sind-dasselbe-14090416.html), accessed July 4, 2016.

18 | Original in German: *Nein zum Heim*.

19 | Cf. Tilman Steffen (2016): Landtagswahlen: NPD dient sich der AfD an [Federal State Elections: NPD Offers Its Services to AfD]. In: Die Zeit Online, March 7, (http://www.zeit.de/politik/deutschland/2016-03/landtagswahlen-npd-afd-allianz-koalition-erststimme), accessed July 4, 2016.

20 | Cf. Alexander Jürgs (2016): Im Windschatten der AFD erzielt auch die NPD hohe Gewinne [In the Wake of AfD also NPD Is Gaining]. In: Die Welt, March 7, (http://www.welt.de/politik/deutschland/article153015408/Im-Windschatten-der-AfD-erzielt-auch-die-NPD-hohe-Gewinne.html), accessed July 4, 2016.

21 | Original name in German: *Christlich Demokratische Union Deutschlands*.

22 | 'We are the People' ('Wir Sind das Volk') was the central parole of the uprising citizens in the German Democratic Republic when they took to the streets to demand freedom in the weekly Monday demonstrations in 1989. This slogan was captured by far-right actors to mobilize old grievances in their very own direction.

23 | See the compilation of blogger Katharina Nocun, January 26, (http://kattascha.de/?p=1923), accessed July 4, 2016.

24 | See interview with Petry by Tim Sebastian (2016): Frauke Petry on Clonflict Zone. In: Deutsche Welle, March 23, (http://www.dw.com/en/frauke-petrys-afd-worried-or-xenophobic-citizens/a-19136333), accessed July 4, 2016.

25 | Cf. Matthew Feldman/Paul Jackson (eds.) (2014): Doublespeak: The Rhetoric of the Far Right since 1945. Stuttgart: Ibidem.

26 | See his interview with Panorama (from min. 05:59 on), Ben Bolz/Johannes Jolmes (2015): Deutsche Frauen: Bedroht von "lüsternen Flüchtlingen"? [German Women: Threatened by "Lustful Refugees"], October 8, (http://daserste.ndr.de/panorama/archiv/2015/Deutsche-Frauen-Bedroht-von-Fluechtlingen,rassismus126.html), accessed July 4, 2016.

27 | Documented in: Bülend Ürük (2016): Interne Anweisung von AfD-Chefin Frauke Petry legt Medienstrategie offen: "Provokante Aussagen unerlässlich, sie sorgen für notwendige Aufmerksamkeit" [Internal Instructions of AfD-Chairperson Frauke Petry Reveal Media Strategy: "Provocative Statements Indispensable, They Create the Necessary Attention"]. In: Kress News, March 7, (http://kress.de/news/detail/beitrag/134284-interne-anweisung-von-afd-chefin-frauke-petry-an-ihre-mitglieder-provokante-aussagen-unerlaesslich-sie-sorgen-fuer-notwendige-aufmerksamkeit.html), accessed July 4, 2016.

28 | Cf. Ruth Wodak (2014): The Strategy of Discursive Provocation: A Discourse-Historical Analysis of the FPÖ's Discriminatory Rhetoric. In: Feldman/Jackson (2014): Doublespeak, pp. 101-22.

29 | Cf. Tom Jacobs (2015): The Persuasive Power of Repeated Falsehoods. In: Pacific Standard, September 17, (https://psmag.com/the-persuasive-power-of-repeated-falsehoods-870853bb9ac#.qk3vzdltu), accessed July 4, 2016.

30 | Original name in German: *Die Republikaner.*
31 | See Knoell (1992): Hondrich, p. 152.
32 | Original name in Hungarian: *Fiatal Demokraták Szövetsége*, in English: *Alliance of Young Democrats.*
33 | This is the short version of the Hungarian original: *Jobbik Magyarországért Mozgalom* which translates as *Jobbik, the Movement for a Better Hungary.*
34 | See Andreas Koob/Holger Marcks/Magdalena Marsovszky (2013): Mit Pfeil, Kreuz und Krone: Nationalismus und autoritäre Krisenbewältigung in Ungarn [Equipped With Arrow, Cross and Crown: Nationalism and Authoritarian Crisis Management in Hungary]. Münster: Unrast.
35 | Cf. Süddeutsche Zeitung (2016): Ministerpräsident Weil: Seehofer ist Kronzeuge für Pegida [Prime Minister Weil: Seehofer is Accomplice Witness for Pegida]. In: Süddeutsche Zeitung, February 13, (http://www.sueddeutsche.de/politik/fluechtlingspolitik-ministerpraesident-weil-seehofer-ist-kronzeuge-fuer-pegida-1.2862356), accessed July 4, 2016.
36 | Original name of this political party in German: *Die Linke.* Cf. Ivo Bozic (2016): Zu Gast bei Linken [Guests of the Left]. In: Jungle World, January 21, (http://jungle-world.com/artikel/2016/03/53344.html), accessed July 4, 2016.
37 | Cf. Martin Kaul (2016): Der Kampf um Connewitz: Großangriff auf einen Stadtteil [Struggling for Connewitz: Major Offensive on a Neighborhood]. In: Taz, January 12, (http://www.taz.de/%215265306/), accessed July 4, 2016.

On Patrol with the New German Vigilantes

Oliver Saal

Germany's political culture is currently facing a shift to the right as anti-immigrant violence and attacks on refugee camps are soon to become daily routine.[1] The right-wing party *Alternative for Germany* (AfD)[2] achieved successes in every recent federal state election.[3] Through their success, right-wing populist and anti-immigration politics acquired a new quality. Anti-immigrant groups such as *Patriotic Europeans Against the Islamization of the Occident* (PEGIDA)[4] in Dresden regularly mobilize hundreds and sometimes thousands of people. The increased number of refugees that came to Germany in 2015 has been instrumentalized to fuel racism and spread nationalist sentiments.

For such groups, it is self-evident that immigrants pose a threat to the security of their homes and children, especially to women, and to the integrity of the state as a whole. Certainly, the events of New Year's Eve 2015 in Cologne and other German cities can be seen as a culmination point for these discussions. During the New Year's celebrations, more than a hundred cases of sexual assault, numerous thefts and at least five rapes were reported.[5] All of these incidents involved women being surrounded and assaulted by groups of men, reportedly of 'Arab or North African appearance'.[6]

While only few vigilante groups[7] were active before the events in Cologne, a comprehensive formation of vigilantes could be observed in the aftermath.[8] The groups organize themselves by way of private Facebook groups and Whatsapp. On Facebook alone, more than 100 groups could be counted in January 2016, with names such as *Fulda takes care, All for one and one for all, Düsseldorf keeping watch, Citizens Initiative for Security Braunschweig* or plainly *Vigilantes Memmingen*.[9] As we will see, most of them never went beyond merely gathering in Facebook groups or ranting about the government. Yet, it is still instructive to observe the fears and sentiments expressed in these groups. Others have indeed become active, carrying out arson attacks and bombings against homes and cars of political opponents as well as refugee camps.

THE VIGILANTES FTL/360 IN FREITAL: FROM VIGILANTISM TO FAR-RIGHT TERRORISM

The small town of Freital in Saxony made it onto national news on account of its vigilante group. From March 2015 on, continuous rallies were held by up to 1,500 local and external racists. They picketed in front of the former hotel *Leonardo* that sheltered no more than 100 immigrants. Not only were stones thrown and arson attacks committed, but immigrants, their supporters, politicians and journalists were attacked on the streets of Freital. This hostile and aggressive atmosphere was supplemented by massive amounts of hate speech and rightist agitation online[10] – foremost by the group *Vigilantes FTL/360*[11]. This group was founded after one alleged case of sexual assault aboard public bus line 360. From that moment on, members of the Facebook group followed and documented almost every footstep made by immigrants in Freital. They patrolled bus line 360 and they carried out attacks.

The group's actions prove that the road from vigilantism to terrorism can be a rather short one.[12] Seven men and one woman face charges of founding a terrorist association.[13] The case covers them carrying out bombings and arson attacks against an alternative community project in Dresden and an immigrant accommodation in Freital. Bus driver Timo S., the alleged leader of the group, is also charged for chasing a local politician, beating him up with a baseball bat and threatening witnesses of the incident. During raids, police found several explosives, fireworks and swastika banners. The Facebook site of the group is still online, amassing 2,500 likes and still harassing its political enemies of *Freital Against Nazis*[14] – case in point for a group of neo-Nazis in the disguise of vigilantism.

For protagonists of the far right, the self-portrayal as vigilantes is very attractive: it helps them appear as 'men of action' and they know well that alleged mass crimes perpetrated by immigrants are a reliable factor for mobilization. In 2014, vigilante members of the Dortmund-based *Right-Wing Town-Guard*[15] patrolled in uniforms,[16] handing out pepper-spray to pedestrians – along with leaflets touting "we won't leave you by yourselves" and "where state's power fails, we citizens are in demand!"

Vigilante groups are not a new phenomenon in Germany: in Bavaria and Saxony, police cooperate with so-called 'security watch groups'. They rely on the right to perform 'citizen's arrests', which are permitted on the basis of paragraph 127 of the German code of criminal procedure – if the arrestee is caught *in flagrante delicto*, anyone observing a crime is granted the right to apprehend the offender. Since the fall of the iron curtain, members of such groups have patrolled voluntarily – advised and accepted by the police – primarily in rural areas close to the Czech and Polish borders.[17]

MIXED SCENES

The boundaries between groups such as the Freital *FTL 360* and a regular neighborhood watch are not always clear-cut. First, even members of the latter groups probably have a rather disputable understanding of law and order and are likely to have an affinity for the use of guns. Second, it is at times unclear who is responsible for organizing a group and what his/her true motivations are. Third, vigilante groups often emanate from rather mixed scenes – as was the case for *Vigilantes Munich*. Members of *a.i.d.a.*[18] – the Munich-based center for the documentation of and information about modern Nazism – monitored the foundational meeting of the group.[19] As *a.i.d.a.* stated, members of security corporations, doormen, soldiers, bikers and neo-Nazis such as Peter Meidl from the German neo-Nazi-party *The Right*[20] were among the men who met in a Munich restaurant. Previously, they had mingled in a private Facebook group named *Vigilantes Munich*, sharing racist and anti-Islamic posts. This is also where they arranged their meeting.

The role that Facebook is playing in allowing like-minded people to find each other and spread rumors[21] about factual or alleged crimes committed by immigrants can hardly be overstated. Inside their private groups, users feel free to express even their most drastic violent phantasies. On January 23, 2016, when one user of the group *Vigilantes Berlin ST* posted a newspaper report about forty Dresden hooligans chasing immigrants in the streets and looting shops, he added the comment: "It begins! Best regards from intervention group Dresden!" Another user commented: "That's the right thing to do here. Beat the bastards to death."

Through such speech-acts, users try to break a feeling of powerlessness and regain the capability to act. In each of those vigilante Facebook groups, immigrants are regarded as a looming threat. What is striking is the frequency with which fear is expressed of being outnumbered by immigrants, who are held accountable for rising crime rates, thefts and sexual assaults. They are not called immigrants, but insulted with terms such as 'rapefugees' or with ironical denominations such as 'skilled laborers' (always in quotation marks) or simply seen as 'invaders'. In every group, the neo-Nazi symbols or content being posted are never met with objections.

The activism of most of these users is limited to the Internet and Facebook, which proves the assumption that their kind of vigilantism supports a political project rather than being an actual attempt to re-establish law and order. The appearance of the new German vigilantes has a temporal, spatial and discursive connection to the so-called refugee crisis. Vigilantes see themselves as saviors of Germany, as those who fight to re-establish order where the state has retreated – the events in Cologne were widely seen as an example of such a withdrawal.

However, the withdrawal of the state from its responsibilities is not a rumor, it is a fact – not only in matters of domestic security, but also in other political fields such as welfare, health care and education. By highlighting this neoliberal development, vigilantes attempt to legitimize themselves; they want to prove that the state is either in the hands of criminals or that it fails to fulfil its obligations of maintaining stability and order, guaranteeing the rule of law and protecting property.[22] Based on this assumption, the necessity for self-defense is being constructed, a situation in which vigilante violence serves as a legitimate political instrument.

ANNOTATIONS

1 | Recent data from the German Federal Criminal Police Office *(Bundeskriminalamt)* count 563 criminal acts against refugee camps and 824 attacks on refugees outside of their camps just within the first half of 2016. This number is higher than in 2015 – when Germany experienced an all-time high of anti-immigrant violence. See Frank Jansen (2016): Zahl der rassistischen Gewaltdelikte "erschreckend" hoch [Number of Racist Violent Crimes "Alarmingly" High]. In: Tagesspiegel, June 20, (http://www.tagesspiegel.de/politik/bka-zu-uebergriffen-auf-fluechtlinge-zahl-der-rassistischen-gewaltdelikte-erschreckend-hoch/13759764.html), accessed June 26, 2016; cf. Paul Blickle/Kai Biermann/Philip Faigle/Astrid Geisler/Götz Hamann/Lenz Jacobsen/Anna Kemper/Martin Klingst/Karsten Polke-Majewski/Stefan Schirmer/Hannes Soltau/ Julian Stahnke/Toralf Staud/Tilman Steffen/Sascha Venohr (2015): Gewalt gegen Flüchtlinge: Es brennt in Deutschland [Violence Against Refugees: It Is Burning in Germany]. In: Die Zeit, December 3, (http://www.zeit.de/politik/deutschland/2015-11/rechtsextremismus-fluechtlingsunterkuenfte-gewalt-gegen-fluechtlinge-justiz-taeter-urteile), accessed June 26, 2016.
2 | Original name in German: *Alternative für Deutschland.*
3 | Cf. Philip Oltermann (2016): German Elections: Setbacks for Merkel's CDU as Anti-Refugee AfD Makes Big Gains. In: The Guardian, March 14, (https://www.theguardian.com/world/2016/mar/13/anti-refugee-party-makes-big-gains-in-german-state-elections), accessed June 26, 2016.
4 | Original name in German: *Patriotische Europäer gegen die Islamisierung des Abendlandes.*
5 | Cf. Damien McGuiness (2016): Germany shocked by Cologne: New Year Gang Assaults on Women. In: BBC News, January 5, (http://www.bbc.com/news/world-europe-35231046), accessed June 26, 2016.
6 | The 'abusive foreigner' is a racist and colonial trope, cf. Heike Radvan/Simone Rafael/Enrico Glaser (2016): Das Bild des "übergriffigen Fremden": Warum ist es ein Mythos? Wenn mit Lügen über sexuelle Gewalt Hass geschürt wird [The Image of the

"Abusive Foreigner": Why Is It a Myth? When Lies about Sexual Violence Are Used to Stir Up Hatred]. Berlin: Amadeu Antonio Stiftung.

7 | For the history, significance and typology of vigilante groups in Germany, see Matthias Quent (2016): Bürgerwehren [Vigilantes]. Berlin: Amadeu Antonio Stiftung.

8 | For an analytical and comparative exploration of the conditions in which vigilantism generally emerges, see Ray Abrahams (1998): Vigilant Citizens: Vigilantism and the State. Cambridge: Polity Press.

9 | Cf. Christoph Hasselbach (2016): Civilian Defense Groups on the Rise in Germany. In: Deutsch Welle, January 14, (http://www.dw.com/en/civilian-defense-groups-on-the-rise-in-germany/a-18980998), accessed June 26, 2016.

10 | See Netz gegen Nazis (2015): In Freital eskaliert der Hass gegen Flüchtlinge: geschürt wird er im Internet [In Freital Hate against Refugees Is Escalating: It Is Stirred Up on the Internet], June 24, (http://www.netz-gegen-nazis.de/artikel/freital-eskaliert-der-hass-gegen-flüchtlinge-geschürt-wird-er-auch-im-netz-10446), accessed June 26, 2016.

11 | Original name in German: *Bürgerwehr FTL 360*.

12 | Matthias Quent brings forward the argument that all those phenomena – anti-immigrant violence, the organised actions of the 'Freital group' and even the German right-wing terrorist organization *National Socialist Underground* (NSU) – should be summarized under the designation "vigilante terrorism", see Matthias Quent (2016): Selbstjustiz im Namen des Volkes: Vigilantistischer Terrorismus [Street Justice in the Name of the People: Vigilante Terrorism]. In: Aus Politik und Zeitgeschichte, 24–25/66, pp. 20–26, here: p. 20.

13 | Cf. Timothy Jones (2016): German Counterterrorism Unit Arrests Far-Right Terror Suspects. In: Deutsche Welle, April 19, (http://www.dw.com/en/german-counterterrorism-unit-arrests-far-right-terror-suspects/a-19197547), accessed June 26, 2016.

14 | Original name in German: *Freital gegen Nazis*.

15 | Original name in German: *Rechter Stadtschutz*.

16 | See Oliver Saal (2016): "Die Rechte": Maschendrahtzäune und Pfefferspray gegen Geflüchtete ["The Right": Wire-Netting Fence and Pepper Spray Against Refugees]. In: Netz gegen Nazis, March 10, (http://www.netz-gegen-nazis.de/artikel/die-rechte-die-maschendrahtzaunpartei-hetzt-im-wahlkampf-gegen-fluechtlinge-10942), accessed June 26, 2016.

17 | See Kurt H. G. Groll/Herbert Reinke/Sascha Schierz (2008): Der Bürger als kriminalpolitischer Akteur: Politische Anstrengungen zur Vergemeinschaftung von Sicherheit und Ordnung [The Citizen as Criminal-Political Actor: Political Effort to Communitize Security and Order]. In: Hans Jürgen Lange (ed.): Kriminalpolitik [Criminal Politics]. Wiesbaden: VS Verlag für Sozialwissenschaften, pp. 343–360, here: p. 349. See also Christian Bangel (2014): Bürgerwehren in Brandenburg: Die Angst geht auf Streife [Vigilantes in Brandenburg: Fear Is Patrolling]. In: Die Zeit, May 12, (http://www.zeit.de/politik/deutschland/2014-05/buergerwehr-in-deutschland), accessed June 26, 2016.

18 | The full name in German is: *Antifaschistische Informations-, Dokumentations- und Archivstelle München e. V.* In English: *Antifascist Information, Documentation and Archive Center Munich.*
19 | a.i.d.a (2016): Chronik [Timeline]. In: a.i.d.a., January 15, (https://www.aida-archiv.de/index.php/chronik/5323-15-januar-2017), accessed June 26, 2016.
20 | Original name in German: *Die Rechte.*
21 | Cf. Jan Heidtmann (2016): Bürgerwehren: die innere Unsicherheit [Vigilant Groups: The Inner Anxiety]. In: Süddeutsche Zeitung, January 23, (http://www.sueddeutsche.de/politik/buergerwehren-in-deutschland-buergerwehren-die-innere-unsicherheit-1.2830313), accessed June 26, 2016.
22 | See Mike Davis/Justin Akers Chacon (2006): No One Is Illegal: Fighting Racism and State Violence on the U. S.-Mexico Border. Chicago: Haymarket, p. 18.

Casapound Italia
The Fascist Hybrid

Heiko Koch

Changing political and economic situations generate new types of political protagonists – and the far right is no exception to this. Whether their structures and organizational forms endure, whether they diffuse (trans)nationally and whether their models prove successful, depend on various factors. A particular model that is soon to serve as a flagship for the far right in Europe is the neo-fascist movement party *CasaPound Italia* (CPI)[1].

Why has this organizational model within the far right in Italy and Europe been so successful? This chapter intends to shed light on the hybridity of CPI and the resulting force for the renewal of fascism. To carry out my argument, I first describe the evolution of CPI from a movement to a party. I then discuss strategies and practices in terms of organizational and ideological hybridization, and finally outline the European dimension of the self-proclaimed 'fascists of the third millennium'.

'FASCISM FOR THE THIRD MILLENNIUM'?
THE EVOLUTION OF CASAPOUND ITALIA

In December 2003, the neo-fascist movement titled *CasaPound* was founded in Rome. Under the pretext of allegedly anti-capitalist critique, members of various national-revolutionary groups, the Roman *White Power Music* scene and the neo-fascist *Italian Social Movement – Tricolour Flame* (MSI-FT)[2], occupied a six-story apartment building in the Esquilino district of Rome, in the immediate vicinity of the main station, Termini. The occupation was named 'Casa Pound' – a reference to the antisemitic, US-American writer Ezra Pound. Until 2008, *CasaPound* was closely linked to the traditional fascist party MSI-FT, but, following an internal dispute in 2008, it split and became a social association. In 2012, *CasaPound* registered as an official political party and has thereafter officially been known as *CasaPound Italia*. Since then, CPI has not only operated as a movement on social, political and cultural levels, but also as a party within the institutional framework. In 2013, it participated in Rome's local elections for the first time – and nationwide in 2015. The party attained some seats on local councils under the umbrella of the Sovereignty *(Sovranita)* electoral alliance with the *Northern League*[3]. In 2010, CPI announced that it had 2,200 members and today it boasts a membership of nearly 5,000.

Carried forward by a general swing to the right in Italy, flanked by the revaluation of the fascism under Berlusconi,[4] and supported through right-wing party structures – which saw CPI as a welcomed and useful youth movement – this new actor succeeded in establishing itself in far-right contexts and beyond. Partially successful occupations in Rome and other cities followed, and a scene for right-wing social centers was born in Italy – the *Centri Sociali di Destra*. Their illegal and oftentimes violent actions were barely punished by the authorities. In early 2016, a report by the Prevention Police of the Ministry of Interior was drafted, certifying the neo-fascists of CPI with fundamental legal compliance and a high ethical disposition. The report ignored their pronounced racism and reduced the violence they committed to a singular problem of individual members.[5] As such, CPI has remained largely undisturbed by authorities and state bodies, despite the fact that its aggressive appearance and numerous acts of violence have openly shaped its structures and promoted its growth.

'PENETRAZIONE FASCISTA': THE PENETRATION OF EVERYDAY SPACES

Parallel to the occupations, CPI founded a variety of social and cultural organizations. This socio-cultural sphere includes theater, art and cultural circles, social and health centers, civil defense organizations and right-wing NGOs – which are even active abroad –, an animal and nature protection organization, a scouting organization, a mothers association, and, last, but not least, a trade union. Approximately 20 bars, restaurants, various tattoo shops and 15 bookstores serve as socio-political meeting points. All of this is tied to the approximately 100 party offices across Italy. *CasaPound Italia's* socially oriented activation strategy is in line with traditions of the 'social right' *(destra sociale)*[6]; it serves a large network, and uses these organizations to penetrate social and cultural areas – the so called 'fascist penetration' *(penetrazione fascista)*.

With over a dozen music bands in line with the party, various football supporter-groups *(ultras)*, and many leisure and sports associations, it also influences the subcultural milieu to ensure a close link between sporting and music events and political activism. Furthermore, CPI has operated in the education sector by establishing its own organizations: the *Student Bloc*[7], its student organization, is active in over 40 cities. According to their speaker[8], the *Student Bloc* received more than 27,000 votes for the school and student councils nationwide in December 2015, including 11,000 in Rome and the surrounding provinces. In terms of (social) media, CPI possesses a large number of publications and propaganda organs. In addition to several small print media outlets, they operate a large number of websites, Facebook pages, video channels, an Internet radio station with various editors and an online newspaper. The party's degree of professionalization in the media sector is considerable.[9]

In addition to this diverse infrastructure, CPI organizes a large number of both small and large events, festivals, concerts, protest activities, rallies, demonstrations, conferences, conventions and campaigns, all of which take place throughout the year across Italy and are attended by up to several thousand members and sympathizers.

THE NEO-FASCIST POLITICS OF POLARIZATION

The campaigns of CPI reflect upon traditional fascist positions as well as current debates within the European far right. Its main point of contention has been migration to Italy and Europe. Here, CPI speaks of an invasion and promotes a stop to all forms of immigration.[10] It opposes the *ius soli* and propagates its own Italian identity in opposition to all non-Italians. *CasaPound Italia's* rhetoric is extremely aggressive and actions taken against refugee housing, such as in the Roman district of La Storta in 2015, have been carried out very violently in part.[11]

A recurring theme within CPI is the alleged social and cultural decay of Italy and the consequent decline of praised values such as nation and state, people and family – seen a process of weakness and decadence for which CPI mainly blames leftist, liberal and democratic policies and immigration. Further campaigns testify to strong ultra-nationalism and promote Italian irredentism and territorial claims on neighboring nations. *CasaPound Italia* provocatively pushes this position, such as through the demonstrations in 2011 in the South Tyrolean city of Bolzano with the motto 'Bolzano is Italy', or in 2015 with a national demonstration in the border town of Gorizia with the slogan 'Stand up, fight, victory', to mark Italy's entry into the First World War in 1915.

Through concerted national-revolutionary acts, CPI portrays itself as the savior of 'national employment' and the 'national industry', in response to the economic crisis and the impact of austerity policies in the EU. As for many far-right groups, the banks and the government are responsible for the crisis: they either obey the dictates of the EU, the USA or international finance capital, or exploit and suppress the people and the nation. In response, CPI promotes a classic fascist-style autarkic economy, all-encompassing national sovereignty and a cooperative community within an organic nation. The forms of action taken up at protests are often inspired by repertoires of emancipatory and left-wing groups; however, in the context of CPI, they appear nationalized and aggressive.

BLURRING REALITIES – THE HYBRIDIZATION OF CASAPOUND ITALIA

CasaPound Italia can be described as a political hybrid: as a movement that has succeeded in combining different, sometimes antagonistic, theories and logic from differing cultural and social spheres of society to establish new patterns of action and thought. The use of right-wing social centers and the general socio-cultural infrastructure to create new spaces has been especially attractive for young people; here, a fusion of different social strata, right-wing scenes and subcultures emerged within the everyday fascist routine. Members and sympathizers become radicalized in this parallel universe, and CPI creates new generations of neo-fascist activists through the constant penetration of their projects. Hence, CPI has partially managed to transform the heterogeneous nature of its members and sympathizers to own their symbiotic identity. The diversity of socio-cultural influences in CPI acts synergistically and creates innovative cultural initiatives and new forms of political cooperation – be it music projects, fashion brands, sporting events, transnational organizations, campaigns or conventions.

CasaPound Italia brings together various, and sometimes conflicting, currents in their approach. As a movement, it uses the flexible level of lobbying for direct action in far right-parties combined with an array of resources, access and effective forces possessed by grassroots organizations and subcultures. As a party, CPI is protected by its status as an official party and tries to take advantage of the mechanisms of the rigid, regulated level of parliaments and administrative power. The existing party status (as of late 2012) also allows other social structures access to CPI and widens its possibilities for influence and access to power.

Additionally, a contemporization of traditional fascist images, aesthetics and public forms of action – a new staging of the Italian fascism – takes place within CPI by way of New Right cultural approaches and the adoption of a so-called 'right-wing Gramscianism' – i.e., the focus on achieving hegemony in civil societies rather than just politics[12]. The strategies and methods applied by CPI are thus modernizing antiquated patterns of argumentation and rhetoric held by Italian fascism. Familiar political forms of discourse and dichotomous political localizations are undermined by CPI's aesthetic camouflage, communication strategies and ethnopluralism within the broader public.[13] A new fascist image is being created, lowering democratic resilience. The professional use of new media and social networks complete the implementation of media strategies and CPI's campaigns.

CasaPound Italia:
A Role Model for the Far Right in Europe?

Despite its ultra-nationalism, CPI considers its ideas to be explicitly European and has been seeking exchange and cooperation with other far-right movements and parties in Europe – especially neo-fascist, national-revolutionary and New Right groups and trends. In this sense, a lively exchange exists between CPI and other right-wing structures in Europe. The exchange of strategies, tactics and solutions to problems – i.e., the transfer of ideology, economic, ideological and political support, and export of its organization model – is of utmost concern to CPI. The group has appointed its own representative to take care of its foreign contacts. Since 2006, the network *Zentropa* has served as a transnational forum to convene CPI, French New Right figures, and other international far-right projects. Over the last ten years, they networked with likeminded people in just over a dozen European countries, thereby managing, among other things, to establish a basis for a national-revolutionary conference, held at the end of each year since 2014 in Paris. The conference was used by Ukrainian neo-Nazi, *Azov Regiment*[14], and their international branch *Reconquista*[15] to openly promote its violent acts in the Donbass region.

European participation in the Italian *White Power Music* scene – and martial arts tournaments called *Tana delle Tigri*, established by CPI around 2008 in Rome – can be ascribed to this cooperation. Another form of transnational cooperation is the *Nonprofit Organization Solidarity Identity* (Sol.id)[16], created in 2011. Sol.id is a right, ethno-pluralistic[17] NGO with projects operating in Burma, Palestine, Kosovo, the Crimea, Kenya, South Africa and Syria. Two of them that particularly stand out are the long-running project for the Karens population in Burma and charitable solidarity actions with the Syrian Baath regime, held since 2013.

In geopolitical terms, CPI participates in the transnational *European Front for Syria* that was founded to support the regime of Bashar al-Assad. Likewise, CPI organized the first *International Congress of Identity-Solidarity* in Rome in September 2015; representatives from Syrian government organizations, Islamic associations, *Hezbollah* and the *Social Nationalist Party of Syria*[18] participated in this congress. Thus, even on the international, geopolitical terrain, CPI's hybridity is recognizable.

The party's appeal and fascination for other right-wing movements in Europe has been inevitable considering the diverse synergistic processes and innovative projects. It should not be surprising that CPI is conceived as an engine of renewal by many of its sympathizers: in the small Saxon town of Pirna, the NPD office calls itself *House Monday*[19], referring to CPI's first occupation. Similarly, in Spain, admiration of a group of far-right militants, called *Hogar Social*[20], began to exactly emulate the practice of house occupations carried out by CPI. However, it remains unclear whether the model put forth by CPI will witness long-term success outside of Italy.

Annotations

1 | The original Italian name will be used throughout the text because the original goes back to a personal name that cannot be translated.
2 | Original name in Italian: *Movimento Sociale – Fiamma Tricolore*.
3 | Original name in Italian: *Lega Nord*. The electoral alliance *Sovranita* (Sovereignty) was built in January 2015 as a *CasaPound* group with the intention of culture-political collaboration with the *Lega Nord*, also in the question of elections.
4 | Cf. Aram Matteoli (2010): "Viva Mussolini!" – Die Aufwertung des Faschismus im Italien Berlusconis [The Revaluation of Fascism in Berlusconi's Italy]. Paderborn: Schöningh.
5 | The report originated from a lawsuit in which the daughter of Ezra Pound, Mary de Rachewiltz, sued the party for using her father's name. A copy is available at: https://insorgenze.net/2016/01/30/il-documento-shock-del-ministero-dellinterno-Casa Pound-solo-bravi-ragazzi/, accessed June 27, 2016.
6 | The *destra sociale* ('social right') is a self-imposed term by a part of the Italian neo-fascist milieu that supposedly follows social and syndicalist approaches of historical fascism.
7 | Original name in Italian: *Blocco Studentesco*.
8 | Blocco Studentesco (2015): Blocco Studentesco: Ottenuti oltre 27 mila voti nelle scuole d'Italia, decine di consiglieri eletti nelle consulte provinciali [The Student Bloc Obtained More than 27,000 votes in the Italian Schools, Dozens of Councilors Are Elected in the Provincial Councils], December 15, (http://www.bloccostudentesco.org/news/393-blocco-studentesco-ottenuti-oltre-27mila-voti-nelle-scuole-ditalia-decine-di-consiglieri-eletti-nelle-consulte-provinciali.html), accessed August 3, 2016.
9 | See Samuel Bouron in this volume.
10 | See Caterina Froio in this volume.
11 | Il Messaggero (2015): Roma, Manifestazione Anti-Immigrati di Residenti e Casa-Pound a Casale San Nicola: Scontri con la Polizia 14 Feriti [Rome: Anti-Immigrant Manifestation of Residence and CasaPound in Casale San Nicola: 14 Injured in Clashes with Police], July 17, http://www.ilmessaggero.it/roma/cronaca/roma_protesta_casale_san_nicola_CasaPound_immigrati-1148109.html, accessed June 27, 2016.
12 | Tamir Bar-On (2013): Rethinking the French New Right: Alternatives to Modernity. New York: Routledge, p. 22. See also Tamir Bar-On in this volume.
13 | See Natascha Strobl and Julian Bruns in this volume.
14 | Original name in Ukrainian: *Полк Азов*. It is also called *Azov Battalion*. See also Matthew Kott, Graham Macklin and Mathias Schmidt in this volume.

15 | The Reconquista network presents itself on its website as "an international movement of the Great European Reconquest and at the same time a network of international support for the founder and the avant-garde of this movement – the 'AZOV' Civil Corps." They consider themselves "a new generation of the fighters for a genuine Europe that arose under conditions of the undeclared war on Ukraine by the neo-Bolshevik Russia, and on Europe – by the multicultural EU, both united by their contempt for Ukrainian nationalism and the European identity."
16 | Original name: *Solidarité Identités*.
17 | For the concept of ethno-pluralism see Natascha Strobl and Julian Bruns in this volume.
18 | Original, transliterated name: *Al-Ḥizb Al-Sūrī Al-Qawmī Al-'Ijtimā'ī*.
19 | Since October 2013, the building *Haus Montag* has been used as the local office of the far-right *National Democratic Party of Germany* (original name in German: *Nationaldemokratische Partei Deutschlands*, NPD) in Pirna-Copitz. According to the media, the owner of the property is the Norwegian neo-Nazi Eirik Ragnar Solheim. The building was reshaped by Thomas Sattelberg, the former leader of the legally banned Kameradschaft *Skinheads Sächsische Schweiz* and current chair of the cadre of the NPD.
20 | This can roughly be translated with social housing or home.

Who are 'They'?
Continuities and Changes in the Discourse of CasaPound Italia on Migration and Otherness

Caterina Froio

Numerous observers have stated that the arrival of refugees from foreign countries increases the popularity of far-right organizations. According to these interpretations, electoral and political support can be promoted through the societal resonance of ethnocentric discourses in the European Union (EU). Recent data from the Eurobarometer illustrates that, in EU member states, migration from non-EU countries is now considered to be the primary concern. In November 2015, 58 percent of European citizens considered immigration to be the most important problem, coming before terrorism (25 percent) and the economic situation (21 percent). This represents a sudden shift with respect to the results from the 2013 Eurobarometer, when, in the middle of the euro crisis, EU citizens seemed to be more concerned about the economy (45 percent), unemployment (36 percent) and the public finances of member states (26 percent).[1]

This chapter explores the arguments developed by far-right organizations in politicizing migration. It focuses on a peculiar representative of the Italian far-right scene: *CasaPound Italia* (CPI)[2], an organization torn between extremism, radicalism and populism. Following Cas Mudde,[3] CPI can be considered as ideologically extreme – it opposes democracy and believes in creating a new authoritarian order (akin to Mussolini's fascism) – but it is procedurally radical populist in the sense that it runs for elections, opposes minority rights and criticizes the functioning of representative institutions. *CasaPound Italia's* rhetoric on immigration mirrors this tension between an extreme ideology and radical electoral ambitions. This is particularly hazardous as, through this process, CPI risks losing the anti-systemic appeal that constitutes its 'trademark', especially on an issue such as immigration, which touches upon a key ideological feature of the far right: nativism.[4] Within the far right, not only do groupuscular actors face these tensions, but (some) more established political parties do as well. To shed light on these questions, this chapter explores the factors that fuel CPI's anti-migrant discourse by highlighting continuities and changes with respect to classic nativist far-right rhetoric.

EXTREME AND RADICAL:
CASAPOUND ITALIA ON THE FAR-RIGHT STAGE

The difficulty in defining what constitutes the far right (and what does not) has to do with a threefold difference that exists among these organizations that pertains to ideological references and ambitions, organizational structure and preferred strategies of mobilization. Ideologically, the spectrum of far-right activism ranges from organizations that believe in creating a new authoritarian order (the extreme right), to ones that accept liberal democracy but oppose minority rights and the functioning of representative institutions (the populist radical right).[5] From the organizational point of view, the far right includes organizations that differ in terms of their size and internal structures; these range from conventional political parties to less-established and (often) loosely organized social movement organizations, subcultural groups, sport clubs and intellectual circles.[6] Finally, diversity likewise emerges in terms of their strategies of mobilization: while some organizations engage in conventional politics and mainly invest in the electoral arena and electoral campaigning, others privilege the subcultural arena of symbolic and violent politics, comprised of concerts and targeted aggressions towards buildings and/or people.[7] Still, hybrid actors often navigate between the two poles on this spectrum, engaging in both types of activities and arenas.[8]

CasaPound Italia is a hybrid in the far-right scene.[9] It behaves much as a social movement does but also runs for elections. Its references include the fascist dictator Benito Mussolini and the anarchist sailor-adventurer Corto Maltese. It is made of 'men of law and order' who occupy buildings. While one of its sympathizers killed two Senegalese street vendors in Florence, at the same time, the organization advertises activities for international cooperation. Since CPI was born (with the occupation of one building close to the main train station in Rome in 2003), this contradictory combination of references and repertoires of action has been the main source of the group's popularity in Italy and abroad.

Starting with the campaign for the 2014 European elections, the self-proclaimed 'fascists of the third millennium' approached the better-known *Northern League*[10]. This alliance enabled the group to address topics such as migration, which, until then, had been relatively marginal in the rhetoric of CPI. Before, CPI used to be focused around the economy and the right to housing for Italian citizens.[11] Even if political agendas of far-right organizations should not be reduced to immigration issues[12], migration politics do play a prominent role in the discourse of the far right.[13] *CasaPound Italia's* rhetoric on migration results from the combination of classic nativist and nationalistic arguments such as 'identity threats' along with more unusual forms of prejudice inspired by the reframing of anti-globalization arguments and 'Third Position' stances less common in the far-right milieu.

THE CLASSIC SHADES OF FAR-RIGHT ANTI-IMMIGRATION RHETORIC: ECONOMY, CULTURE AND SECURITY

CasaPound Italia shares elements of nativism with other far-right organizations, including the idea that states should only be inhabited by their native group and that non-native elements are a threat to the homogeneity (and development) of the nation-state.[14] The main 'foes' are ethnic minorities, even if this does not exclude ethnic minorities without a migrant background. In line with the classic Schmittian friend-foe distinction that characterizes the identity politics of far-right organizations, CPI delineates boundaries between natives and non-natives, between the in-group ('us') and the outgroups ('them'). Both categories are, quoting Mudde's reference to Benedict Anderson[15], "imagined", in the sense that they are socially constructed. This means that 'foes' refer to real existing groups (such as the Roma people in Italy), though the characteristics that CPI attributes to them are stereotypical constructs. As in classic arguments common to most extreme and radical right populist parties,[16] migration is predominantly framed as a threat to the native people in economic, cultural and security terms, according to the discourse of CPI.

Given the primary importance that socio-economic issues occupy in the ideology of CPI,[17] it comes as little surprise that migration is, first of all, framed as a threat to the economy of the nation, to native workers and to natives' housing rights. Three major arguments are used to illustrate these alleged pieces of evidence. First, migrants supposedly steal the jobs of natives even though in times of economic hardship, the national priority, employment (only) for Italians must prevail. Second, migrants are portrayed as being ready to accept working conditions and standards that would be unacceptable to native workers. Third, migrants are the primary beneficiary of public housing at the natives' expense – not considering that inhuman working (and living) conditions are also signs of discrimination by the majority population.[18] In its 2013 electoral program, CPI writes that:

"[immigrants] are a resource for the General Confederation of Italian Industry[19] and for the employers who are the primary beneficiary of this new slavery-based economy and of an 'industrial reserve army' made of growing unprivileged masses looking for jobs [...]"[20]

In the same document, CPI adds:

"We must stop exposing our [Italian] corporations to this competition [from immigrant workers]. This will make useless the contribution of immigrant workers, and it allows the protection of our workers, now bypassed by 'the competitive workers' par excellence: immigrants."[21]

Migration is also perceived as a threat to the homogeneity and distinctiveness of the natives' culture as well to the traditional values of the 'Italian nation'. The groups that are targeted, according to this argument, are mainly migrants from outside the EU, who, according to CPI, do not belong to the 'Europe of Nations' or to the 'People(s') Europe'. These expressions make reference to an alleged homogeneous pan-European identity based on shared history and traditions that are supposedly at the origins of Europe's cultural distinctiveness. A book written by one of the leaders of CPI contains a section that is dedicated to diversity and its challenges.[22] Here, CPI writes:

"We fight for a plural world where differences- under whatever form- are protected and incremented. We want a world with people that are different, with different languages, different cultures, different religions and different food. [...] We oppose the model of a multiracial society [...] and the ethno-masochism of the idiots."[23]

In this framework, CPI's 2013 platform for the general elections proposed "to stop the flows of migrants"[24].

Like most contemporary far-right organizations (including more mainstream political parties), CPI's discourse on the 'cultural threats' brought about by migration disavows biological racism and emphasizes cultural and historic differences among human beings. While traditional racist far-right organizations embrace biological conceptions of race, cultural racist organizations adopt an 'ethnopluralist' version of it. However, these two are not necessarily disconnected: CPI's ethnopluralist interpretations emphasize the need for preserving the uniqueness and 'purity' of the cultural identities of different ethnic groups. This conception presupposes the existence of incompatible cultural differences that disappear through the mixing of different ethnic groups within the same society.[25] On this ground, CPI portrays migrants as a threat to 'cultural differentialism' and 'ethnopluralism' in line with theories derived from the experience of the French New Right.[26]

Moreover, among the classics of far-right nativist rhetoric, CPI associates migrants with criminality, drug dealing, prostitution and street fights. Migrants are also portrayed as being primarily responsible of urban decay, since they are considered as being "foreign to our [Italian] land and history"[27]. The groups targeted may vary; these include both non-European ethnic (more recently the refugees) and domestic minorities (the Roma in particular). In CPI's discourse, special emphasis is placed on the Roma people, commonly referred to by the offensive term 'Gypsies', against whom the CPI frequently mobilizes. Roma are portrayed as criminal, social parasites who exploit state anti-discrimination benefits – a position strongly shared with the more institutional *Northern League*.

Last, but not least, after the attacks in Paris and Brussels in 2016, CPI's interpretation of these massacres is not consistent with Samuel Huntington's theory of the *Clash of Civilizations*. In CPI's online magazine, *Il Primato Nazionale*, the group explains that cultural incompatibility has not to do with Islam per se, but rather with immigration and the multiculturalist ideology[28]. European countries should not rally to defend the 'fake progressive values' of Charlie Hebdo, but rather ally with the social-nationalist Arabs to resolve the issues of immigration.[29] In this interpretation, the two instances of carnage are not only the result of the war between 'Islam' and the 'West' but also a war within Islam. While CPI recognizes that "there is a problem with Islam"[30] it also argues that "[t]he real problem is that Oriana Fallaci's[31] theories have led us to embark in a senseless crusade that ended up hurting the last strongholds of secular and nationalist Islam, such as Saddam, Ghaddafi and Assad."[32]

REFRAMING CLASSIC NATIVIST ARGUMENTS: GLOBALIZATION AND 'PEOPLE'S UPROOTING' RHETORIC

In addition to classic nativist arguments, CPI's propaganda offers some unusual perspectives on xenophobic discourse. These originate from a reframing of another leitmotiv of extreme right rhetoric: anti-globalization combined with 'Third Position' arguments advocating equidistance from both the Marxist left and the conservative right. For CPI, globalization is seen as an economic and cultural process of deterritorialization, denationalization and technological interconnectedness. It is associated with the increasing homogenization of ethnic and cultural differences deriving from the movement of peoples, but also from the diffusion of similar consumption and communication standards on a global scale. The group calls for the re-establishment of the authority (and borders) of the nation-state to stop international free markets, while simultaneously proposing to keep a market-based economy within the nation-state.

CasaPound Italia adds a specific argument inspired by 'Third Position' rhetoric, which rejects both communism and capitalism, and that CPI calls the 'fascist alternative'. This type of discourse is especially common among Italian fascist and neo-fascist organizations, particularly the *Italian Social Movement – Tricolour Flame*[33], *New Force*[34] and initially *National Alliance*[35]. In the European far-right scene, 'Third Position' discourses are rarer and mainly spread among non-party and subcultural organizations. In this interpretation, without expressing solidarity, CPI sees migrants as the victims of globalized capitalism and labels migrant movements to the West a form of "new slavery"[36]. Always in ethno-differentialist terms, migrants are also described as the victims of processes of "peoples' eradication"[37] that "impoverish"[38] both migrants and the arrival countries from social, cultural and existential points of view.

Conclusions

The rhetoric on migration by a group like CPI cannot be considered innovative in the far-right panorama. On the one hand, when it comes to nativist interpretations of migration in economic, cultural and securitarian terms, CPI is similar to more established populist radical right parties.[39] On the other, the 'fascists of the third millennium' pair this classic nativist rhetoric with a rather unusual one that combines more extreme elements of anti-globalization and 'Third Position' arguments. Even if the far right might be 'atypical' when it comes to migration, the boundaries between the nativist rhetoric of party and non-party organizations in this area seem to be fading. It is hard to tell whether this will impact the group's political success. However, some of the frames used by CPI to politicize migration (economic, cultural and securitarian) are not exclusively a priority of such marginal neo-fascist organizations and do not only appeal to old-style skinheads, whereas other more extreme frames actually are (anti-globalization and 'Third Position').

In current times, it is hard for the far right to capitalize (only) on old racist ideas, especially if the organization has to combine an extreme ideology with radical electoral acceptability. The combination of classic and more extreme frames of migration creates a discourse in which – without expressing compassion or empathy – opposition to migration is built on a rhetoric that portrays migrants as victims of the same processes that natives oppose. In this way, CPI seems to reconcile both extremism and radicalism, a strategy that, so far, has allowed the group to invest, more or less successfully, in the subcultural as well as electoral arenas.

Annotations

1 | European Commission (2013; 2015): Data from Eurobarometer 79, 80, 83, 84, What Do You Think are the Two Most Important Issues Facing the EU at the Moment? (http://ec.europa.eu/public_opinion/archives/eb_arch_en.htm), accessed June 23, 2016. For an overview of the political debate on migration in Italy cf. Pietro Castelli

Gattinara (2016): The Politics of Migration in Italy: Perspectives on Local Debates and Party Competition. Abingdon, New York: Routledge.
2 | The Italian name and the short version will be used throughout the text because the original goes back to a personal name that cannot be translated.
3 | Cas Mudde (2007): Populist Radical Right Parties in Europe. Cambridge: Cambridge University Press, pp. 11-59.
4 | Ibid., pp. 22-23.
5 | Hans-Georg Betz (1993): The Two Faces of Radical Right-Wing Populism in Western Europe. In: The Review of Politics, 55/4, pp. 663-686; Paul Taggart (2002): Populism and the Pathology of Representative Politics. In: Yves Mény/Yves Surel (eds.): Democracies and the Populist Challenge. London: Palgrave Macmillan, pp. 62-80; Cas Mudde (2007): Populist Radical Right Parties; Andrea Mammone/Emmanuel Godin/Brian Jenkins (2013): Varieties of Right-Wing Extremism in Europe. Abingdon, New York: Routledge.
6 | Michael Minkenberg (2005): From Party to Movement? The German Radical Right in Transition. In: Xavier Casals (ed.), Political Survival on the Extreme Right. European Movements between the Inherited Past and the Need to Adapt to the Future. Barcelona: ICPS, pp. 51-70; Michael Minkenberg (2008): The Radical Right in Europe: An Overview. Bertelsmann Stiftung; Sivan Hirsch-Hoefler/Cas Mudde (2013): Right-Wing Movements. In: David A. Snow/Donatella della Porta/Bert Klandermans/Doug McAdam (eds.): The Wiley-Blackwell Encyclopedia of Social and Political Movements. Oxford: Oxford University Press, pp. 1-8; Roger Griffin (2003): From Slime Mould to Rhizome: An Introduction to the Groupuscular Right. In: Patterns of Prejudice, 37/1, pp. 27-50.
7 | Manuela Caiani/Donatella della Porta/Claudius Wagemann (2012): Mobilizing on the Extreme Right: Germany, Italy, and the United States. Oxford: Oxford University Press; Daniel Koehler (2015): Contrast Societies: Radical Social Movements and their Relationships with their Target Societies. A Theoretical Model. In: Behavioral Sciences of Terrorism and Political Aggression, 7/1, pp. 18-34; Caterina Froio/Pietro Castelli Gattinara (2015): Neo-Fascist Mobilization in Contemporary Italy: Ideology and Repertoire of Action of CasaPound Italia. In: Journal for Deradicalization, 1/2, pp. 86-118.
8 | Nicolas Lebourg (2015): Le Front National et la Galaxie des Extrêmes Droites Radicales [The National Front and the Extreme Right Galaxy]. In: Sylvain Crépon/Alexandre Dézé/Nonna Mayer (eds.): Les Faux-Semblants du Front National: Sociologie d'un Parti Politique [The Pretexting Attempts of the Front National: Sociology of a Political Party]. Paris: Presses de Sciences Po, pp. 121-140; Matteo Albanese/Giorgia Bulli/Pietro Castelli Gattinara/Caterina Froio (2014): Fascisti di un altro Millennio? Crisi e Partecipazione in CasaPound Italia [Fascists of Another Millennium? Crisis and Participation in CasaPound Italia]. Acireale: Bonanno.
9 | See Heiko Koch in this volume.
10 | Original name in Italian: *Lega Nord*.
11 | Pietro Castelli Gattinara/Caterina Froio (2014): Discourse and Practice of Violence in the Italian Extreme Right: Frames, Symbols and Identity Building in CasaPound Italia. In: International Journal of Conflict and Violence, 8/1, pp. 154-170.

12 | Cas Mudde (1999): The Single-Issue Party Thesis: Extreme Right Parties and the Immigration Issue. In: West European Politics, 22/3, pp. 182-197.
13 | David Art (2011): Inside the Radical Right: The Development of Anti-Immigrant Parties in Western Europe, Cambridge: Cambridge University Press.
14 | Cf. Cas Mudde (2007): Populist Radical Right Parties.
15 | Ibid., p. 65.
16 | Marc Helbling (2014): Framing Immigration in Western Europe. In: Journal of Ethnic and Migration Studies, 40/1, pp. 21-41.
17 | *CasaPound Italia* defines itself as the heir of the fascist social tradition, cf. Pietro Castelli Gattinara/Caterina Froio/Matteo Albanese (2013): The Appeal of Neo-Fascism in Times of Crisis: The Experience of CasaPound Italia. In: Fascism: Journal of Comparative Fascist Studies, No. 2, pp. 234-258.
18 | Cas Mudde (2007): Populist Radical Right Parties, p. 78.
19 | Original name in Italian: *Confederazione generale dell'industria italiana*.
20 | CasaPound Italia (2013): Programma Politico CasaPound Italia [CasaPound Italia's Political Program], January 11, (http://www1.interno.gov.it/mininterno/export/sites/default/it/assets/files/25_elezioni/17_CASAPOUND_ITALIA.PDF), accessed June 30, 2016.
21 | Ibid., p. 3.
22 | Adriano Scianca (2011): Riprendersi Tutto: Le Parole di CasaPound [Let's Take Everything Back: CasaPound's Words]. Cusano Milanino: Società editrice Barbarossa.
23 | Ibid., pp. 107-108.
24 | CasaPound Italia (2013): Programma Politico CasaPound Italia [CasaPound Italia's Political Program], p. 3.
25 | João Carvalho (2013): Impact of Extreme Right Parties on Immigration Policy: Comparing Britain, France and Italy. Abingdon, New York: Routledge.
26 | Tamir Bar-On (2011): Transnationalism and the French Nouvelle Droite. In: Patterns of Prejudice, 45/3: pp. 199-223; Tamir Bar-On (2013): Rethinking the French New Right: Alternatives to Modernity. Abingdon, New York: Routledge; see also Tamir Bar-On in this volume.
27 | CasaPound Italia (2013): Sul Fronte dell'Essere: Le Proposte di CasaPound Italia sull'Immigrazione [Being on the Edge: CasaPound Italia's Proposals on Immigration], September 13, (http://www.casapoundlombardia.org/images/IMMIGRAZIONE/immigrazionepdf.pdf), accessed July 7, 2016.
28 | Adriano Scianca (2015): Perché è giusto dire: "basta con la Fallaci" Soprattutto oggi [Why it is Right to Say: "Enough with Fallaci." Especially Today], November 14, (http://www.ilprimatonazionale.it/politica/basta-fallaci-34188/), accessed July 7, 2016.
29 | Redazione Il Primato Nazionale (2015): Charlie Hebdo: Verso un "Patriot Act" alla Francese? [Charlie Hebdo: Towards a French style "Patriot Act"], January 22, (http://www.ilprimatonazionale.it/esteri/charlie-hebdo-verso-un-patriot-act-alla-francese-14705/), accessed July 7, 2016.

30 | Redazione Il Primato Nazionale (2015): Noi e l'Islam: Meno Fallaci e più Filippani Ronconi [Us and Islam: Less Fallaci, More Filippani Ronconi], November 19 (http://www.ilprimatonazionale.it/cultura/meno-fallaci-piu-filippani-ronconi-34560/), accessed July 7, 2016.

31 | Oriana Fallaci was a controversial Italian journalist and writer. Betwen 2001 and 2004, she published three books: *The Rage and the Pride*, *The Force of Reason* and *Oriana Fallaci Interviews Herself – The Apocalypse* that denounced the presumed 'Islamization' of Europe. For a discussion on Fallaci's role in the development of an intellectual Islamophobia in Italy, cf. Bruno Cousin/Tommaso Vitale (2013): Italian Intellectuals and the Promotion of Islamophobia after 9/11. In: George Morgan/Scott Poynting (eds.): Global Islamophobia and Moral Panic in the West. Burlington: Ashgate, pp. 47–66.

32 | Eugenio Palazzini (2016): Siria, Assad: Francia e Gran Bretagna Appoggiano il Terrorismo [Syria, Assad: France and Great Britain Support Terrorism], March 30, (http://www.ilprimatonazionale.it/esteri/siria-assad-francia-e-gran-bretagna-appoggiano-il-terrorismo-sanzioni-causa-dei-profughi-42643/), accessed July 7, 2016.

33 | Original name in Italian: *Movimento Sociale Italiano – Fiamma Tricolore*.

34 | Original name in Italian: *Forza Nuova*.

35 | Original name in Italian: *Alleanza Nazionale*. Guido Caldiron (2009): La Destra Sociale da Salò a Tremonti [The Social Right from Salò to Tremonti]. Roma: Manifesto-Libri/Contemporanea.

36 | CasaPound Italia (2013): Programma Politico CasaPound Italia [CasaPound Italia's Political Platform], p. 4.

37 | Ibid.

38 | Ibid.

39 | See Stijn van Kessel in this volume.

What's in the Mind of the Neo-Nazi Next Door?
A Personal Reflection on the Rise and Persistence of Golden Dawn in Greece

Angélique Kourounis

How could a racist party, which long received less than 0.2 percent of the national vote, win representation in the Greek Parliament with 18 seats? How could a party that promotes violence, hate, sexism and murders amplify its reach with each pogrom it wages? How has *Golden Dawn* (XA)[1] managed to remain the third political power in Greece for four years? And what's in the mind of a Golden Dawner? These were the questions I wanted to probe as I began filming *Golden Dawn: A Personal Affair*[2] in late 2009.

Now, why is *Golden Dawn* a *personal* affair for me? Well, I was born into a French immigrant family, I am a feminist, my partner is Jewish, one of my three sons is a homosexual, another an anarchist. If these fascists seize power, the only remaining question would be which wagon our family would be put on. So, the more research I did to answer the questions mentioned above, the more I realized that my motive was fear. With a father-in-law and a grandmother in the *Resistance*, a mother-in-law that had to take off the yellow star in order to pass through enemy's lines and bring back food to her family, and with an uncle and an aunt who returned from Auschwitz, I was brought up with stories of the War. I was told, growing up, that this world of war would never exist again. But does it really belong to the past?

BEING A GOLDEN DAWNER

My doubts were increasing in tandem with the growing amount of footage I gathered. The men in black became an obsession: "How could someone be a Golden Dawner today?" I thought about this question every single day. And to this day still, after five years of research, the question remains unanswered. Greece's lingering financial crisis is certainly not the only explanation. Those who choose to vote for XA have varied and differing motives. In order to try to understand the reasons, it was not enough to just go to them and ask; I had to try to gain their trust, or at least break down some of the barriers.

As a journalist, my habit is always to get right to the source of information; and this is how I did things as a filmmaker. Listening to the speeches, declarations and testimonies of others is fine, but sharing the everyday life of the Golden Dawners is something quite different. I had to enter their minds. I did not want to make a film as an outside observer from the sidelines but from within – a film about them, reaching as deep inside as I could without lying or having to actually embed myself within the group.

It was important for me to maintain a distant eye, the eye from without. I was not after the thoughts of the everyday, normal people voting for XA nor was I open to their arguments, I wanted to understand what was going on inside of the minds of those at the center. In short, I was after the thoughts of the hard-core individuals who are convinced of the rightfulness of their ideas, not out of need but out of conviction. Those who vote XA because they are starving and have been given a certain amount of food were not my target group, they were and still entail, the collateral damage of the country's austerity programs. They may feel humiliated, left aside – we have heard about them many times.

In the film, Mrs. Stella, an unemployed woman in her late 50s, represents these people. They are not the ones who are the decision-makers or ideologists. It is comparably easy to meet them and get them to talk. If the left had delivered on their promises, there wouldn't be any voters of the likes of Mrs. Stella opening their bags for XA food distributions. But getting the Golden Dawners of high rank, the people in charge, to talk outside of press conferences or parliamentary debates is an entirely different matter. So I laid the cards on the table; I wasn't going to judge them, I told them I just wanted to learn. I told them: "I want to understand what makes you tick, what is the key to your success, who you are!"

DELVING INTO THE FUNCTIONING OF A NEO-NAZI PARTY

There were neither leading questions nor hidden cameras. Everything else was about taking time – it took me five years to complete. There is no way to make such a film in a couple of weeks. Every morning, I started browsing their agenda: demonstrations, gatherings, press conferences, any event: I was there. I wanted them to get used to my camera. And though they eventually did, they were also conscious of the lens. They would often send me away, deny me access or not allow me to shoot.

The reason that this film could be made at all is closely related to a change in XA's media strategy after the killing of the anti-fascist musician Pavlos Fyssas in September 2013. XA tried to open up to the media in order to prove that it was no group of 'elephants' – an expression used in Greece for blatant neo-Nazis, racist, sexists and antisemites. Haris M., a former high-ranking military officer and current candidate for XA, debunks himself when he forgets his microphone is still on. I was lucky to be there at the right moment, with the right person. This happened after the third year of filming. At the time, I had another two years of shooting with this leading XA member, with whom I established a 'good relationship'. Stubbornness and persistence eventually paid off.

A major difficulty I faced was that the story line changed several times during shooting because of events like local elections, the killing of Pavlos Fyssas, etc. That is why this film is in its fourth version, while three separate and shorter versions with different story lines aired on TV earlier. During the years of shooting, there were periods when I had serious doubts, which I mention in the film. So did the Golden Dawners, who, every time we met, would ask me: "What about your movie, still not finished?"

I told them the truth: events had happened too fast and overran my narration; I had to start all over several times and I told them that if XA did not allow me to film within the group, there was no purpose in pursuing the film. I'm in no rush, I would tell them, I can wait. In the meantime, I continued my journalistic work. They might have listened to the pieces I aired: I never called the Golden Dawners anything else than that which they are: a neo-Nazi movement – a term they aggressively deny in public. The risk was to compromise the film for the sake of the security of my team and myself. At some point, though, each of us involved had to cope with their violent aggressiveness.

Ironically, a significant source of help was the sexism of the Golden Dawners: women, they think, are stupid – fat women twice as stupid. As a woman, 70 pounds overweight at the time, I took advantage of the double dose of discrimination, meaning that I was estimated to be a negligible security risk. I even pushed my luck, asking silly questions all the time – remarks that yielded snarky smiles from them. Haris, in fact, was so convinced that he told supporters with a running microphone: "Don't worry, I made a fool out of her." My teammate, Thomas Iacobi, acted as a counterweight: A blond, blue-eyed German; he was the entry ticket and the pretext at the time. All security guards ever had to do was look at him and my presence was quickly diminished, if not lost entirely.

ETHICS AND SELF-PROTECTION

It takes a lot of self-control to bring this kind of a shooting project to completion; you constantly have to remind yourself: "Hang in there, shoot, gather footage." This endeavor would deliver to the audience all the elements they require to make up their minds. It was a tricky project, though: often you have to pick a priority, let go of something in order to assure the other. For instance, there was a moment when I spotted a German neo-Nazi who had joined the Golden Dawners for a mass demonstration. I deliberately turned the camera away, I knew if they spotted me shooting the scene, they would get wild. I preferred to lose a precious and telling scene rather than jeopardize the whole film.

Another moment was when Haris M. showed us the two editions of Hitler's *Mein Kampf* on his bookshelf and declared that Greece today had similar problems to Germany in the Second World War. The question that burned at the tip of my tongue was: "And, are you going to apply the same solutions?" I didn't ask this question, of course, fearing that the oyster may close and not open again. Sometimes, less is more in the long run. Yet, every time I see the film, I feel that this was a missed opportunity and wonder what may have happened if I did utter my burning question.

I admit my film isn't objective. But it is fair. It isn't propaganda. I was afraid that such a film would have been counter-productive and miss its purpose of reaching as broad of an audience as possible, bringing them to ask themselves questions. Sections of the Greek leftist movement claim I should have done so – been more forceful, more combative. I admit, I consider militant films counter-productive and limiting to the audience. Something that all of us involved wanted the project to achieve was to stoke greater debate and discussion.

The purpose was to show that these neo-Nazis are neither aliens nor monsters, but awfully ordinary people, people you may meet every day – neighbors, rich, poor, simple-minded or academic, people with two arms, two legs, a head; everyday people. I don't believe Mrs. Stella is a Nazi, and I doubt she is aware of the genuine aggression fomented by Golden Dawners. Maybe she would start thinking twice if she saw the film. I dream of making a screening for a Golden Dawner audience, observe their reaction and ask them: Are you aware of all of this?

Limits and Prospects

The film has a significant flaw: I only deal with elements I can prove. Therefore, I fall well short of getting to the root of XA's funding because I simply don't have rock-solid proof of its origin. I do have clues, hints and information I share with people in discussions, but I didn't include them in the documentary because I can't prove them. I still ponder over the same questions as when I began shooting. I haven't gotten an answer, even if I now have a better understanding of how they tick. What is clear, however, is that there is no blanket or collective cause for XA membership. Crisis doesn't explain everything, as each and every person has his/her own reasons for joining XA.

What I am sure of after 5 years shooting is that these people are extremely dangerous, mainly because most people do not take them seriously. This is very worrying since, in the meantime, they are preparing to take the control and they are getting closer to this goal. The Greek left is shattered; people are more and more disillusioned and bored while the only other group gaining strength in the elections besides XA is that composed of those who reject voting. Meanwhile, Golden Dawners vote with one voice, united.

So, we are at a point at which we finally have to resist this pan-European threat. As different as their structures, strategies and domains of success may be – *Jobbik* in Hungary[3], *PiS* in Poland[4], the Dutch *Party for Freedom* in the Netherlands[5], the *Northern League* in Italy[6], the *Front National* in France[7], *UKIP* in Great Britain[8], not to mention the far right in Austria and Germany. The far right is no longer an exotic phenomenon but heavily on the move.

I may not have found the answers in my film, but I hope to have delivered enough illustrations to consider the danger that XA represents and to raise awareness of the fact that we have to resist this; the need for resistance is imminent, now, every single day, and in general. Getting informed is part of resisting. That is why we schedule screenings all over Europe wherever we can and talk to people. Because, in the end, there is no difference whatsoever in the Golden Dawners slogan, "Greece belongs to Greeks, Foreigners out", and a sign bearing the word 'Juden' that Nazis used to affix on Jewish stores during the Third Reich. In both cases, society missed the opportunity to react properly. Today, we are no longer in the Thirties. We do not have the luxury to say that we don't know what is going to happen once they take power. We have sufficient knowledge of their goals and methods.

That means *today* is when we have to stand up and resist – or not. This is our choice.

Annotations

1 | Original name in Greek: Χρυσή Αυγή.
2 | The film *Golden Dawn: A Personal Affair* is being screened as of spring 2016 in Europe and beyond. More information at: goldendawnapersonalaffair.com.
3 | This is the short version of the Hungarian original: *Jobbik Magyarországért Mozgalom* which translates as *Jobbik, the Movement for a Better Hungary*.
4 | The abbreviation is used here because it is better known than the official *Prawo i Sprawiedliwość*. This means *Law and Justice* in English.
5 | Original name in Dutch: *Partij voor de Vrijheid*.
6 | Original name in Italian: *Lega Nord*.
7 | To avoid confusion with groups from other countries that carry the name *National Front*, the original is used throughout the text.
8 | The short version is used for being better known than the official name *United Kingdom Independence Party*.

Paradox: Facebook page of the *Identitarian Generation*, known for their social media savvy. The photo posted here shows a person holding the Identitarian flag over an ancient village in the French province of Normandy. (Original photograph taken by Nicolas Hecker, edited by Deniz Beşer, 2016).

... Over Cultural Hegemony

Preparing for (Intellectual) Civil War
The New Right in Austria and Germany

Natascha Strobl and Julian Bruns

In the spring of 2016, activists of the *Identitarian Movement Austria*[1] entered the stage during a performance of Elfriede Jelinek's play *The Wards (Die Schutzbefohlenen)* in the main hall of the University of Vienna.[2] Some among the 30 participants displayed a banner soaked in artificial blood that read: 'You hypocrites!' *(Ihr Heuchler!)*. The actors – among them refugees and children – were shocked; intervention on the part of some anti-fascist audience members finally ended the disruption. This act, which attracted media coverage, is one of several incidents incited by New Right actors that have received increasing attention among the German and Austrian public. From the early 2000s on, the New Right started establishing new specialized forms of media and institutions, and increasingly took to the streets. The *Identitarians* are the spearhead of this new strategic development. At first glance, this might appear to be a contradiction, as the very definition of New Right is one of a movement which has shifted from action to intellectual debate: but this is only one side of the story.

Ever since 2012, when *Identitarians* entered the political scene, their claims have become action-oriented. They have successfully brought New Right ideology to the streets and have also created new spaces for the entire spectrum to operate. Since then, we have witnessed huge demonstrations: first, the *Vigils for Peace*[3], then demonstrations by the *Hooligans Against Salafists* (Ho.Ge.Sa)[4] and, finally, *Patriotic Europeans Against the Islamization of the Occident* (PEGIDA)[5]. While each of them have their own unique history, they share the commonality that key players from the New Right have assumed major roles within these groups, both in the foreground and behind the scenes. Finally, with the emergence of *Alternative for Germany* (AfD)[6] the New Right has managed to turn their ideology into a political party program.

So what's going on in the New Right circles in Austria and Germany? This article portrays a new generation of New Right actors, placing its focus of interest on three main levels of action: intellectual work, street action and party politics. It argues that the New Right has taken its ideology to the streets as well as into several parliaments since 2012. In this study, we aim to show the group's specific strategies, its main institutions and its players.

DEFINITION – WHAT IS THE NEW RIGHT?

One unique trait of the New Right is its inclusion of both conservative and right-wing extremist elements. In fact, it transcends the (fictitious) border between conservatism and right-wing extremism and proves that right-wing extremist ideas float freely between these poles; it is a distinctively bourgeois and elitist spectrum. The New Right can be described as a modernized form of right-wing extremism. It strives for cultural and political hegemony which is to be obtained through a strategy referred to as *metapolitics*: the New Right rejects political parties and favors the intellectual level in fighting a 'cultural war' aimed at reversing the socio-political changes of 1968. Opinion leaders in the areas of culture, media and politics spread its ideas and shape its discourse.

Ideologically, there is little difference between the Old Right and the New Right. Strategic innovations have, however, been important: its language has become softer while racist ideas have been reformulated through concepts such as ethnopluralism. This latter concept sees cultures as homogeneous and static entities; adherents of ethnopluralism argue that every culture is a combination of ethnic and cultural elements and has its own soil, on which it 'naturally' belongs. When one culture is mixed with another, conflicts arise that eventually lead to violence and war. In order to avoid such conflict, ethnopluralists demand a sort of 'worldwide apartheid'. It does not leave any room for counter-cultures, class struggles or other forms of contradiction.

A closer look at self-declared ethnopluralists, such as the *Identitarians*, reveals that they still view a strong hierarchy to exist between cultures, with, for example, 'European' culture being superior to 'Muslim' culture. As such, ethnopluralism is akin to racism, but with cultures taking the place of races. This has been a strategic decision that is a consequence of the Holocaust and other crimes committed by National Socialist Germany – open racism and antisemitism were discredited and could no longer be maintained. Instead, the so-called 'Conservative Revolution' and its anti-democratic and elitist ideas serve as the role model for the New Right.[7] They can freely distance themselves from National Socialism, even invoking a history of resistance (for instance, by declaring the mutinous Wehrmacht officer Stauffenberg to be a role model), while, at the same time, holding on to an anti-pluralist, nationalist and racist worldview.

A NEW GENERATION OF THE NEW RIGHT

Between 2000 and 2013, the New Right made significant developments. Since then, new magazines and Internet platforms have emerged, and a new generation has taken over. Leading figures such as Götz Kubitschek (associated with the think tank *Institut für Staatspolitik*, magazine *Sezession*, the publishing house *Antaios* and the NGO *Ein Prozent*)[8] have coined new ideas such as "pre-civil war"[9]. Kubitschek and others, such as Karlheinz Weißmann[10], have worked out a new strategy: to implant their ideas onto the streets. They found inspiration from the left and copied leftist forms of action. This new generation of the New Right looked to younger adherents to put their ideas into practice. After a number of experimental actions under the banner of *Conservative Subversive Action* (KSA)[11], the idea of an activist branch first took shape in France. Inspired by the Italian neo-fascist youth organization *CasaPound Italia*[12], French activists of the *Identitarian Generation*[13] (a youth organization affiliated with the party *Identitarian Bloc*[14]) occupied the building site of a mosque in Poitiers in southern France – where Karl Martell had fought off a Moorish army in 732. This inspired the founding of several offshoots all across Europe; strong national *Identitarian* organizations were formed in Austria, Germany, the Czech Republic and Italy.

In 2014, the New Right took several opportunities to spread its ideas on the streets of Germany. The *Vigils for Peace* were organized with the help of Jürgen Elsässer, editor of the New Right magazine *Compact*. Elsässer gave speeches beside other main speakers, such as radio host Ken Jebsen and pop musician Xavier Naidoo. They all spoke about their racist and/or nationalist ideas in front of thousands of people. In May 2014, the *Identitarians* held their first ever demonstration, which took place in Vienna. In October 2014, Ho.Ge.Sa held one of the largest right-wing demonstrations in years. Though the demonstration quickly escalated into violence against minorities, political enemies and the police, players of the New Right, such as Elsässer, Akif Pirinçci (an author) and Tatjana Festerling (then part of the AfD Hamburg, PEGIDA, and now *Fortress Europe*[15]) showed their approval. The *Identitarians* marched side by side with hooligans and neo-Nazi skinheads to promote their anti-Muslim racism. In the same month, a group of like-minded people started the PEGIDA demonstrations in Dresden, mobilizing up to 20,000 people for their rallies against Islam, feminism and the 'multicultural society'. Important players such as Kubitschek, Elsässer and Martin Sellner[16] fostered a hateful climate against refugees in Germany, while Austrian and German *Identitarians* blocked border crossings to stop refugees. Kubitschek used PEGIDA to propagate his ideas of 'civil disobedience', blocking, occupying and eventually torching refugee shelters. The *Identitarians* continued their demonstrations through Vienna in 2015 and 2016, both times facing huge anti-fascist counter-protests. In 2016, they also tried to march through Berlin, and were confronted with counter-protests once again.

Active on Three Levels

When considering the present situation, we can see a highly diversified New Right. In the case of Austria and Germany, this does not comprise two separate groups but rather one transnationally organized spectrum. The actors involved focus on one or more levels of action, as described in the following.

Intellectual work: This remains the very core of the New Right. Many blogs, magazines and books provide the intellectual framework for the movement. Ideas and articles are discussed at many networking events, from summer universities to conferences. Magazines such as *Sezession, Blaue Narzisse* or *Compact* are full service providers, publishing daily updates on their blogs and magazines and frequently hosting events.

Street action: In the past three and a half years, the *Identitarians* took New Right ideology to the streets. Some journalists and scholars have made the mistake of simply labeling them as 'neo-Nazi' rallies. This misses the point, in our opinion: the *Identitarians* do not use neo-Nazi methods, but, instead, they draw from leftist and NGO approaches. This sets them apart from known right-wing extremist street action and calls for a different set of tools for analyzing them as well as for organizing anti-fascist counter-protests. Apart from the *Identitarians*, the PEGIDA rallies still meet every Monday in Dresden. One of its main actors was Götz Kubitschek. With the formation of *One Percent* by Kubitschek along with Karl Albrecht Schachtschneider (a lawyer), Hans-Thomas Tillschneider (AfD), Jürgen Elsässer (*Compact* Magazine) and Philip Stein (co-speaker of the right-wing student fraternities), a new organization came into play. *One Percent* functions as a New Right NGO; its members document street action, collect donations and carry out public relations work.

Party politics: The AfD has created new opportunities for the leaders of the New Right. The journal *Junge Freiheit*, for example, took the stance of fully supporting AfD and declaring the party to be the sole future for the New Right. This led to many debates within the spectrum, as other groups, such as *Sezession*, preferred pursuing intellectual work and possibly street action in the future. Many within the New Right see AfD as an opportunity, especially Björn Höcke, the popular leader of AfD in Thuringia. Höcke, Elsässer and Kubitschek maintain a close personal relationship. As the *Austrian Freedom Party* (FPÖ)[17] is very strong in Austria, an independent New Right spectrum never fully diversified there as it did in Germany. The Austrian *Identitarians* proved to be one of the most successful *Identitarian* groups in Europe, maintaining close ties with key figures in the New Right as well as with FPÖ and AfD. In Austrian counties such as Burgenland, the youth organization of the FPÖ and the *Identitarians* are almost identical.

CONCLUSION

The New Right has gained momentum and formed alliances. Their main goal is still to achieve a cultural revolution in favor of the right. In 2011, Kubitschek said that he believed the New Right needed to win the intellectual civil war that was going on in Germany. Now, five years later, the New Right no longer limits itself to mere words but has taken its ideology to the streets. The *Identitarians* have encroached into leftist territory by adopting leftist forms of struggle for themselves, with PEGIDA serving as the largest stage for the main players on the New Right. With the emergence of AfD, the paradox of a New Right party formed, representing a new stage for its main actors. Time will tell if the party's logic and 'intellectual civil war' can be reconciled. The balancing act of both cultivating their elitist and antidemocratic ideology and, at the same time, organizing mass protests and trying to win parliamentary elections will be a critical test in proving whether all three levels of action can be maintained.

ANNOTATIONS

1 | Original name in German: *Identitäre Bewegung Österreich*. *Identitarian* is used as a synonym for *Identitariam Movement* in this text.
2 | Der Standard (2016): Theaterstück Gestürmt: Verfassungsschutz Ermittelt Gegen Identitäre [Theater Play Raided: Secret Service Investigating Identitarians], April 15, (http://derstandard.at/2000034939397/Identitaere-stuermten-Theaterstueck-Verfassungsschutz-ermittelt), accessed July 2, 2016.
3 | Original name in German: *Montagsmahnwachen*. The *Vigils for Peace* were weekly gatherings of hundreds of people in the center of the German capital of Berlin, pronouncing their support for Russia along with their skepticism towards liberal democracies. Open to conspiracy myths and to actors from the far right, this mobilization was prompted by the conflict in eastern Ukraine since early 2014.
4 | Original name in German: *Hooligans gegen Salafisten*.
5 | Original name in German: *Patriotische Europäer gegen die Islamisierung des Abendlandes*.
6 | Original name in German: *Alternative für Deutschland*.
7 | See Tamir Bar-On in this volume.
8 | *Institut für Staatspolitik* (Institute for State Governance, IfS) is a New Right think tank; *Sezession* is the monthly magazine by the IfS and one of the most important organs of the German New Right; *One Percent for our Country* is a nationalist NGO, original name in German: *Ein Prozent für unser Land*.
9 | In German this means: "Vorbürgerkrieg". Kubitschek coined the term to describe a state of underlying conflicts in which societal fracture lines can be found everywhere. Nonetheless, this conflict is not obvious – fault lines can be seen by those who are

willing to believe them. In contrast to other forms of war, there is no declaration of war. The "pre-civil war" just becomes more obvious day by day. Kubitschek sees the reason for this conflict to be in the multicultural character of German society. The danger is embodied by young male migrants, whom Kubitschek describes as aggressive and violent. The German 'folk' are said to have to fight back against ethnic minorities to sustain their hegemony. C.F: Götz Kubitschek (2007): Vorbürgerkrieg [Pre-Civil War]. In: Sezession, No. 20, p. 56.

10 | Weißmann is a co-founder of IfS. He fell out with Kubitschek and the IfS because of their different opinions about the relationship between the New Right and the AfD. He now works for the *Junge Freiheit (Young Freedom)* which is weekly German newspaper and part of the New Right spectrum, even though it calls itself as 'conservative'.
11 | Original name in German: *Konservativ Subversive Aktion*.
12 | See Heiko Koch and Caterina Froio in this volume.
13 | Original name in French: *Génération Identitaire*.
14 | See Samuel Bouron in the volume.
15 | Original name in German: *Festung Europa*. This organization was founded by Tatjana Festerling in 2015 and is a PEGIDA spin-off operating in Dresden.
16 | He used to be part of the *Identiarian Movement Vienna* and is now the chairman of *Identitarian Movement Austria*.
17 | Original name in German: *Freiheitliche Partei Österreichs*.

The Strategy of the French Identitaires
Entering Politics through the Media

Samuel Bouron

French far-right activism has experienced tremendous changes in recent years. Besides traditional far-right party politics, new patterns of street-based mobilization have been attracting action-oriented youths in particular. This trend is epitomized by the growing popularity of the *Identitarian Bloc*[1]. Its ideology rests on the idea of an existent struggle between different political factions with the aim of becoming the legitimate representative of the people, a struggle that the far-right is winning. Behind the scenes, the recurring idea of the *Identitarian Bloc* is to occupy a cultural and 'meta-political' territory over which the left once held a monopoly. Their aim is to gradually become associated with the only possible alternative to change the world[2]. They try to frame a maximum of popular needs and present themselves as substitutes for the time when the economy and the state will be bankrupt. One can participate in financing the *Identitarian Movement* by eating their food, drinking their beer (the *'Desouchière'*), buying their clothes, listening to their music or reading their books. For Philippe Vardon, a cofounder of the *Identitarian Bloc* in 2003,

"the idea of a meta-political type of project is to attract people who would never come, or only with difficulty, to political action through classic activism. The objective then is to act on the perception that individuals have of the world and the society in which they live in order to create currents of opinion favorable to the struggle between political movements or groups implementing these projects."[3]

In approaching this movement, one must understand that they do not have any kind of army or even any small group of activists that would directly invest the field of party politics. They deploy a communication strategy which, despite its limitations, makes them true professional politicians. It is therefore useful to describe the contours of this professionalization process particularly mobilized by the far right with claims of 'meta-political' ideas.

STRIVING TO REPLACE THE LEFT ON THEIR TRADITIONAL TERRITORIES

In this way, the ideal activist should be able to speak the language of the 'apolitical' institutions (including those whose goals are not directly political) in which he or she is integrated, while diverting its objectives to the benefit of the militant group. When in training, activists learn diverse communication skills: writing press releases, developing websites, creating graphic models to create a banner or a stencil, and making public speeches – the priority is to avoid appearing amateur. The group aims at offering products whose quality should equal that of professionals which, in turn, should lead the group to being taken more seriously by media outlets and by other political groups.

The *Identitarians* took up the repertoire and aesthetics from different groups classified on the left of the political spectrum. On environmental issues, they support de-growth narratives and have participated in the creation of the Associations for Maintaining a Peasant Agriculture, equivalent to the Community Supported Agriculture. The movement also declares itself feminist, an idea it supports by the creation of groups such as *Beautiful and Rebellious*[4] or the *Antigones* (anti-Femen), in which *Identitarian* activists are predominant. In the cultural field, they invest in the creation of rock bands such as *Hotel Stella*, always with the aim of disseminating beyond the small world of far-right activists. *Greenpeace, Act Up* and even the radical anti-fascist movement constitute an important source of inspiration for them.

To raise awareness, the themes selected by managers largely draw on popular culture and are sometimes inspired by consumer films such as *Braveheart, 300, Fight Club* or *The Lord of the Rings*. For example, an *Identitarian* training camp devoted to Tolkien's trilogy was created in 2012, in which a reinterpretation of the work was carried out. During the camp, they asked activists to identify the character with which they felt more affinity. In the event of *Fight Club*, Parisian activists from *Identitarian Youth*[5] (the youth group of the *Identitarian Bloc*) were inspired by "Project chaos" in the film and chose to accordingly name their section "Apache Project"[6]. Despite the fact that the novel makes explicit reference to anarchism, they engaged with the film's scenario in order to learn from its style and aesthetics to construct political movements.

The *Identitarians'* strategy is very similar to that of the Italian neo-fascist movement *CasaPound Italia*[7] through its investment in the associative sector. The latter has occupied a building in Rome since 2003, which serves as an anchor point for their various 'meta-political' actions. They were able to create their own media, including a radio station, as well as a restaurant, a theater company, sports clubs, music groups and an art gallery. The objective of this movement has been to give fascism a young and trendy image, far from the cheesy and aging representation of an extreme right which is out of touch with today's world. It consists of activists who are mostly students or graduates in major cities and who put their cultural and artistic skills to benefit their political movement.

PROFESSIONAL COMMUNICATION

For now, new technologies have been the major area in which *Identitarian* leaders have invested, including Fabrice Robert, one of the founders of the movement, and Damien Rieu, the main spokesman of the Lyon chapter (the third-largest city in France). Several unfulfilled projects have been discussed for the coming years, such as an *Identitarian* Wikileaks, a Novopress (their press agency) app for tablets and smartphones, the creation of a petition website, a survey website, a dating site to find 'native French' partners, a tutoring website and opening of their very own online social network. The leaders attach great importance to such communication strategies. Each activist is trained to be able to speak to the press and to carry out symbolic acts in order to 'generate a buzz'. Even if the actions are considered wrong by the media, the point is for them to make an impression and to hold public debates. In so doing, they forsake the scandalous bonehead clothing range, composed of military apparel and shaved heads, which is becoming increasingly marginal among their ranks. The activists now prefer 'casual' looks that do not directly identify them with the far right. Here, again, of paramount importance is infiltrating society rather than scaring it.

Like the movement created by Alain Soral[8] (a French far-right essayist with close ties to the comedian Dieudonné), the *Identitarians* are very active on the Internet, which is the preferred venue for their ideology. Unlike newspaper columns, for which they are likely to be denied and their words potentially presented in their political context, owning their own media give them the opportunity to issue propaganda aimed at blurring the political divide between the left and the right. Social networks also allow them to broadcast their own videos, the fun and spectacular dimensions of which often initially shroud their ideological flavor. It even happens that some journalists themselves fall into the trap set for them: this happened in 2009, when the *Identitarian Bloc* created a female character who was supposed to live in the neighborhood of La Goutte d'Or in Paris, claiming to have suffered from the invasion of Muslims to the area – where she had supposedly lived for generations. This was the starting point of the 'buzz' of a "cocktail sausage-plonk"[9]. Despite the attempt of the *Identitarians* to innovate ways to communicate, their ideological background remains quite homogeneous. It opposes "French from the roots"[10] activists who would be at war against the invasion of a Muslim population.

LIMITS OF THE MOVEMENT

However, this type of organization also has limitations. Activists generally find little interest in campaigning. Meeting the people of their district to defend their ideas, inventing slogans, organizing awareness campaigns, towing markets or finding a financial agent to manage finances are all steps that paradoxically appear to be unappealing 'dirty work'. Conversely, participating in the political game involves a form of submission that leads to a loss of the feeling of radicalism conquered within a limited space, only ever together with the other activists. It is also a way for some women activists to exist away from virile sociability. But most remain anonymous and extend the autonomy of the *Identitarian* training camp experience to the so-called 'identity houses' *(maisons de l'identité)*, with the nightly hanging of posters, concerts, private parties or boxing classes. The pleasure of belonging to a community of action and belief seems to be sufficient in itself.

The efficiency of the *Identitarian* political strategy thus proves to be, at the moment, very limited. The will to implement itself locally to run for municipal elections and take control of the territories which are most favorable to them has not worked from an electoral point of view. For example, the ambition of the group *Nissa Rebela* to become the third political force in Nice was a failure, and the candidates of the *Identitarians* rarely score in the double digits when they appear under this political label. In general, the *Identitarians* have not actually recorded any successes other than media agitations; and in the political arena, it is the party *Front National*[11] which seems to reap the fruits of their labor. Those who would like to make a career in politics indeed see few prospects within the *Identitarian Bloc*, while at the same time, the creation of *Rassemblement bleu marine*[12] allows the integration of those whom the party considers to be the best elements of *Identitarians*. Nevertheless, these positions will rarely be the most prestigious ones. While parts of the left no longer joins forces against a common enemy – especially as it has abandoned a reading of the social world in terms of class struggle – this far right has not abandoned the old story of the struggle of races.

ANNOTATIONS

1 | Original name in French: *Bloc Identitaire*, also shortened to *Les Identitaires*.
2 | Antonio Gramsci analyzes the political failure of the Maurasian fringes of the far-right in restoring an old world of the Old Regime, monarchy and Catholicism on account of a political abstraction deficit and the inability to impose their own worldview and history. This would result in a popularity deficit and in relegation to the sidelines of

politics along with sectarian isolation. See Vito Carofiglio/Carmela Ferrandes (1986): The Adventures of the French Right and Gramsci Avatars. In: Mots, No. 12, pp. 191–203.
3 | Philippe Vardon (2011): Eléments pour une contre-culture identitaire, Nice: Idées, p. 275.
4 | Original name in French: *Belle et Rebelle*.
5 | Original name in French: *Jeunesses Identitaires*.
6 | In the film *Fight Club*, created by David Fincher in 1999, Project Chaos brings together an activist group that wants to sabotage the capitalist world. The name Apache Project is extracted from the film and by the Apaches, a Parisian street gang of the Belle Epoque.
7 | The original Italian name will be used throughout the text because the original goes back to a personal name that cannot be translated. See Caterina Froio and Heiko Koch in this volume.
8 | Alain Soral founded the movement party *Reconciliation in France and in Belgium* (Original name in French: *Reconciliation Nationale*). Once a member of the *French Communist Party* (original name in French: *Parti Communiste Français*), Soral joined the *Front National*, which he left in 2009. Jean-Marie Le Pen is the godfather of Dieudonné's son.
9 | On July 18 2010, *Bloc Identitaire* organized a giant *aperitif* that was to bring together all the people hostile to Islam. It was cancelled by the authorities.
10 | The far right opposed the 'French from the roots' to the category of French individuals of immigrant origin. This opposition is increasingly used in the public debate (former French President François Hollande used it on February 23, 2015).
11 | The English translation is *National Front*. However, to avoid confusion with groups or parties from other countries carrying the same name, the original name French is used in this text.
12 | The *Rassemblement Bleu Marine* is a French political coalition of sovereigntist parties close to Marine Le Pen that was created in 2012 in the context of the parliamentary elections.

Arguing with the Nouvelle Droite
Substantive Debate, Partisan Polemics or Truth-Seeking?

Tamir Bar-On

In 2014, I published a piece entitled *The French New Right: Neither Right, nor Left?*[1]. Surprisingly, the French *Nouvelle Droite's* (ND)[2] main figure Alain de Benoist responded with a polemical article[3]. I, in turn, replied with an essay titled *A Response to Alain de Benoist*[4]. I neither identify with a political party, nor a political movement. De Benoist does. He cannot claim intellectual objectivity. He is self-described as "a man of the right", as highlighted by his most famous book, *Vu de Droite*[5], which won de Benoist France's most important literary award.

In this piece, I offer some comments on my debate with de Benoist. I argue that, while we should strive towards intellectual objectivity, we cannot be silent in the face of falsehoods. In this respect, the ND plays a dishonest game. Its leader and other ND intellectuals feign intellectual objectivity and the platitudes of transcending right and left[6]; but in a Gramscian vein, they seek cultural hegemony and the triumph of their decidedly revolutionary right-wing ideals. Or, as de Benoist put it, "the French right [...] hasn't realized the importance of Gramsci. It hasn't seen that cultural power threatens the apparatus of the state"[7]. Considering this, was my unusual exchange with a renowned French intellectual a substantive debate, a case study of partisan polemics, or an exercise in truth-seeking? I want to suggest that the exchange included all three of these elements.

I take the debate with de Benoist as an opportunity for learning. Some people told me not to respond to de Benoist. How can you respond to a neo-fascist? Perhaps I am a real liberal and believe in the clash of radically divergent ideas. The exchange reminded me of de Benoist's debate with the French scholar of the ND, Pierre-André Taguieff, in the mid-1990s[8]. Taguieff noted that the ND advances a new "cultural racism", but also asked the question of whether French media and intellectual elites had treated de Benoist to a real discussion or an "inquisition"[9]? Moreover, I demonstrate that the ND leader is a neo-fascist with a human face. As Umberto Eco noted, neo-fascists (or 'Ur-Fascists') maintain fascist core values, but do not subscribe to the violent tactics or annihilationist goals of the National Socialists or Fascists of the past[10]. Eco points out that, in a post-Second World War, post-Holocaust and anti-fascist age, one cannot openly state a desire to "re-open Auschwitz"[11]. In addition, he notes that we must be vigilant of the return of a new type of fascism that "can come back under the most innocent of disguises"[12]. The Holocaust survivor and renowned chemist Primo Levi warned of "a new fascism, with its trail of intolerance, abuse, and servitude, can be born outside our country and imported into it, walking on tiptoe and calling itself by other names."[13]

Moreover, in 1961, the French neo-fascist Maurice Bardèche argued that the single party, secret police and even the cult of the leader "are not necessarily fascist attributes"; "the famous fascist methods are constantly revised"; and, one day, fascism would be re-born "with another name, another face"[14]. In my debate with de Benoist[15], I argued that the ND worldview has similarities with some of the core aims of historical fascism, but it does not use open violence or invoke the same expansionist and annihilationist goals of some fascists of the past[16].

THE NOUVELLE DROITE: NEO-FASCISM WITH A HUMAN FACE

Politics with a human face was a part of a political program announced by Alexander Dubček of Czechoslovakia's Communist Party in April 1968. 'Socialism with a human face' was a reaction to the worldwide events in May of 1968, but also a criticism of dogmatic Soviet Communism. The Warsaw Pact invasion of Czechoslovakia on August 20–21, 1968 ended the hopes of 'socialism with a human face' and demonstrated the sheer brutality of the Soviet Union.

There are no tanks to stop de Benoist's 'neo-fascism with a human face'; he can operate freely through the dissemination of his works. He helped inspire other intellectuals through the ND, especially in Western Europe and later in Central and Eastern Europe and Russia. Interestingly, de Benoist's ND project began in 1968, the year of the Warsaw Pact invasion of Czechoslovakia and massive student and worker protests in France in May 1968. De Benoist and the ND were influenced by both events, insisting that a revolution is possible in advanced industrialized societies without using violence.[17] If we want to better understand de Benoist's 'neo-fascism with a human face', we must see through what Feldman and Jackson view as the "doublespeak" of the far right: its disdain for liberal democracy since 1945 and its attempts at "repackaging" contemporary ultra-nationalism in order to make it more palatable to a mainstream European audience.[18] This explains de Benoist's unusual intellectual evolution towards the left and New Left, his search for allies on the left and right and beyond, and his turn from open support for racism and colonialism in the 1960s to a radical embrace of cultural ethno-pluralism in the 1970s until today.[19]

The ND combined approaches from inter-war Conservative Revolution (CR), New Left (NL) and various other influences.[20] CR thinkers undoubtedly influenced the National Socialists.[21] The use of NL influences was designed to re-think the sterile legacy of fascism, reconstitute the right after the debacle of losing French Algeria, and win supporters in a cultural climate that was decidedly left-wing in the 1960s and 1970s. The ND saw itself as an intellectual vanguard in winning cultural hegemony from the liberal left. It differentiated itself from political parties and extra-parliamentary (or terrorist) movements on the radical right.

The ND is a complex phenomenon. In my work, *Rethinking the French New Right*[22], I proposed four interpretations of the ND: first, the ND as a neo-fascist movement created for anti-fascist times; second, a challenge to the traditional right-left political spectrum; third, a variant of alternative modernity within a broader modernist framework – i.e., ND thinkers seek revolutionary alternatives to liberal and socialist variants of modernity, rather than seeking to destroy all aspects of modernity – and, last, a species of the 'religion of politics' in the context of a more secular age. It is my claim that ND thinkers embody all four conceptual tools. The aim of *Rethinking the French New Right* was to move beyond the debates around the ND that related to neo-fascism and, instead, expand the ambit of possible interpretations of the ND.

DEBATE, PARTISANSHIP, OR TRUTH-SEEKING?

Here are some learning points from my debate with de Benoist, which highlight that the debate was simultaneously substantive, polemical and aimed at intellectual truth-seeking:

1. The battle of ideas matters. Revolutions are made by material factors, but likewise by the battle of ideas. Both Gramsci and de Benoist would agree: De Benoist's ND project has been dubbed "Gramscianism of the right"[23].
2. In a polemical debate, our message is distorted; there are opportunistic lies that are spread in order to discredit the researcher (e.g., de Benoist falsely claimed that I had not had any contact with him); and one is pinned with labels such as 'citizen of the world' or 'neo-fascist'[24]. I did not label de Benoist a 'neo-fascist' in order to discredit him, but to show historical continuity between his ideas and CR thinkers of the inter-war years, as well as the ND's exclusionary ethnic particularism and "multiculturalism of the right"[25].
3. Are we ever fully objective in an intellectual or political debate? We can try, but I doubt it. This debate reinforced this view. Yet, in my classes as a

lecturer and as a writer, I highlight and analyze a wide-range of perspectives and ideologies. We must ultimately think critically rather than be the slaves of any political camp.
4. De Benoist is intellectually brilliant, but also demeaning. When I noted in my response to de Benoist that the ND's 'anti-racist' stance echoes xenophobic political parties, de Benoist mocked me. De Benoist and ND writings must be analyzed in terms of what is said in their texts – their 'code words', such as "Indo-European" (instead of Aryan), "European culture" (instead of white), and "Judeo-Christian tradition" (instead of Jews) – what they often no longer write about (Jews, Zionism, support for conspicuous racism), and their, not too veiled, sarcasm that is directed at their supporters as much as at their opponents.[26]
5. I still hope to change the world, not merely Europe, which is also the case for de Benoist. I still believe in administrative equality, unlike de Benoist. I want to get rid of poverty and social injustice. I am for women's rights, not a club of old European men. He only wants to 'liberate' a part of humanity: 'original' European ethnic groups. He forgets that direct democracy is a scam when it excludes those who supposedly do not belong to the political community. He wants to use referenda in order to stop immigration, refugees and asylum-seekers, and even expel non-Europeans from Europe.

Conclusion

This paper sought to reconstruct an intellectual debate between myself and Alain de Benoist. I suggested that our debate contained elements of a substantive clash of irreconcilable ideals, polemical posturing and truth-seeking.

Despite the ND's fall from the media and intellectual spotlight in France, the ideas of the ND on immigration, national identity and the loss of national sovereignty are increasingly accepted by many Europeans. The question we might ask today is why the cultural climate has shifted so dramatically rightwards since 1968, the year that the ND was created. Is it the post-9/11 climate? The Paris terrorist attacks? The refugee crisis? The rise of radical right-wing political parties in the 1980s and, especially, 1990s? The co-optation of radical right-wing ideas by mainstream parties and through coalition governments? The dramatic decline of the radical left, as Slavoj Žižek[27] suggested? Problems of the EU? Capitalist globalization and its excesses? Is it the slow cultural change in mentalities engineered by the ND? Or the increasing orthodoxy of neoliberal or Anglo-American New Right solutions worldwide?

For the ND, the authentic right is neither neoliberal, nor republican. It is a right that harkens back to Europe's dark past, a right of homogeneous regions and nations, a right in which internal homogeneity will be achieved through cultural and legal means. We need to be aware that fascism, as Eco warned us, can return under the most innocent of disguises. Copsey writes that neo-fascism, including the ND as one such permutation, "represents a continual evolution of fascism away from its dominant inter-war manifestations"[28]. Sunshine argues that the ND aims at "rebranding fascism" using "sophisticated" left-wing critiques of society, and their goal is "to create a new form of fascism, with the same core values of a revitalized community that withstands the decadence of cosmopolitan liberal capitalism"[29]. Should the ND project be implemented, it would mean the end of liberal Europe.

Annotations

1 | Tamir Bar-On (2014): The French New Right: Neither Right, nor Left? In: Journal for the Study of Radicalism, 8/1, pp. 1-44.
2 | In English it means 'New Right', but the French name is used as an exception, as it is known internationally.
3 | Alain de Benoist (2014): Alain de Benoist Answers Tamir Bar-On. In: Journal for the Study of Radicalism, 8/1, pp. 141-168.
4 | Tamir Bar-On (2014): A Response to Alain de Benoist. In: Journal for the Study of Radicalism, 8/2, pp. 123-168.
5 | Alain de Benoist ([1977] 1979): Vu de Droite: Anthologie Critique des Idées Contemporaines [View from the Right: Critical Anthology of Contemporary Ideas]. Paris: Copernic, p. 16.
6 | Alain de Benoist (1995): End of the Left-Right Dichotomy: The French Case. In: Telos, No. 102 (Winter), pp. 73-90.
7 | Alain de Benoist (1979): Vu de Droite, p. 19.
8 | Pierre-André Taguieff (1994): Sur la Nouvelle Droite: Jalons d'une Analyse Critique [About the Nouvelle Droite: Yardstick of a Critical Analysis]. Paris: Descartes et Cie; Pierre-André Taguieff (1994): The New Right's View of European Identity. In: Telos, No. 98/9 (Winter-Spring), pp. 34-54; unknown Author (1994): Origins and Metamorphoses of the New Right: An Interview with Pierre-André Taguieff. In: Telos, No. 98-99 (Winter-Spring), pp. 159-172.
9 | Pierre-André Taguieff (1990): The New Cultural Racism in France. In: Telos, No. 83, pp. 109-122; unknown Author (1994): An Interview with Pierre-André Taguieff, pp. 159-172.
10 | Umberto Eco (1995): Eternal Fascism: Fourteen Ways of Looking at a Blackshirt. In: New York Review of Books, 42/11, p. 15.
11 | Ibid.
12 | Ibid.
13 | Primo Levi (1986): Primo Levi's Heartbreaking, Heroic Answers to the Most Common Questions He Was Asked About 'Survival in Auschwitz'. In: New Republic,

February 16, (https://newrepublic.com/article/119959/interview-primo-levi-survival-auschwitz), accessed June 23, 2016.
14 | Maurice Bardèche (1961): Qu'est-ce que le Fascisme? [What Is Fascism?]. Paris: Les Sept Couleurs, pp. 175-176.
15 | Tamir Bar-On (2014): A Response to Alain de Benoist.
16 | Using the definition of Stanley Payne [(1995): A History of Fascism: 1914-1945, London: UCL Press, p. 7], I identified 12 similar characteristics: 1. Antiliberalism 2. Anticommunism 3. Anticonservatism 4. An attempt to create a new, modern, self-determined and secular culture 5. A highly regulated, multiclass and integrated national economic structure. 6. An economic framework that uses the state to restrain capitalism, banks and multinational corporations 7. A desire for nationalist (or regionalist) states 8. The goal of empire 9. The desire for European grandeur in the geopolitical realm 10. A positive evaluation of authors that legitimize violence, such as Carl Schmitt and Julius Evola 11. A stress on the emotional and mystical aspects of life, including traditions, Indo-European symbols and primordial ties to the region, nation or Europe 12. An organic view of society and extreme stress on the masculine principle.
17 | Alain de Benoist (1979): Les Idées à l'Endroit [The Ideas Are in Place]. Paris: Libres-Hallier, pp. 258-259.
18 | Matthew Feldman/Paul Jackson (2014): Introduction. In: Matthew Feldman/Paul Jackson (eds.): Doublespeak: The Rhetoric of the Far Right Since 1945. Stuttgart: Ibidem Press, p. 23.
19 | Tamir Bar-On (2007): Where Have All the Fascists Gone?, Aldershot: Ashgate; Tamir Bar-On (2013): Rethinking the French New Right: Alternatives to Modernity. Abingdon: Routledge.
20 | Tamir Bar-On (2007): Where Have All The Fascists Gone?, pp. 9-10; Tamir Bar-On (2013): Rethinking the French New Right, pp. 10-11.
21 | Jeffrey Herf (2002): Reactionary Modernism: Technology, Culture, and Politics in Weimar and the Third Reich, Cambridge: Cambridge University Press; Roger Woods (1996): The Conservative Revolution in the Weimar Republic. New York: St. Martin's Press.
22 | Tamir Bar-On (2013): Rethinking the French New Right, p. 1.
23 | Antonio Gramsci (1982): Selections from the Prison Notebooks, London: Lawrence and Wishart; Rob van Craenenburg (1998): Whose Gramsci? Right-Wing Gramscism. In: International Gramsci Society Newsletter, No. 9 (March), pp. 14-18, (http://www.internationalgramscisociety.org/igsn/articles/a09_5.shtml), accessed July 8, 2016.
24 | Arthur Versluis/Alain de Benoist (2014): A Conversation with Alain de Benoist. In: Journal for the Study of Radicalism, 8/2, p. 102; Tamir Bar-On (2014): A Response to Alain de Benoist, p. 128.
25 | Alberto Spektorowski (2012): The French New Right: Multiculturalism of the Right and the Recognition-Exclusionism Syndrome. In: Journal of Global Ethics, 8/1, pp. 41-61.
26 | Tamir Bar-On (2014): A Response to Alain de Benoist, pp. 125-126.

27 | Slavoj Žižek (2000): Why We All Love to Hate Haider. In: New Left Review, No. 2 (March-April), (https://newleftreview.org/II/2/slavoj-zizek-why-we-all-love-to-hate-haider), accessed June 24, 2016.

28 | Nigel Copsey (2013): Fascism... But with an Open Mind: Reflections on the Contemporary Far Right in (Western) Europe, First Lecture on Fascism by Institute for War, Holocaust and Genocide Studies (NIOD), Amsterdam, April 25. In: Fascism: Journal of Comparative Fascist Studies, 2/1, p. 16.

29 | Spencer Sunshine (2008): Rebranding Fascism: National Anarchists. In: PublicEye, 23/4, p. 5, (http://www.publiceye.org/magazine/v23n4/rebranding_fascism.html), accessed June 24, 2016.

Black Sheep in a Far-Right Zoo?
Fethullah Gülen's Strategy of 'Non-Violence'

Laura Lotte Laloire

As if to support Charles Tilly's aphorism, in the Turkish far right, "political violence occurs when actors have few opportunities[1], yet enough resources to mobilize for violence"[2]. Already since the summer of 2015, the killing of civilians and demolition of entire towns has re-intensified in the majority Kurdish-populated south-east[3]. After the attempted coup d'état on July 15, 2016, this violence and emergency rule have also been extended throughout the rest of Turkey[4]. President Recep Tayyip Erdoğan and his autocratic measures are perhaps the most severe but far from being "Turkey's only problem"[5]: indeed, large parts of a nationalistic-minded population and various organized groups have supported these developments up to now and have always employed violence, an archetypal tool in the far right's repertoire. The ultra-nationalist *Grey Wolves*[6], youth gangs such as the *Ottoman Hearth*[7] and *Alperen Hearth*[8], and Islamist street fighters called *Lions of Allah*[9] are all elements of the so-called 'three-legged' Turkish right. This is "composed of the center-right, nationalists, and Islamists"[10] who all accord to the broad definition of the *far* right in this volume: they base their

"ideology and action on the notion of inequality among human beings, combining the supremacy of a particular nation, 'race' or 'civilization' with ambitions for an authoritarian transformation of values and styles of government"[11].

Another actor that fulfills these criteria is the *Gülen Movement* (GM)[12], which has recently garnered a great deal of attention. Except for, as yet unproven, allegations by President Erdoğan[13], this group has hardly been suspected of actively employing violence. The Western media, in particular, has been portraying the GM as a victim of the Turkish government's repressive measures[14]. However, it shares most of the ideological ingredients that pave the way for violence carried out by the groups mentioned above and is rooted in the same era. Taking ideology as well as the historical context as important preconditions for a long-term analysis, this chapter asks how we might explain the GM's development over the decades and its apparently exceptional relationship with violence?[15]

ONE LITTER: NATIONALISM AND ISLAMISM IN TURKEY

The Gülen Movement, originating in Turkey in 1968, was founded by the Sufi[16]-inspired, Sunni Muslim preacher Fethullah Gülen. The external perception of it being a predominantly religious movement – referred to as *Hizmet*[17] by adherents and as *Cemaat*[18] by the broader Turkish-speaking public – corresponds to the image that its official statements[19] aim to convey. Nevertheless, it should be noted that Fethullah Gülen's conservative interpretation of Islam is inextricably linked with Turkish nationalism: having grown up in a political climate dominated by nationalism, he frequently claimed a "superiority of the Turkish culture"[20]. A quote from 1997 illustrates his ideology of Turanism (also Pan-Turkism) quite clearly:

"Turkey [...] today encompasses 60 million. Together with the Turks in Central Asia it is 120-130 million. If it manages to break down the Chinese wall and to unite with the Turks there, it will be 300 million."[21]

Directly derived from his ultra-nationalist ideology – typical for a Pan-Turkist – Fethullah Gülen had directed his hate "against Kurds, Jews, women, and dissident thinkers"[22]. Furthermore, he had announced a "struggle against communism, atheism, and evolutionary theory"[23]. Scholars on the far right call these rather plain rhetorical moves "scapegoating", "vilification and demonization"[24], important (socio-)psychological preconditions on the path to violence. Another element of GM's ideology used to be the rejection of "Westernization and all connected social norms or lifestyles [...] dooming all westernizers in the country"[25].

These roots exhibit strong parallels to those of the violent group *Grey Wolves*, founded in the same time (1961). Both movements combine nationalism with an Islamic identity; slight shifts in emphasis either towards Islam or the nation usually depend on the target audience (urban/rural, educated/uneducated, young/old, etc.). In a historically so-called secular state, the generally strong bind between Islam and politics may seem contradictory but has been a central ingredient of Turkish politics since the founding of the Republic in 1923[26]. With the "Turkish-Islamic synthesis"[27] in the 1970s, at the very latest, this conjunction has become a central paradigm and strategy of the Turkish (far) right.

Non-Violent Black Sheep? Gülen's Herding Strategy

In this context, Gülen's recipe for success has been to mobilize the masses through preaching, despite occasional repression by the government. Starting as a one-man show, strongly based on Fethullah Gülen's charisma, it attained a bottom-up dynamic and finally achieved social hegemony[28]: Gülen managed to politically mobilize listeners in a very receptive, pious society, fed up with the so-called secular elites and hungry for a share of Turkey's wealth. This civil society-oriented approach – partly borne out of the structural constraint of a ban on Islamist political parties and partly just a clever strategic choice by Gülen – can be considered the first pivotal step towards unleashing a process of path-dependent development. In fact, his adherents today account for at least 10 to 15 percent of the Turkish population[29]. They comprise the largest Islamic group not organized by the state and, for some authors, constitute the very reason why a civil society exists in the country at all[30].

The GM reproduces a specific moral consensus, such as through educational institutes that have a high social and cultural impact in Turkey, where private funds are indispensable for university admission. In so-called 'light houses' *(ışık evleri)*, hierarchically organized student dormitories, obedience to God is merged with a strong respect for the worldly shepherd, Fethullah Gülen. By way of very persistent networking, Gülen gradually managed to establish closer economic ties with and among Turkey's conservative Muslim entrepreneurs. In so doing, he has accumulated an enormous amount of capital: this ranges from Gülen-owned newspapers, such as *Zaman*[31], *Today's Zaman* or *Aksiyon*, to TV stations, such as *Samanyolu*, the *World Media Group*, and even entire trade associations, such as *TUSKON*. This has created direct and indirect dependencies on the network, structures and dynamics resembling that of a 'sect'[32].

Having said this, however, a close look at the GM's past reveals that violence has likewise been part of its repertoire. As he rather convolutedly admits on his website, in 1963, Gülen co-founded a *Club for the Combat of Communism*[33] together with far-right militants. In plain terms, this merely constituted a professional organization which attacked left-wing youth on the streets. Moreover, in 1991, he indirectly donated 3.5 billion Turkish lira to the *Grey Wolves*, thus financing a violent group[34]. Apart from this instrumental dimension of violence, Gülen also rhetorically identifies himself with this violent group, such as when expressing his condolences for the late Member of Parliament, Muhsin Yazıcıoğlu, a former member of this group[35]. In an aesthetic dimension, Gülen's language contains countless allusions to violence: he addresses his followers as "soldiers" or "recruits", and emphasizes "our Jihad is education"[36].

Spotted in Black and White: A Movement Rife with Contradictions

Contradictions inherent in the movement – such as between tradition and modernity, hierarchy and network, or Islam and secularism – became even more glaring during a turn in the 1990s, which I consider to be a "strategic opening"[37]. Very popular among the far right, the tool of "double speak"[38] has since been employed in particular, which means that official 'front stage' and inofficial 'back stage' rhetoric widely differs. In the case of GM, only one side of the coin has particularly been stressed: 'open-mindedness', 'modernity' and 'tolerance'. In official documents, Gülenists have explicitly distanced themselves from violence and aped the language of 'Western' liberal democracy (unlike the *Grey Wolves*, incidentally)[39]. This "strategic de-radicalization"[40], Fethullah Gülen's attempt at appearing 'normal' to the public, strongly resembles European far-right actors that employ a strategy of normalization and are currently flourishing (the German AfD[41], the Austrian FPÖ[42], etc.). The reasons for this strategic change of the GM can be put into three different perspectives:

First, the Turkish Left was largely demobilized and exhausted on account of the military coup of 1980 and the global demise of communism. The Turkish state had done most of the repression on its own, and Gülen's openly violent troops, such as of the *Club for the Combat of Communism*, were left without much to fight against. Second, after the 1980 military coup, Gülenists suddenly found themselves under broader persecution by the Turkish state than ever before. Facing the threat of isolation, and due to the realization that globalization/Westernization cannot be stopped, Gülen, unlike other Islamists, decided to embrace this development as an opportunity. From a cultural viewpoint, Bozay argues that, paradoxically, Gülen assumed the movement could only maintain its Islamic identity by opening up[43]. Third, and from a more materialist view, others claim that altered mid-term goals within Gülen's class base were the reason behind this 'opening' process. Formerly a project of an excluded Anatolian middle class, this group had, by then, become the ruling elite of the country, or, at least, an important part of it. The accumulated capital needed to be reinvested but this could not be easily achieved with an ideology confined to the cultural and geographical borders of Turkey. As such, the new strategy has meant that, in order to attract international economic contacts, dialogue and exchange, the GM has been forced to cast its net beyond its own adored nation-state. Ever since, Fethullah Gülen – who himself has since lived in the USA, allegedly to receive better health care – has put a great deal of effort into spreading the GM transnationally.

In spite of this development, the GM had also infiltrated state authorities, especially the judiciary and police[44], which is an unobtrusive, yet effective sphere of political violence. An example here is the carefully planned and systematically conducted killing of the Armenian journalist Hrant Dink in 2007, which several authorities had been informed about in advance[45]. Among others, also Gülenists positioned in state authorities and the police have supported or at least tolerated the murder that was ultimately conducted and professed by a member of the *Alperen Hearth*. From the 1970s onwards, Fethullah Gülen secretly told his members to wait for the right moment "to reach the switching points of power without attracting attention"[46]. Due to Turkey's peculiar situation of hosting a very complicated and dense network of state elites, secret service, military, judiciary, criminals and far right – often referred to as a 'deep state' – it is difficult to assess how exactly Gülen instrumentalized these institutions for his ends[47]. It is, however, clear that the GM has had particular success using an officially non-violent repertoire of action. At the same time, these achievements should be evaluated against the backdrop of a division of labor between the mass movement and more openly militant organizations, such as the *Grey Wolves*, who created an atmosphere conducive for Gülen's 'politics' to resonate. At least until 2013, their ideology and the function that both movements had fulfilled for state and economic elites were similar, only differing in their strategic paths.

A MODERN KING OF THE JUNGLE

To conclude, the movement's relationship with violence can only fully be grasped if structural and historical conditions are taken into account, while acknowledging the relative agency of its leader. His achievement of officially disassociating the movement from violence (strategic de-radicalization), while concurrently relying on indirect and state channels, went hand in hand with a 'strategic opening' to 'modernity'. The effort to maintain its identity despite state repression in the 1980s ironically led to the 'modernizing' of Gülen's entire movement, which owed to processes of diffusion, such as by way of intensified interactions and experiences with 'the West'. Further investigation is needed into the extent to which this strategic decision, which guaranteed organizational survival, has transformed Gülen's ideology to its core over the years.

Critical observers are convinced that a leopard cannot change its spots, and the GM's ideology has remained 'anti-Western' and 'anti-modern' since he still advocates a conservative form of Islam and even compliance with *sharia* regulations[48]. However, the GM's Islamism is, at the same time, inherently modern: not only the fact that initial anti-Western slogans have disappeared, indicates an ideological adjustment, a modernization. Some may eventually regard the movement as harmless since it is not as 'anti-Western' as other Islamist groups. Based on the analysis above, however, it is reasonable to conceive of the GM as a threat to a pluralistic society, also outside of Turkey. For once, the self-portrayal of this Janus-faced movement does not amount to whitewashing: it is indeed a modern movement; and as is typical of modern projects, it officially condemns violence while relying on it behind the scenes.

Annotations

1 | "Few opportunities" means that before the coup attempt in July 2016, President Recep Tayyip Erdoğan had found himself in a stalemate and the Turkish state has been in crisis, marked by: a declining economy, a left and pro-Kurdish opposition party attaining the 10 percent threshold in the parliamentary elections of 2015 – endangering the introduction of a presidential system –, foreign relations at rock bottom, Western criticism for tolerating ISIS, and allegations of corruption.
2 | Cf. Charles Tilly (1978): From Mobilization to Revolution. New York: McGraw-Hill.
3 | Tom Stevenson (2016): Im Belagerungszustand: Militäreinsatz gegen die PKK im Südosten der Türkei [In State of Occupation: Military Operation against PKK in the South-East of Turkey], February 4, (https://de.qantara.de/node/22631), accessed July 1, 2016.
4 | Deniz Yücel (2016): "Der eigentliche Putsch beginnt erst jetzt" ["The Actual Coup is Only Starting Now]. In: Die Welt, July 16 (http://www.welt.de/politik/ausland/article 157090810/Der-eigentliche-Putsch-beginnt-jetzt-erst.html), accessed July 16, 2016.
5 | "The outsize personality of President Erdoğan obscures the systemic dynamics that sustain his exercise of power. [...] The main opposition party, the Republican People's Party (CHP), rails against the government, not because Kurdish cities are laid to rubble, but because it waited too long with allowing the military to take action.", Halil Karaveli (2016): Is Erdoğan Turkey's Only Problem? April 5, (http://www.turkeyanalyst.org/publications/turkey-analyst-articles/item/528-is-erdoğan-turkey's-only-problem?.html), accessed June 30, 2016.
6 | The *Grey Wolves* are also called Ülkücü or *Idealists* and used to be considered the *Nationalist Movement Party's* (*Milliyetçi Hareket Partisi* – MHP) youth organization or armed wing. Under its leader, Devlet Bahçeli, MHP has tended to deny them, trying to gain a more statesman-like reputation, see e. g. Tanıl Bora (1991): Der "Nationale Reflex": Die fundamentalistische Disposition des Nationalen in der Türkei und der proto-faschistische Nationalismus der MHP [The "National Reflex": Fundamentalist Dispositions of the National in Turkey and the Proto-Fascist Nationalism of MHP]. In: Sociologus, 51/1-2, pp. 123-139.
7 | Nikolaus Brauns (2015): Erdoğans Bürgerkriegstruppe [Erdoğan's Civil War Corps]. In: Junge Welt, September 22, (http://kurdistan.blogsport.de/2015/09/22/erdogans-buergerkriegstruppe/), accessed March 13, 2016.

8 | Original name in Turkish: *Alperen Ocakları*. The youth organization of the fascist *Great Unity Party (Büyük Birlik Partisi* – BBP) is one of the most violent far-right groups in Turkey.
9 | The Arabic name is *Esedullah Timleri*, see Orhan Kemal Cengiz (2015): Who are 'Allah's lions'? (translation by Sibel Utku Bila). In: Al Monitor, September 15, (http://www.al-monitor.com/pulse/originals/2015/11/turkey-pkk-clashes-who-are-terrorizing-kurds.html#ixzz43YbihUMg), see also Cihan Başakçıoğlu (2015): Teşkilat-ı Mahsusa'dan Esedullah Timi'ne devlet aklı: Kontrgerilla [The Esedullah Team And The History Of State-Directed Mass Violence In Kurdistan]. In: Özgür Gündem, English version available at: https://rojavareport.wordpress.com/2015/12/05/the-esedullah-team-and-the-history-of-state-directed-mass-violence-in-turkey/, both accessed June 26, 2016.
10 | E. Burak Arıkan (2002): Turkish Ultra-Nationalists under Review: A Study of the Nationalist Action Party. In: Nations and Nationalism, 8/1, p. 361; see also Tanıl Bora (1998): Türk Sağının Üç Hali: Milliyetçilik – Muhafazarkarlık – İslamcılık [Three States of the Turkish Right: Nationalism – Conservatism – Islamism], 2nd edn. Birikim: İstanbul.
11 | See Maik Fielitz/Lotte Laloire in this volume.
12 | For Fethullah Gülen and his adherents different labels circulate: movement, sect, network, etc., which will be used interchangeably in this text.
13 | Up until their falling out in around 2013, Gülen was an ally of Recep Tayyip Erdoğan and his movement was the 'soft-power instrument' of the ruling *Justice and Development Party*, original name in Turkish: *Adalet ve Kalkınma Partisi* (AKP).
14 | See e. g. Frank Nordhausen (2016): Erdogan attackiert Gülen-Bewegung [Erdoğan Attacking the Gülen Movement]. In: Frankfurter Rundschau, March 5, (http://www.fr-online.de/tuerkei/tuerkei-erdogan-attackiert-guelen-bewegung,23356680,30040938.html), accessed June 27, 2016.
15 | This text was already completed prior to the attempted coup on July 15, 2016 and aims to provide a long-term analysis of the GM.
16 | 'Sufism' is an umbrella term for currents in Islam that emphazise the inner mystical dimension of it and often feature ascetic tendencies.
17 | This means 'service' in English.
18 | This means '(religious) community' in English.
19 | Guelen-Bewegung.de (2014): Ist Hizmet eine politische Bewegung? [Is Hizmet a Political Movement?], January 23, (http://www.guelen-bewegung.de/ist-hizmet-eine-politische-bewegung/), accessed July 3, 2016.
20 | Fethullah Gülen according to Günter Seufert (2013): Überdehnt sich die Bewegung von Fethullah Gülen? Eine türkische Religionsgemeinde als nationaler und internationaler Akteur. Berlin: SWP, p. 14.
21 | Fethullah Gülen according to Kemal Bozay/Fikret Aslan (eds.) (2012): Graue Wölfe heulen wieder: Türkische Faschisten und ihre Vernetzung in Deutschland [Grey Wolves Are Howling Again: Turkish Fascists and Their Network in Germany], 3rd edn. Münster: Unrast, p. 211.

22 | Ibid.
23 | Nikolaus Brauns (2009): Dritte Kraft in der Türkei [Third Force in Turkey]. In: Junge Welt, June 19, (http://www.nikolaus-brauns.de/Fethullah_Gulen.htm), accessed June 26, 2016.
24 | Chip Berlet 2014: Heroes Know which Villains to Kill: How Coded Rhetoric Incites Scripted Violence. In: Matthew Feldman/Paul Jackson (eds.): Doublespeak: The Rhetoric of the Far Right since 1945. Stuttgart: Ibidem, pp. 314, 316.
25 | Seufert (2013): Gülen, p. 7.
26 | Presidency of Religious Affairs (Diyanet) (n. d.): Establishment and a Brief History, (http://www.diyanet.gov.tr/en/kategori/kurumsal/1), accessed July 1, 2016.
27 | See Ünal Bilir (2004): Der Türkische Islam als politisches und religiöses Weltbild in seinem historischen Kontext von der II. Mesrûtiyyet-Periode bis zur Gegenwart [Turkish Islam as Political and Religious Philosophy in its Context from the Mesrûtiyyet Period up to the Present]. Hamburg: University Hamburg, pp. 41–69, (http://ediss.sub.uni-hamburg.de/volltexte/2005/2311/pdf/05_Kapitel2.pdf), accessed June 26, 2016.
28 | See Joshua D. Hendrick (2009): Globalization, Islamic Activism, and Passive Revolution in Turkey: The Case of Fethullah Gülen. In: Journal of Power, 2/3, pp. 343–368.
29 | Helen R. Ebaugh (2009): The Gülen Movement: A Sociological Analysis of a Civic Movement Rooted in Moderate Islam. Heidelberg, London, New York: Springer, pp. 4, 46.
30 | See Hakan M. Yavuz (2015): Toward an Islamic Enlightenment: The Gülen Movement. New York: Oxford University Press.
31 | At the time of this volume's publication, however, the newspaper has come under the control of the AKP government and President Erdoğan.
32 | Friedmann Eißler (2015): Die Gülen-Bewegung (Hizmet): Herkunft, Strukturen, Ziele, Erfahrungen [The Gülen Movement (Hizmet): Origins, Structures, Goals, Experiences]. In: EZW, No. 238, p. 4.
33 | See Nikolaus Brauns (2013): Der Puppenspieler [The Puppet Master]. In: Junge Welt, January 31, a copy is available at: http://www.ag-friedensforschung.de/regionen/Tuerkei1/guelen.html, accessed May 23, 2016.
34 | See Bozay/Aslan (2012): Grey Wolves.
35 | Bozay/Aslan (2012): Grey Wolves, p. 215.
36 | Guelen-Bewegung.de (2014): Unser Dschihad ist die Bildung [Our Jihad is Education], January 24, (http://www.guelen-bewegung.de/p99/), accessed July 3, 2016.
37 | Inspired by Bozay and Aslan's observation of the movement's 'opening' or 'modernization' process (Bozay/Aslan (2012): Grey Wolves, p. 216).
38 | See Feldmann/Jackson (2014): Doublespeak.
39 | Fethullah Gülen (2012): Violent Responses Are Not in the Tradition of the Prophet. In: Financial Times, September 27, a copy is available at: http://fgulen.com/de/homepage/887-fgulen-com-deutsch/presseraum/autoren/33291-gewalt-ist-nicht-in-der-tradition-des-propheten, accessed July 21, 2016.

40 | Anton Shekhovtsov (2015): How the European far right became mainstream: Strategic 'Deradicalization' Is the Key to Winning Euroskeptic Votes. In: Politico, April 22, (http://www.politico.eu/article/euroskeptics-far-right-became-mainstream/), accessed June 26, 2016.
41 | See also Holger Marcks in this volume.
42 | See also Bernhard Weidinger in this volume.
43 | Bozay/Aslan (2012): Grey Wolves, p. 214–215.
44 | Most prominently revealed by Ahmet Şık (2011): İmamın Ordusu [The Imam's Army], released as (ed. version): 000Kitap [000Book]. Istanbul: Postacı; see also Rachel Sharon-Krespin (2009): Fethullah Gülen's Grand Ambition Turkey's Islamist Danger. In: Middle East Quarterly, 16/1, pp. 55–66.
45 | See Brauns (2013): The Puppet Master.
46 | Bozay/Aslan (2012): Grey Wolves, p. 214, according to: Kozmopolit (2003): German-Turkish Online Magazine, No. 9.
47 | President Erdoğan had been unveiling proof of this in court proceedings against the GM, which he had labeled as "Fethullahist Terrorist Organization (FETÖ)" already before the coup attempt. One charge is, for example, that Gülen tried to checkmate adversaries such as the small religious Tahşiye movement in a "plot by police officers and prosecutors linked to the Gülen Movement", both quotes derived from: Daily Sabah (2016): Fethullah Gülen No-Show at His First Trial in Turkey. In: Daily Sabah, December 22, (http://www.dailysabah.com/investigations/2015/12/23/fethullah-gulen-no-show-at-his-first-trial-in-turkey), accessed July 3, 2016. As these sorts of trials are part of a rat race between the former party comrades, of course, information presented therein will have to be considered with caution.
48 | See Friedmann Eißler (2010): Für die Scharia: Die Gülen-Bewegung gibt sich modern – und ist antiwestlich eingestellt [In favor of Sharia: The Gülen Movement Pretends to Be Modern – and Is Opposed to the West]. In: Zeitzeichen, July, pp. 20–22, (http://www.diakonierwl.de/cms/media/pdf/publikationen/newsletter/migration_und_flucht/5-Eissler-Fuer_die_Scharia.pdf), accessed June 26, 2016.

Women and their Rights in the Nationalists' Strategies
Abortion as a Contentious Issue in the Polish 'Culture War'

Halina Gąsiorowska

In Poland, the long-lasting 'culture war'[1] over gender roles and religion is often linked to Samuel Huntington's concept of the *Clash of Civilizations*[2] in far-right discourse. The well-known juxtaposition used in far-right propaganda of "civilization/culture of life versus civilization/culture of death", which is used in reference to anti-abortion and pro-choice movements, respectively, has been extended to Christians and Muslims. For example, one of the internet memes published by the anti-abortion *Foundation PRO – the Right to Life* (Foundation PRO)[3] as well as by the *National Organization of Women* (NOK)[4] on their Facebook sites depicts doctors performing abortion and Muslims as killers. The meme includes the following 'information': "Islamists killed 128 French people on November 13, 2015. Doctors performing abortion kill 600 of them every day"[5]. The picture alludes to the concept of a "culture of death"[6], connecting abortion, terrorism and Islam. Although Polish nationalists rarely talk about abortion at their anti-immigration rallies, or express Islamophobia at anti-abortion pickets, the two issues are vital for the far right in Poland and remain at the center of the conflict over 'modernity' in the country.

In Europe, the far right has instigated moral panic propelled by a fear of terrorism, and points to Muslims as a threat to 'European' liberties, especially women's and LGBTQ[7] rights. The assaults on women celebrating New Year's Eve 2015 on the streets of Cologne, serve *Patriotic Europeans Against the Islamization of the Occident* (PEGIDA)[8] and many other nationalist organizations in Europe as a proof of an allegedly negative 'Arab attitude' towards 'Western' expressions of femininity[9]. This argument in the anti-immigration discourse of the far right is well-grounded in the nationalists' ideal of a strong man defending 'his' woman. Although the task might be understood literally, in the context of the assaults in Cologne, protecting wives, mothers, sisters and daughters of the nation has a broader symbolic meaning. Scholars interested in the relationship between gender and nation state that, in nationalists discourse, women symbolize the nation and are the bearers of its values.[10] Within Islamophobic discourse, female citizens of Europe signify Europeans' equality and freedom.

It is self-evident that nationalists perceive a woman as a mother who plays a vital role in reproducing the nation as well as its culture, encouraging women to bear more children – mainly in order for (Christian) Europeans to outnumber Muslims. Although more of 'our own' children are wanted, restricting abortion is not the priority of today's nationalist parties and organizations in Western Europe. In fact, Marine Le Pen, leader of the French *Front National*[11], supports abortion on demand until the 22nd week of pregnancy;[12] and most European far-right actors do not seek to ban abortion completely. The European far right focuses on fighting what they label the 'Islamization of Europe' by protesting against immigrants and refugees and opposing multiculturalism on various levels.

In Poland, which still is a supposedly homogenous society, nationalists have started organizing anti-refugee demonstrations and, at the same time, continue their struggle to delegalize abortion; in fact, anti-abortion organizations supported by far-right women have just launched yet another campaign. This action indicates the importance of the law regulating abortions for shaping the national character of the Poles. Polish nationalists perceive Catholicism as its defining component; according to their worldview, one cannot be really Polish if one is not Catholic and does not follow the commandments of the Catholic Church. As such, the far right believes that, since the Church views abortion as a sin and akin to murder, it should not be legal in Poland.[13]

THE RECENT BATTLE OVER ABORTION

In April 2016, the anti-abortion organizations *Ordo Iuris Institute for Legal Culture* (Ordo Iuris)[14] and the *Foundation PRO* drafted a bill, which, if enacted, would ban abortion in Poland almost without exception. The current law allows for abortion if the pregnancy poses a danger to the life or health of the prospective mother, if it results from rape or incest, or if the fetus is malformed[15]. A person who performs or helps perform an illegal abortion can be sentenced to three years in prison.[16]

The authors of the proposal only accept the termination of pregnancy if it is the result of a doctor's attempt to save the pregnant woman's life. However, the draft also introduces longer prison sentences (of up to 10 years) for those who perform abortions against the pregnant woman's will, and a five-year sentence if she asks for help with terminating her pregnancy. The threat of such penalties would effectively discourage specialists from undertaking a medical treatment that could result in the termination of a pregnancy. According to the draft, a pregnant woman who performs an abortion herself could also be sentenced to three months to five years of imprisonment, though a court could refrain from ordering such punishment. A woman who is raped or one who has a malformed fetus would be forced to carry and bear the child.[17]

The draft was discussed in the media and many right-wing politicians, including Prime Minister Beata Szydło, expressed their support for the delegalization of abortion. Protests against the planned restriction of women's rights were organized by a coalition of feminist groups and organizations titled *Coalition Reclaim Choice*[18]. The grassroots women's social media initiative, *Gals for Gals*,[19] was partially responsible for the large turnout at a demonstration held in front of the Parliament of Poland on April 9, 2016, organized by the *Coalition Reclaim Choice*. The protests included several demonstrations and sending clothes hangers (as the symbol of illegal abortion) to the Prime Minister. As a result of this, far-right politicians began mitigating their initial statements. The *Foundation PRO* keeps collecting signatures, while pro-choice activists supported by left-wing political parties have answered with a draft which would introduce abortion on demand; this entails the *Stop abortion*[20] committee battling the *Women Rescue*[21] committee for signatures.

Although anti-abortion organizations do not necessarily need to be nationalist, *Foundation Pro* in Poland has been supported by female activists of the *National Movement* (RN)[22] for many years. For example, female nationalist activists used to help *Foundation PRO* create anti-abortion exhibitions. Men and women from organization such as *All-Polish Youth* (MW)[23] and the *National Radical Camp* (ONR)[24] formed anti-abortion pickets along the planned route of *Manifa* – the name of feminist demonstrations organized in many Polish cities on International Women's Day. The growing number of women in the far-right movement drew media attention a few years ago: in 2012, several of them were featured in the women's magazine *Wysokie Obcasy*[25], owned by the influential liberal daily, *Gazeta Wyborcza*.

NATIONALIST WOMEN ON THE FRONT LINES

In 2013, *National Movement Women's Section* (RN-SK)[26] and the organization *Women for the Nation* (KDK)[27] were founded. Their activists, mostly comprised of young women in their early 20s, continued their previous activism in the field of promoting a traditional role for women as mothers along with anti-abortion and anti-feminist propaganda. Two of their actions, aimed at confronting feminists, made it into mainstream news. *Women for the Nation* came to *Manifa* with an anti-abortion banner; after being asked to leave the demonstration, they accused its organizers of discrimination and intolerance against women who have a different worldview[28]. The *Women's Section* of the RN has employed a similar strategy, appearing at the Congress of Women, where they started collecting signatures for the delegalization of abortion.[29] In both instances, the anti-feminists claimed that they felt invited to the events as women and were surprised by the hostility of feminists and their lack of tolerance.[30] Anna Holocher – leader of the *Women's Section* at the time – called feminists "femi-Nazis"[31] in an interview she gave in the aftermath of their actions at the Congress of Women.

These actions could be understood as an element of a broader strategy by the nationalists aimed at changing their negative public image as racists, neo-Nazis, fascists or hooligans prone to physical violence, attacking people and causing damage on the streets. The negative image was reinforced by the nationalists' behavior during their Independence March on November 11, 2011 in Warsaw. That day, some of the participants at the demonstration damaged the Constitution Square in Warsaw, burned a car belonging to the TVN television station, and engaged in fights with police.[32] Two years later, participants of the March attacked the Przychodnia Squat located in the center of Warsaw, breaking windows in the building and burning cars parked in the backyard.[33] Holocher, using the label "femi-Nazis",[34] attempted to overturn the accusations of intolerance, brutality and murderous intentions. The struggle carried out by the women to create a positive image for the RN is exemplified by commercials, ads and some of the banners they produced.

In one of the videos advertising their organization and the RN, far-right women rhetorically ask if a viewer believes the mainstream media, which present nationalists as hooligans and barbarians, and which would like to introduce a "Catholic *sharia*" in Poland[35]. The women themselves serve as an answer to the question: appearing feminine and innocent with their make-up, high heels and short skirts adorned in folk patterns. The young women were meant to attract new members to the national movement and promote the nationalist and anti-feminist 'lady' as model of femininity.[36]

The 'ladies' manifested their attachment to motherhood and anti-abortion views during "In the Name of Ladies"[37] pickets and a "Ladies Walks" that they organized to celebrate International Women's Day. In pictures taken at the event, participants held banners that read: "I know the worth of my sex"[38] or "St. Mary – the masterpiece of femininity"[39]. The slogans reflect the nationalists' belief that men and women have discrete tasks to perform as part of their destiny, that of the female being motherhood. In this system of beliefs, abortion contradicts the natural order; moreover, abortion not only threatens the constitution of a woman as a mother, but also Polish culture. The 'ladies', in some of their speeches, claim to embody 'real' Polish women, in contrast to feminists; nationalists perceive abortion as an anti-Polish (anti-Catholic) act. When explaining the neologism: "femi-Nazis", Holocher stresses that it was the National Socialists who allowed Polish women to have abortions[40]; (Polish) nationalists like to compare abortions to the Holocaust.

ARE WOMEN IN THE NATIONAL MOVEMENT TREATED INSTRUMENTALLY?

Nationalist women and their organizations have been criticized for mainly serving as a propaganda tool for the hard-core members of the RN. Some journalists have suggested that young women in far-right organizations are exploited by older men.[41] Nevertheless, the use of women as symbols in marketing is nothing unusual; in *Pretty Radical: A Young Woman's Journey into the Heart of Poland's Far Right*[42], the recent documentary by *The Guardian*, a male member of the ONR openly admits that 19-year-old Paulina was chosen to run as the candidate of the organization in local elections in Wocławek in order to soften and warm its image. Paulina claims to accept her role.

Moreover, some of the decisions made by nationalist women show that they are active agents in their movement. For instance *Women for the Nation* in Bielsko-Biała dissolved their organization in 2013, rejecting the male leadership that the RN had attempted to impose on them.[43] Last year, the *Women's Section* seceded from the RN and set up a separate organization, the *National Organization of Women*. However, the secession could also be interpreted as part of the rivalry between two main fractions of the ONR and the MW.

Regardless of their actual level of independence, the nationalist women, just like their male colleagues, perceive Catholicism as a shield against the influence of the 'Other': the non-clerical civic culture of the European Union and Islam ascribed to refugees who are suspected of terrorism. As such, the delegalization of abortion and promotion of a Catholic nuclear family remain important goals of the far right in Poland, especially since nationalists understand the nation to be a traditional family.

ANNOTATIONS

1 | By 'culture war' I mean the conflict of worldviews between progressivists/liberals and traditionalists/conservatives. The concept was developed by James Davidson Hunter (1991): Culture Wars: The Struggle to Define America. New York: Basic Books. The notion of 'culture war' has been applied to descriptions and interpretations of cultural changes in post-communist Poland. Cf. Jo Harper (2016): Poland's Culture War: Let the Abortion Battle Commence. In: Deutsche Welle, April 15, (http://www.dw.com/en/polands-culture-war-let-the-abortion-battle-commence/a-19191002), accessed May 16, 2016.
2 | Samuel Huntington (1993): The Clash of Civilizations? In: Foreign Affairs, 72/3, pp. 22, 29, 31-32, 40-41, 48.
3 | Original name in Polish: *PRO – Prawo do życia*.
4 | Original name in Polish: *Narodowa Organizacja Kobiet*.

5 | Fundacja PRO (2015): Mem. In: *Fundacja Pro – Prawo do Życia* – Facebook, November 14, (https://www.facebook.com/FundacjaPro/photos/a.10150241757838631.33752 4.300745193630/10153775213273631/?type=3&theater), accessed May 16, 2016.

6 | The terms "culture of life" and "culture of death", willingly employed by the far right, come from Pope John Paul II (1995): Evangelium Vitae, (http://w2.vatican.va/content/john-paul-ii/pl/encyclicals/documents/hf_jp-ii_enc_25031995_evangelium-vitae.html), accessed May 16, 2016.

7 | LGBTQ is the acronym of Lesbian, Gay, Bi-Sexual, Trans-Gender, Queer and expresses the diversity of sexuality and gender identities and/or subsumes subjects typically excluded from the heterosexual mainstream.

8 | Original name in German: *Patriotische Europäer gegen die Islamisierung des Abendlandes.*

9 | Dziennik Narodowy (2016): Festerling: Codziennie w Niemczech gwałcone przez imigrantów są dziewczynki, chłopcy, kobiety, a nawet pederaści [Festerling: In Germany Girls, Boys and even Pederasts are Raped by Immigrants Every Day]. In: Dziennik Narodowy, April 14, (http://www.dzienniknarodowy.pl/189/festerling-codziennie-w-niemczech-gwalcone-przez-i/), accessed May 16, 2016. Cf. (2016): Lej żonę, bo tak nakazuje Allah! [Beat your Wife becasue Allah Says So!]. In: Dziennik Narodowy, May 26, (http://www.dzienniknarodowy.pl/661/lej-zone-bo-tak-nakazuje-allah/), accessed May 26, 2016.

10 | Anne McClintock (1995): Imperial Leather: Race, Gender and Sexuality in the Colonial Contest. New York: Routledge. p. 354–355, quoted in: Agnieszka Graff (2008): Rykoszetem: Rzecz o płci, seksualności i narodzie [Ricochet: On Gender, Sexuality, and Nation]. Warszawa: WAB, pp. 16, 35–36, 81–85.

11 | The English translation is *National Front*. However, to avoid confusion with groups or parties from other countries carrying the same name, the original name in French is used in this text.

12 | Annika Hamrud/Christina Wassholm (2014): Patriotism and Patriarchy: The Impact of Nationalism on Gender Equality. Johanneshov: Kvinna till Kvinna, p. 29.

13 | Agnieszka Graff (2008): Rykoszetem, pp. 33–35. The views are also expressed in the popular nationalist slogan: 'Great Catholic Poland'.

14 | Original name in Polish: Ordo Iuris Instytut Na Rzecz Kultury Prawnej.

15 | ISAP (1993): Dz. U. 1993, 17/78, p. 3, (http://isap.sejm.gov.pl/DetailsServlet?id=WDU19930170078Lj.pdf), accessed May 16, 2016.

16 | ISAP (1997): Dz. U. 1997, 88/53, p. 60, (http://isap.sejm.gov.pl/DetailsServlet?id=WDU19970880553Lj.pdf), accessed May 16, 2016.

17 | Inicjatywa Stop Aborcji (2016): Projekt in Stop Aborcji, (http://www.stopaborcji.pl/wp-content/uploads/2016/03/projekt_2016.pdf), accessed May 16, 2016.

18 | Original name in Polish: *Porozumienie Odzyskać Wybór.*

19 | Original name in Polish: *Dziewuchy Dziewuchom.*

20 | Original name in Polish: *Stop aborcji.*

21 | Original name in Polish: *Ratujmy kobiety.*

22 | Original name in Polish: *Ruch Narodowy*.
23 | Original name in Polish: *Młodzież Wszechpolska*.
24 | Original name in Polish: *Obóz Narodowo-Radykalny*.
25 | Grzegorz Szymanik (2012): Maszerowanie jest podniecające: Rozmowy z dziewczynami z radykalnej prawicy [Marching is Exciting: Conversations with Girls from the Far Right.]. In: Wysokie Obcasy, December 27, (http://www.wysokieobcasy.pl/wysokie-obcasy/1,96856,13039353,_apos__apos_Maszerowanie_jest_podniecajace_apos__apos__.html), accessed May 16, 2016.
26 | In 2015, the Women's Section transformed into *National Organization of Women*, original name in Polish: *Narodowa Organizacja Kobiet*.
27 | This organization is inactive today.
28 | Kobiety dla Narodu (2013): Oświadczenie Kobiet dla Narodu na temat zajść na Manifie 10.03.2013 [Statement of the Women for the Nation on the incident during Manifa on March 10, 2013]. In: Stopaborcji.pl, March 18, (http://www.stopaborcji.pl/oswiadczenie-kobiet-dla-narodu-na-temat-zajsc-na-manifie-10-03-2013/), accessed May 16, 2016.
29 | Janusz Schwertner (2013): Anna Holocher: To mężczyźni są dyskryminowani przez feministki [Anna Holocher: These Are Men who Are Discriminated by Feminists – an interview]. In: Onet.pl, July 21, (http://wiadomosci.onet.pl/tylko-w-onecie/anna-holocher-to-mezczyzni-sa-dyskryminowani-przez-feministki/lg2x7), accessed May 16, 2016.
30 | Kobiety dla Narodu (2013): Oświadczenie Kobiet dla Narodu na temat zajść na Manifie 10.03.2013. [Statement of the Women for the Nation on the incident during Manifa on March 10, 2013]. In: Stopaborcji.pl, March 18, (http://www.stopaborcji.pl/oswiadczenie-kobiet-dla-narodu-na-temat-zajsc-na-manifie-10-03-2013/), accessed May 16, 2016; Schwertner (2013): Anna Holocher.
31 | Schwertner (2013): Anna Holocher.
32 | Pszl/kf (2011): Marsz Niepodległości pod znakiem zadymy [Independence March under the sign of a riot], November 11, TVP Info, (http://www.tvp.info/5644982/marsz-niepodleglosci-pod-znakiem-zadymy), accessed May 16, 2016.
33 | Wkk (2013): Dlaczego bojówkarze zaatakowali squat Przychodnia [Why Did Louts Attack Przychodnia Squat?]. In: Gazeta Wyborcza, November 12, (http://warszawa.wyborcza.pl/warszawa/1,34889,14936295,Dlaczego_bojowkarze_zaatakowali_squat__Przychodnia_.html), accessed May 16, 2016.
34 | The term was popularized by Rush Limbaugh (1992): The Way Things Ought to Be. New York: Pocket Books.
35 | J. Jastrzębski/Ludwika Kleist (2014): *Ruch Narodowy Sekcja Kobiet* [National Movement: Women's Section], June 2, (https://www.youtube.com/watch?v=V6JGA7emq8k), accessed May 16, 2016.
36 | Ibid.
37 | Original name in Polish: *W imieniu Dam*.

38 | W Imieniu Dam (2013): Photography. In: W Imieniu Dam – Facebook, 19 February, (https://www.facebook.com/NOKwarszawa/photos/a.785521108155922.107374182 8.781208515253848/866437486730950/?type=3&theater), accessed May 16, 2016.
39 | Narodowa Organizacja Kobiet – Warszawa (2016): Photography. In: Narodowa Organizacja Kobiet – Warszawa Facebook, March 6, (https://www.facebook.com/NO Kwarszawa/photos/a.1072833046091392.1073741885.781208515253848/10738 58462655517/?type=3&theater), accessed May 16, 2016.
40 | Schwertner (2013): Anna Holocher.
41 | The instrumentalization of women in the *National Movement* is suggested by: Marta Kasztelan/Marta Soszynska/Agnieszka Liggett/Mustafa Khalili/Charlie Phillips/Juliet Riddell (2015): Pretty Radical: A Young Woman's Journey into the Heart of Poland's Far Right. In: The Guardian, January 19, (https://www.theguardian.com/world/video/2015/jan/19/pretty-radical-young-woman-poland-far-right-video), accessed May 16, 2016.
42 | Marta Kasztelan et al. (2015): Pretty Radical.
43 | Koserwatyzm.pl (2013): Maria Piasecka-Łopuszańska nie jest już szefową Kobiet dla Narodu, za to mężczyzna znalazł się w zarządzie kobiecej organizacji [Maria Piasecka-Łopuszańska Is not the Boss of Women for the Nation Any Longer: A Man Appeared in the Governing Board of the Feminine Organization]. In: Koserwatyzm, October 8, (http://konserwatyzm.pl/artykul/11017/maria-piasecka-lopuszanska-nie-jest-juz-sze fowa-kobiet-dla-narodu-za-to-mezczyzna-znalazl-sie-w-zarzadzie-kobiecej-organiza cji/), accessed May 16, 2016.

Accused: Beate Zschäpe on her way to the court room in Munich holding the trial for serial killings by the German *National Socialist Underground* (NSU). This photo was taken on the fourth day of the trial on May 16, 2013. (Original photograph taken by Theo Schneider, edited by Deniz Beşer, 2016).

... Underground

A Warfare Mindset
Right-Wing Extremism and 'Counter-State Terror' as a Threat for Western Democracies

Daniel Koehler

Terror from the far right has again gained wider public attention since the devastating attacks carried out by Anders Behring Breivik in Norway in 2011 and the detection of the German far-right terrorist cell called *National Socialist Underground* (NSU)[1], whose members committed at least ten murders, three bombings and a dozen bank robberies in Germany for over the span of more than a decade. In many Western countries, violence motivated by racism, anti-government hate, antisemitism or other aspects of right-wing extremism[2] appears to have become a normal part of criminal activities. Hate-crime legislation and statistics vary greatly but show that, next to large-scale terrorist attacks such as 9/11 and the attacks in London, Madrid and Paris, far-right violence and terrorism is the most dangerous politically motivated threat. In the United States, for example, Perliger[3] counted 4,420 right-wing terrorist incidents between 1990 and 2012, which caused 670 fatalities and 3,053 injuries. In Germany, official statistics counted 69 right-wing attacks between 1990 and 2015, leading to 75 casualties, while civil society watchdog groups count up to 184 deaths[4]. In Russia, some experts[5] speak of approximately 450 right-wing motivated killings between 2004 and 2010.

Nevertheless, this specific form of political violence remains largely under-researched and it is misunderstood as being non-terroristic. Additionally, various differing concepts and understandings of right-wing violence exist while a coherent theory of far-right militancy is still lacking. As a consequence, the threat posed by the far right is continuously downplayed, with severe consequences for victims and internal security. But just how exactly does this threat look and what tactical or strategic characteristics can be found among terrorist actors from the far right? Do right-wing terrorists have their own strategic concepts, and, if so, do they follow them? What consequences do authorities and civil society face in countering this form of political violence?

STRATEGIC CONSIDERATIONS

In this article, far-right terrorism is understood to be the use or threat of specific forms of middle to high-distance violence (e.g., explosives, shooting, arson) which are executed on the ideological premise of inequality among human beings and in order to challenge the political status quo – namely, the monopoly of force – through the act of violence as a form of psychological and physical warfare. Additional common motives may have the following intents: demonstrating the weakness of authorities achieved by deliberately instigating chaos; criminally framing left-wing groups and bringing about government crack-downs; exterminating key individuals of the 'enemy'; destroying infrastructure perceived as vital to the 'enemy'; proving the movement's vitality to its members; and, gaining political or social power by resorting to a reign of fear.

Experts have observed that far-right terrorism differs from other types of terrorism in a number of dimensions, most notably the regular absence of any public communication policy connected to the attack.[6] This silence has prompted some scholars to argue that this form of organized clandestine violence from the far right cannot be called 'terrorism' per se. Nevertheless, one particular aspect worth exploring here is the specific far-right terrorist strategy and doctrine adopted by Italian neo-fascists and researchers as a "strategy of tension"[7]. In this concept, Italian right-wing terrorists are dedicated to

"inciting violence and disorder so as to create the state of anarchy, from which public demand for the restoration of law and order will spring and enable the neo-fascists to assume power and govern Italy as a totalitarian state"[8].

The similarity to the Russian concept of 'counter-state terror' is obvious, which also aims to destabilize the political system and create panic in order to achieve a "neo-Nazi Revolution"[9]. While the Italian concept sees the (conservative parts of the) government as its allies and aims at creating a political climate favorable for right-wing parties, the Russian model takes the whole government to be its target. Aiming to destroy government legitimacy (e.g., the safeguarding of the population) through terror and violence, 'counter-state terror' from the far right is, in essence, a form of low-intensity guerrilla warfare.

'SAVING THE RACE AND BRINGING BACK THE REICH': FAR-RIGHT TERRORISM IN GERMANY

Most countries do not provide detailed information about their far-right terrorist structures, such as in the form of comprehensive statistics or research. One of the few countries that offers at least some data is Germany, which makes it possible to gain insights into this form of political violence in the German context and understand the particular nature of that threat.

Looking at the (estimated) number of active far-right extremists, the Federal Office for the Protection of the Constitution[10] counted 21,000 activists in 2014[11]. German authorities regard 50 percent, or 10,500, of those activists to be "violence oriented", meaning they are prepared to use political violence to advance their goals. Although the number of activists has slightly decreased in the last years (to 22,150 in 2012, for instance), the number of right-wing motivated crimes certainly has not. In 2014, German authorities counted 1,029 violent hate crimes ("right-wing politically motivated"), including more than 900 cases of criminal assault with a right-wing extremist motive[12]. Overall, compared to 2013, violent hate crimes increased by 22.9 percent and criminal assaults by right-wing extremists increased by 23.3 percent[13]. Although official statistics for right-wing motivated crimes carried out in 2015 still do not exist, the number of violent attacks against refugee shelters will almost certainly guarantee a record high. In 2015, 901 attacks against refugee shelters with a clear right-wing motive (compared to 199 in 2014)[14] show a visible radicalization within the movement.

Looking at data on extreme right-wing terrorism, the German Institute on Radicalization and De-radicalization Studies (GIRDS) has compiled the most extensive database on terrorist violence from the far right after the Second World War; it currently includes qualitative data regarding 91 identified right-wing terrorist actors (groups and individuals) since 1960. According to the Database on Terrorism in Germany (DTGrwx)[15], the main characteristics of right-wing terrorism are the tradition of small-unit tactics, the lack of public communication and the strong role of the government as a target. Almost half of all identifiable actors are between two and nine members in size; an additional quarter are lone actors, meaning that over 70 percent of all far-right terrorist actors between 1963 and 2015 in Germany only had nine or less members. The tactics used by right-wing terrorists mostly include bombings, assassinations and arson, rarely hostage-taking or kidnapping. One of the most distinctive aspects of far-right terrorism in Germany is the lack of public communication regarding the attack, such as through letters, statements or communiqués. Of all the actors who carried out successful or unsuccessful attacks (around 45 percent of all actors in the database), only a quarter used any kind of identifying mechanism. In general, public statements by right-wing terrorist actors rarely contain concrete political claims or programs. In most cases, swastikas or similar symbols and statements that disparage the victims or target groups are found at the crime scene.

The DTG dataset for Germany validates the finding that right-wing terrorists see government representatives and institutions as their main enemies and targets, along with ethnic minorities, immigrants and Jewish people. Two prominent examples would be the right-wing lone actor Frank S., who tried to assassinate politician Henriette Reker (later elected as mayor of Cologne) on October 17, 2015 on account of her pro-immigration policies, and the right-wing terrorist militia group *FTL/360*[16] from the Saxon town Freital, which (among other attacks) carried out an arson bombing against a local left-wing politician's car in the same year. Destabilizing the government's monopoly of force – in concurrence with the 'counter-state terror' or guerrilla warfare strategy – can be seen as one of the main goals of far-right terrorists, which does not require elaborate or sophisticated public communication strategies. In addition, right-wing terrorists exhibit many characteristics akin to guerrilla[17]-style groups in terms of the general tactical use of violence and terror. These tactics, which are carried out by fluid and more or less spontaneous groupings of effectively ideologized[18] individuals, are not a new phenomenon within the militant clandestine far right.

As the DTG database and examples from other countries show, right-wing terrorism is a security threat largely underestimated by Western authorities. The widespread tactical sophistication in deploying small cell and lone actor operations – as proven by the NSU case – should serve as a warning to police and intelligence officials and deter them from solely looking for Jihadist or RAF[19]-like symptoms or characteristics of terrorism in the extreme right-wing movement: they are unlikely to find any. 'Counter-state terror' not only sees the government and state authorities as its prime targets but also their claim to legitimacy and the monopoly of force. Through unhindered attacks and the killing of civilians with immigrant backgrounds, the NSU and other right-wing terrorist groups strive to destabilize that legitimacy – built largely on the premise that the state is incapable of protecting its citizens – and destroy the (immigrant) population's trust in the government and its authorities. This, in turn, increases the risk of misunderstanding far-right violence as mere low-level hate crimes or subcultural disorganized violence, while far-right terrorist actors and incidents are overlooked and downplayed.

WORLDWIDE WHITE SUPREMACIST INSURGENCY?

Looking at other widely known acts of far-right terrorism in Europe and North America, several striking similarities become evident: most incidents were a) carried out by individuals or small groups, b) they involved explosives, c) they targeted 'foreigners', 'Jews', or government representatives, and d) they did not publically make demands afterwards. The bombing of the Bologna train station in Italy on August 2, 1980[20], for instance, which killed 85 and wounded more than 200, was carried out by two members of *Armed Revolutionary Nuclei* (NAR)[21]. The NAR is a splinter cell of the right-wing terrorist group *New Order*[22] that harbors the goal of deflecting public anger and government reactions on left-wing extremists and of creating public chaos, which would allow extreme right-wing parties to capitalize on the population's need for order[23]. In the aftermath, the group did not issue any claims, hoping that this attack would directly discredit the government as being unable to provide security and contain threats from the far-left.

Similarly, the devastating attack on the Alfred P. Murrah Federal Building in Oklahoma City on April 19, 1995, which remains one of the deadliest terrorist attacks in the history of the United States, after September 11, 2001[24], was carried out by anti-government far-right extremist Timothy McVeigh and two accomplices. They used a car bomb and did not express any demands or statements publicly, targeting a federal government building that housed various government agencies. In planning the attack, McVeigh was inspired by the explicitly racist and antisemitic *Turner Diaries*, which has been referred to as "a bible of the extremist right"[25]. As these books explicitly glorify small and leaderless resistance cells fighting against a corrupt government in a "racial civil (or holy) war"[26] without making any public claims in their attacks, the resulting impact on the tactical level of far-right terrorism can hardly be underestimated. As the more detailed analysis of the German NSU case along with these international examples show, militant right-wing movements around the world have largely adopted such approaches that, in fact, invoke the context of waging guerrilla warfare against an 'occupying enemy force'.

In addition to militant anti-government extremism, racism has also been a common theme among other far-right terrorist actors. Four years after the Oklahoma City attacks, in April 1999, the British neo-Nazi David Copeland orchestrated three nail bomb attacks in London over the course of 13 days, resulting in three fatalities and wounding 137[27]. Copeland had been a long-time member of several neo-Nazi organizations in England and targeted homosexuals and immigrants with his attacks. Another (foiled) attempt at right-wing terrorism became public in the United Kingdom in 2009, when neo-Nazi Ian Davison and his son – part of a right-wing terrorist organization, *Aryan Strike Force* – planned attacks against ethnic minorities using chemical weapons, manufacturing a large amount of the poison ricin[28]. On August 5, 2011, the US neo-Nazi Wade Michael Page also fatally shot six and injured four during an attack at a Sikh temple in Oak Creek, Wisconsin[29]. These last examples are part of what far-right extremists refer to as the 'racial holy war' (or RaHoWa), essentially meaning that they see themselves as small clandestine guerrilla units fighting either the government – which is responsible for using immigration to 'eradicate the white race' – or those individuals identified as a biological threat to their 'racial purity'.

Conclusion

This short overview has shown that right-wing terrorism displays unique characteristics and constitutes a highly dangerous and lethal form of political violence. In order to adequately assess this threat and formulate effective counter strategies on all levels – including actions taken by the police, courts and civil society organizations against right-wing extremism –, much more research and analysis needs to be done. Another important step is to recognize the dangers posed by this form of violence that is tactically highly covert, has a long-term orientation and is mainly focused on destroying government structures.

As most Western countries have prioritized jihadist terrorism as the number-one enemy, police and intelligence resources have been reduced and law enforcement agencies in many countries have barely investigated the far right. As the example of the NSU has shown, the focus on high-impact attacks publicized by the perpetrators can prove misleading and even open windows of opportunity for other terrorists who aim to wage asymmetrical warfare against an enemy that they perceive to be an 'occupying force'. Much like guerrilla organizations, these terrorists rarely rely on publicity, as their primary goal is to continue the struggle against their enemies. Violence is their main message and the resulting condition of fear does, in fact, destabilize the authority held by governments and dissolve both the rule of law and trust in democratic culture.

Annotations

1 | Original name in German: *Nationalsozialistischer Untergrund*.
2 | In this paper, the terms 'right-wing extremism'/'right-wing' and the 'far right'/'far-right' are used synonymously.
3 | Arie Perliger (2012): Challengers from the Sidelines: Understanding America's Violent Far-Right. New York: The Combating Terrorism Center at West Point, p. 86.
4 | Erkol Aslan/Nora Winter (2013): 184 Todesopfer rechtsextremer und rassistischer Gewalt seit 1990 [184 Casualties of Right-Wing and Racist Violence since 1990], (http://www.mut-gegen-rechte-gewalt.de/news/chronik-der-gewalt/todesopfer-rechtsextremer-und-rassistischer-gewalt-seit-1990/), accessed June 20, 2016.
5 | Martin Laryš/Miroslav Mareš (2011): Right-Wing Extremist Violence in the Russian Federation. In: Europe-Asia Studies, 63/1, p. 137.
6 | See Daniel Koehler (2014): German Right-Wing Terrorism in Historical Perspective: A First Quantitative Overview of the 'Database on Terrorism in Germany (Right-Wing Extremism) Dtg Rwx'. In: Project Perspectives on Terrorism, 8/5, p. 48-58.
7 | See Franco Ferraresi (2012): Threats to Democracy: The Radical Right in Italy after the War. Princeton. NJ: Princeton University Press.
8 | Bruce Hoffman (1982): Right Wing Terrorism in Europe. Santa Monica: RAND, p. 2.

9 | Laryš/Mareš (2011): Right-Wing Extremist Violence, p. 137.
10 | Original name in German: *Bundesamt für Verfassungsschutz*, official name for the German domestic intelligence service.
11 | Bundesministerium des Innern (2015): Verfassungsschutzbericht 2014 [Report of the Federal Office for the Protection of the Constitution 2014]. Berlin: Bundesministerium des Innern, p. 33.
12 | Bundesministerium des Innern (2015): Politisch motivierte Kriminalität im Jahr 2014 [Politically Motivated Crime in the Year 2014]. Berlin: Bundesministerium des Innern, p. 3.
13 | Ibid.
14 | Jörg Diehl (2016): Gewaltwelle: BKA zählt mehr als Tausend Attacken auf Flüchtlingsheime [Wave of Violence: BKA Counts More than a Thousand Attacks on Refugee Shelters]. In: Spiegel Online, January 28, (http://www.spiegel.de/politik/deutschland/fluechtlingsheime-bundeskriminalamt-zaehlt-mehr-als-1000-attacken-a-1074448.html), accessed June 20, 2016.
15 | Below referred to as DTG. See German Institute on Radicalization and De-Radicalization Studies (GIRDS) (2016): Database on Terrorism in Germany, (http://www.girds.org/projects/database-on-terrorism-in-germany-right-wing-extremism), accessed June 20, 2016.
16 | For more information on this group see Oliver Saal in this volume.
17 | A "guerrilla" is defined by Merriam-Webster as "a person who engages in irregular warfare especially as a member of an independent unit carrying out harassment and sabotage", (http://www.merriam-webster.com/dictionary/guerilla), accessed June 20, 2016; according to dictionary.com, "guerrilla warfare" is "the use of hit-and-run tactics by small, mobile groups of irregular forces operating in territory controlled by a hostile, regular force", (http://www.dictionary.com/browse/guerrilla-warfare), accessed June 20, 2016.
18 | Cf. Kai Biermann/Philip Faigle/Astrid Geisler/Karsten Majewski-Polke/Hannes Soltau/Julian Stahnke/Tilman Steffen/Sascha Venohr (2016): Der Terror der Anderen [The Terror of the Others]. In: Zeit Online, February 23, (http://www.zeit.de/politik/deutschland/2016-02/rassismus-gewalt-notunterkuenfte-gefluechtete-rechter-terror), accessed June 20, 2016.
19 | This is the acronym of *Red Army Faction* (original name in German: *Rote Armee Fraktion*), a West German far-left militant group founded in 1970.
20 | See BBC News (1980): Bologna Blast Leaves Dozens Dead, August 2, (http://news.bbc.co.uk/onthisday/hi/dates/stories/august/2/newsid_4532000/4532091.stm), accessed June 20, 2016.
21 | Original name in Italian: *Nuclei Armati Rivoluzionari*.
22 | Original name in Italian: *Ordine Nuove*.
23 | Ibid.
24 | See Sheryll Shariat/Sue Mallonee/Shelli Stidham Stephens (1980): Oklahoma City Bombing Injuries. Oklahoma City: Oklahoma State Department of Health.

25 | Peter Applebome (1995): Terror in Oklahoma: The Background. A Bombing Foretold, in Extreme-Right 'Bible'. In: The New York Times, April 26, (http://www.nytimes.com/1995/04/26/us/terror-in-oklahoma-the-background-a-bombing-foretold-in-extreme-right-bible.html), accessed June 20, 2016.

26 | Ibid.

27 | See Andrew Buncombe (2000): 'Hate-Filled' Nailbomber Is Jailed for Life. In: The Independent, June 30, (http://web.archive.org/web/20091201133942/http:/www.independent.co.uk/news/uk/this-britain/hatefilled-nailbomber-is-jailed-for-life-706785.html), accessed June 20, 2016; see also Alex Carter in this volume.

28 | See Jeremy Armstrong (2010): Nicky Davison, Son of a Right Wing Extremist, Found Guilty of Part in Plot to Kill Muslims, Blacks and Jews. In: The Mirror, May 1, (http://www.mirror.co.uk/news/uk-news/nicky-davison-son-of-a-right-wing-218203), accessed June 20, 2016.

29 | See Francis Robles/Jason Horowitz/Shaila Dewan (2015): Dylann Roof, Suspect in Charleston Shooting, Flew the Flags of White Power. In: The New York Times, June 18, (http://www.nytimes.com/2015/06/19/us/on-facebook-dylann-roof-charleston-suspect-wears-symbols-of-white-supremacy.html), accessed June 20, 2016.

Right-Wing Terrorism and Hate Crime in the UK
A Historical Perspective

Alex Carter

The threat that the far right poses to civil society changes across time and space. In Britain, this threat has generally assumed the form of hate-crimes and public disorder; in the past two decades, however, there has been a shift towards solo-actor terrorism. By examining far-right groups in the UK in the post-war period, this paper explores the drivers of this shift; namely, how contact with extremist groups combined with the proliferation of far-right networks created by the Internet can produce a pathway to radicalization that ends in acts of terror.

POLITICAL VIOLENCE AND HATE CRIME:
THE RISE OF THE BRITISH POST-WAR FAR RIGHT

The two most significant far-right groups in England in the post-War period have been the *National Front* (NF), founded in 1967, and the *British National Party* (BNP), founded in 1982. Between the growth of the former throughout the 1970s and the decline of the latter since 2009, there has been a largely consistent cycle of street mobilizations, hate crimes and political violence.

The NF gained a great deal of publicity by organizing numerous intentionally incendiary marches through areas with large non-white populations – with predictable results. The counter-demonstrations were often violent, thereby handing the NF propaganda victories. Throughout this period, incidents of racially motivated attacks increased in number. On Friday, June 4, 1976, ten-year-old Gurdip Singh Chaggar was killed in what has been widely seen as a racially motivated attack.[1] That same month, community relations officers in Blackburn released a dossier detailing more than 30 attacks carried out on Asian families and their property; the officers argued that the blame for these attacks lay with the local *National Party* and their activities.[2] Two Bengali men, Altab Ali and Ishaque Ali, were also murdered in East London in April and June

1978, respectively.³ Similarly, in the 1990s, the BNP managed to raise its profile after leading a series of marches – particularly in East London, where they had established their headquarters – that devolved into serious breaches of public order, as they clashed with locals and anti-fascists. Furthermore, between 1991 and 1993, three young people of color, Rolan Adams, Rohit Duggal and Stephen Lawrence, were murdered in the same area.⁴ Even if the murderers were not actually members of NF or other far-right parties, many observers have felt that the incidents were directly linked to these groups. Taylor, for instance, argues that hate crimes could not be

"divorced from the presence of the NF in the East End of London, both indirectly in that racism was given a 'legitimate' outlet, and directly insofar as it was alleged that not only were NF members involved in violence but that the NF's leadership was turning a blind eye to such behaviour"⁵;

the same could easily be said of the BNP.

As such, the main threats to civil society stemming from the presence of the far right in Britain since the 1960s has tended to be public disorder and political violence, rather than acts of terrorism – although there have been some near misses and aborted attempts. In the summer of 1978, a man named Fred Challis and three accomplices were jailed for admitting to having committed 300 racially motivated attacks in Tower Hamlets and to murdering a homeless man. Challis smashed the man's face in with a gas cylinder, before scrawling "NF rules OK" on the wall in blood; although not actually a member of the NF, Challis felt that the party would appreciate his act⁶. In late 1978, two prominent NF members – James Tierney from Devon and Newcastle branch 'security officer' Alan Birtley – were sentenced to three years in prison for the possession of explosives. Birtley admitted in court that several members of his branch were capable of making explosives and they had intended to use them against their political targets.⁷

Furthermore, across the 1980s, there were several incidents involving far-right members collecting or creating materials that could be used for terrorist activities. On November 1, 1985, the BNP organizer for Redbridge, Tony Lecomber, was arrested after a homemade explosive device in his car detonated early near the *Workers Revolutionary Party* headquarters.⁸ On 27 March 1986, seven Chelsea Football Club supporters were "remanded in custody after Police raids uncovered an array of NF literature, an Ulster Loyalist flag as well as various types of weapons",⁹ and, on July 1, 1986, "armed Wiltshire police seized a weapons cache, including nine anti-tank rockets and launchers, as well as guns, ammunition and explosives" and arrested a man who had "extensive links with the extreme Right"¹⁰.

CLANDESTINE POLITICAL VIOLENCE: THE GROWTH OF FAR-RIGHT TERRORISM

These examples notwithstanding, the prospect of real far-right acts of terrorism did not emerge until the 1990s. In 1992, a new far-right extremist group with openly paramilitary pretensions called *Combat 18* (C18) emerged. Throughout the mid-1990s, they engaged in a series of violent attacks that gave them a reputation as being a terrorist group. These included firebombing a number of buildings, printing magazines and fanzines with hit-lists containing the names and addresses of left-wing activists, gay clubs, and people they perceived as race-traitors, and later publishing bomb-making blueprints with instructions to go out and "Bomb the Bastards".[11]

But in 1997, C18 leader Will Browning went further, arranging for a number of letter-bombs from sympathizers in Europe to be sent to political targets in England. Fortunately, acting on information provided by Scotland Yard, Swedish police intercepted the bombs before they could cause any damage.[12] A couple of years after executing their only real attempted terrorist act, the organizations' volatility led to them all but disintegrating.

Yet, just as it seemed the terrorist threat was fading, in April 1999, David Copeland planted three bombs in predominantly non-white and gay areas of London. The bombs killed four people and seriously injured dozens of others, making it the deadliest far-right terrorist attack in British history. After his arrest, Copeland admitted to the police that his aim was to "cause a racial war in this country. There'd be a backlash from the ethnic minorities. I'd just be the spark."[13]

Copeland has been described as a solo-actor terrorist, as it is all but certain that he planned and carried out his attacks without the direct involvement of another person. Since this incident, there have been a number of other attempts to commit terrorist attacks by solo-actors who have connections to the far right or espouse a far-right ideology. In June 2008, Martyn Gilleard was sentenced to 16 years in prison after police found a wide assortment of weapons, including nail-bombs, in his flat, along with a note that read

"I am sick and tired of hearing nationalists talking of killing Muslims, blowing up mosques and fighting back only to see these acts of resistance fail. The time has come to stop the talking and start to act."[14]

The same year, Nathan Worrell, a member of the *Ku Klux Klan* (KKK), was imprisoned for possession of material for terrorist purposes.[15] In the summer of 2009, Neil Lewington was convicted for "planning a racist terror campaign", after police found a "bomb-making factory" at his home;[16] Lewington had been directly inspired by David Copeland. More recently, Pavlo Lapshyn received a

40-year jail sentence in 2013 for the racially motivated murder of Mohammed Saleem and for planting bombs at three mosques.[17]

PATHWAYS TO RADICALIZATION: GROUP AFFILIATION AND THE INTERNET

The threat of mobilizations by far-right groups leading to an increased incidence of hate crimes and public disorder has by no means waned. Indeed, since the decline of the BNP from 2009, a number of more extreme groups, such as *National Action* and *Britain First*, have emerged. Further, the growth of the so-called 'counter-jihad' movement has witnessed the formation of groups, such as the *English Defence League*, which have been capable of bringing thousands of people to the streets in protests; as such groups do not contest elections, they are not susceptible to the moderating effects often accompanied by electioneering.[18]

However, the growth of solo-actor terrorists is not only the newest development in the repertoires of contention for the far right, it is also arguably the most worrying aspect of their mobilization at the moment. One major contribution to this changing pattern of mobilization is likely the development and proliferation of the Internet. A key observation from terrorism studies is that even solo-actor terrorists rarely act entirely alone, in that they "rely on the moral and sometimes tactical support of enablers, which can occur indirectly by people who provide inspiration for political violence."[19]

The Internet has facilitated access to these networks, possibly rendering pathways to radicalization far easier for potential solo-actor terrorists; while David Copeland made these connections in a face-to-face manner – he was a member of the BNP and the *National Socialist Movement* (NSM) – he nevertheless learned how to construct the nail bombs, which he used throughout London, on the Internet. It may now be much easier for people to do both. Far-right sites, such as the *Gates of Vienna* and *Stormfront*, allow for networks to be developed that are international in scope, and through which ideas and tactics may be shared. According to research carried out by the *Southern Poverty Law Centre*, registered users of the *Stormfront* website have been involved in over 100 murders, giving the site the dubious honor of being the "murder capital of the internet".[20]

It should also be borne in mind that membership in extremist organizations can likewise put people on the pathway to radicalization, which may end in terrorism. The social psychologists Clark McCauley and Sophia Moskalenko describe a mechanism of radicalization called "group polarization", whereby groups of people in discussion of "risk taking or political opinion consistently show [...] a shift in the average opinion of group members toward increased extremism" in the direction of the general consensus prior to the discussion.

So, membership in, and frequent contact with, an extremist group may not only lead to "an internalized shift toward more extreme opinions", but also to a deeper understanding of the ideologies that justify violence.[21] However, whereas McCauley and Moskalenko apply this model to explain group radicalization, the foregoing discussion provides at least some evidence that this can happen in an uneven manner, leading to the development of solo-actors who become more radicalized than others in their group. Most of the solo-actors mentioned above had been, or were, members of extremist groups, such as the BNP, KKK and NSM, which were not pursuing a terrorist agenda. This is substantiated by testimony from the editor of the far-right monitoring magazine *Searchlight*, Gerry Gable, who argued that David Copeland's involvement with the BNP facilitated exposure to more extreme hate-materials, thereby directing him down the pathway to terrorism.

CONCLUSION

It appears that a combination of contact with extremist groups *and* the new freedom of access to 'networks of support' provided by the Internet has been a key factor in the relatively recent growth of far-right terrorism in Britain. In 2012, the British Government's Home Affairs Committee released a report on the *Roots of Violent Radicalisation*, in which they stated that they had "received persuasive evidence about the potential threat from extreme far-right terrorism", a view that the foregoing discussion has reinforced.[22] While public disorder and hate crimes remain a very real threat, there is clearly a need for analyses that are more sensitive to the possible pathways to terrorism that engagement with the far right can lead to.

ANNOTATIONS

1 | Anandi Ramamurthy (2013): Black Star: Britain's Asian Youth Movements. London: Pluto Books, pp. 44-46, here p. 26.
2 | The *National Party* was a group created through a schism with the NF in 1975. See Martin Walker (1977): The National Front. Glasgow: Fontana Paperbacks, p. 119.
3 | Ramamurthy (2013): Black Star.
4 | M. Testa (2015): Militant Anti-Fascism: A Hundred Years of Resistance. Edinburgh: AK Press, pp. 231-238.
5 | Stan Taylor (1982): The National Front in English Politics. London: Macmillan Press Ltd, p. 156.

6 | Bethnal Green/Stepney Trades Council (1978): Blood on the Streets: A Report by Bethnal Green and Stepney Trades Council on Racial Attacks in East London. London: Bethnal Green and Stepney Trades Council, p. 44.
7 | Unknown Author: Action Briefing, Association of Jewish Ex-Servicemen & Women, No. 11, May, p. 7, SCH/01/Res/AF/04/003: Box 3: Board of Deputies Reports Box 1, 1970s & 1980s. Northampton: Northampton University Searchlight Archive.
8 | Board of Deputies of British Jews (1986): Confidential Weekly Summary of Events, March 3-10, p. 1, SCH/01/Res/AF/04/003: Box 3: Board of Deputies Reports Box 1, 1970s & 1980s. Northampton: Northampton University Searchlight Archive.
9 | Ibid., p. 2.
10 | Ibid., p. 1.
11 | Nicholas Goodrick-Clarke (2002): Black Sun: Aryan Cults, Esoteric Nazism and the Politics of Identity. New York: New York University Press, p. 46.
12 | Nick Lowles (2001): White Riot: The Violent Story of Combat 18. Bury: Milo Books, pp. 209-218.
13 | BBC (2000): Profile: Copeland the Killer, June 30, (http://news.bbc.co.uk/1/hi/uk/781755.stm), accessed June 21, 2016.
14 | Peter Oborne (2008): The Enemy within? Fear of Islam: Britain's New Disease. In: The Independent, July 4, 2008, (http://www.independent.co.uk/news/uk/home-news/the-enemy-within-fear-of-islam-britains-new-disease-859996.html), accessed June 22, 2016.
15 | The Guardian (2008): Racist Who Had Bomb Kit Jailed for Campaign against Couple, December 13, (https://www.theguardian.com/uk/2008/dec/13/uk-security-nazi-terrorist-jailed), accessed June 22, 2016.
16 | The Guardian (2009): Neo-Nazi Jailed for Planning Racist Bombing Campaign, December 8, (https://www.theguardian.com/uk/2009/sep/08/neil-lewington-racist-bombing-campaign), accessed June 22, 2016.
17 | BBC (2013): Mosque Bomber Pavlo Lapshyn Given Life for Murder BBC, October 25, (http://www.bbc.co.uk/news/uk-england-birmingham-24675040), accessed June 22, 2016.
18 | See Graham Macklin in this volume.
19 | Ramón Spaaij/Mark S. Hamm (2015): Key Issues and Research Agendas in Lone Wolf Terrorism. In: Studies in Conflict and Terrorism, 38/3, p. 4.
20 | Heidi Beirich (2014): White Homicide Worldwide. Montgomery: Southern Poverty Law Center, p. 1.
21 | Clark McCauley/Sophia Moskalenko (2011): Friction: How Radicalisation Happens to Them and Us. Oxford: Oxford University Press, pp. 103-105.
22 | House of Commons Home Affairs Committee (2012): Roots of Violent Radicalisation. London: House of Commons, p. 20.

Militant: Greek far-right activists participating in the so-called Imia March organized by the neo-fascist organization *Golden Dawn* in the center of Athens on February 1, 2014. This annual march is one of the largest in Europe and is regularly attended by neo-Nazis from around the globe (Original photograph taken by Max Rüting, edited by Deniz Beşer, 2016).

... Within

Patterns of Far-Right and Anti-Muslim Mobilization in the United Kingdom

Graham Macklin

Far-right and anti-Muslim politics in Britain have become increasingly fragmented. The *British National Party* (BNP), once the leading far-right party, has largely collapsed. During the 2010 general election, the BNP polled only 1.9 percent of the vote[1] and was overshadowed by the *United Kingdom Independence Party* (UKIP), a far-right, anti-immigration populist party unencumbered by the BNP's debilitating historical baggage. Thereafter, BNP leadership descended into demoralization, bitter recrimination and factional rivalry, which hastened the departure of its activist base; the collapse of its membership ultimately led to the expulsion of its chairman, Nick Griffin, as the party further continued its descent to political irrelevance. The BNP now appears "finished"[2] as a political force, its "quest for legitimacy"[3] at an end.

While the limited local *electoral* challenge of the BNP has been extinguished, that posed by the populist far-right politics of UKIP has fared little better. Despite polling 12.9 percent in the 2015 general election[4], UKIP failed to make a meaningful national breakthrough, although this was arguably due to the vagaries of the British electoral system rather than a lack of support. Leading figures have since publicly been at loggerheads with one another while the party itself has seemingly lost momentum, sometimes struggling to be heard during the 'Brexit' campaign dominated by mainstream *Conservative Party*[5] voices.[6]

Within this overarching context of far-right political failure, the *English Defence League* (EDL), an anti-Muslim street-based movement, which, since 2009, has campaigned against 'militant Islam', has also stagnated and fragmented.[7] While many activists were motivated by a belief that they were on the "front line"[8] in a 'clash of civilizations', the organization went into decline from 2011 onwards, due in part to a combination of infighting and hardline policing strategies which took much of the 'buzz' out of its demonstrations.[9] The group suffered a grievous blow in October 2013 when its founder, Tommy Robinson, resigned, claiming that street demonstrations were "no longer productive" and that "fringe elements" had increasingly gained a foothold within the group.[10] His departure, motivated also by his own on-going legal difficulties, stalled what little momentum the EDL had recouped in the aftermath of the killing of Lee Rigby, a serving soldier murdered outside Woolwich barracks, London, by two Islamist terrorists.[11] The killing generated an unparalleled, though brief, spike in the number of protests staged by far-right groups across Britain.

FRAGMENTED MOBILIZATION: STRENGTH OR WEAKNESS?

Electoral collapse and movement decline have produced an increasingly complex and diverse constellation of far-right, anti-minority and anti-Muslim groups whose organizational structures and patterns of activism are continuing to evolve. Though the EDL continues to exist, it has been joined on the anti-Muslim hinterland by a kaleidoscopic array of like-minded groupuscules. Many of these 'groups' are in fact little more than flags of convenience for disparate clusters of activists, structurally disenfranchised by the fragmentation of the EDL but still networked through the dense web of personal and social media ties that underpins the anti-Muslim protest movement.[12] They enable activists from different groups, localities and tendencies to come together as 'affiliates' under a common 'banner', often just for a one-off protest in a particular geographical location or on a particular issue. Such temporary and permeable 'structures' blur the lines of activity between groups, especially at the grassroots where demonstrators from one group are often interchangeable with those from another.

Within a fragmented scene, the porous and polyvalent nature of anti-Muslim mobilization – wherein 'group' loyalties and identities are less fixed – has helped obviate the organizational entropy engulfing political parties such as the BNP, whose regimented, sectarian boundaries preclude co-operation between ostensibly like-minded groups; this has resulted in that party continuing to wither. While political mobilization within the anti-Muslim scene has continued to devolve downwards to a local level (though the remnants of the EDL still hold the occasional 'national' demonstration), its organizational evolution suggests a continued inner coherence and resilience to the movement.

Despite this broader organizational fragmentation, the various anti-Muslim groups continue functioning as a 'network of networks' – a microcosm of the wider transnational 'counter-jihad'[13] movement of which they form a part. This evolution towards more decentralized organizational activity enables the activists who comprise this 'scene' to continue mobilizing on a regular basis. Indeed, while large 'set-piece' demonstrations might be increasingly hard for activists to stage, small, local demonstrations involving handfuls of militants are held week after week across Britain. These have been disruptive and, moreover, financially draining for local authorities and police forces, who spend vast sums of public money policing them in an 'age of austerity'.

One consequence of the changing structural dynamics of the anti-Muslim movement set in motion by the EDL's disintegration as a 'national' organization has been the development of an increasingly militant 'local' scene, which, as one recent report observed, is becoming increasingly violent.[14] The *North West Infidels* (NWI) and the *South East Alliance* (SEA) are, at present, the two most structurally viable organizations to have emerged from the profusion of groups spawned by the decaying EDL. Notably, in seeking to establish themselves, both groups have sought to 'outbid'[15] others within the wider anti-Muslim milieu with whom they are in competition for limited financial and human resources. This competition has fueled processes of ideological radicalization, leading both groups to (re)define themselves as ostensibly far-right groupuscules. Tactically, both groups have also pursued increasingly confrontational strategies with political opponents, staging provocative and increasingly violent demonstrations in towns such as Liverpool[16] and Dover.[17]

This increased militancy of these 'infidel' groups has provided the broader context for the revitalization of older violent grouplets, including the *National Front* and *British Movement*, founded in 1967 and 1968, respectively.[18] It has also generated groups such as National Action, a small, youth-focused, National Socialist group which has come under official scrutiny for holding 'self-defense' training camps in the Brecon Beacons.[19] Its activists have engaged in ever-more provocative antics, including one protest in Newcastle ahead of Holocaust Memorial Day, during which they displayed banners reading "#HITLERWAS RIGHT".[20] The group's own demonstrations have been vastly outnumbered, yet the broader societal impact of their militancy is reflected in the jailing of one activist on its periphery for an attempted racist murder.[21]

Transnational Networks

While far-right and anti-Muslim campaigns are often localized in their focus – mobilization converging upon specific towns such as Rotherham[22] and Rochdale[23] over 'Muslim grooming' or, increasingly, the arrival of Syrian refugees – the groups themselves are embedded within broader transnational networks. Far-right and anti-Muslim transnational 'networks' are not – nor have they ever been – monolithic entities, however. They are multiple, variegated and constantly evolving; sometimes overlapping with one another, sometimes not.

Anti-Muslim groups are increasingly utilizing the 'counter-jihad' network as a focus for mobilization – Tommy Robinson's internationalized activities being a case in point. Robinson's return to activist politics in 2016 – following a spell in jail for mortgage fraud – highlighted his wider networking within the broader 'counter-jihad' movement. Having spoken at *Patriotic Europeans Against the Islamization of the Occident* (PEGIDA)[24] rallies in Utrecht (the Netherlands)[25], and Dresden (Germany)[26], and attended a rally in Prague addressed by Czech President Milos Zeman – in part to foster a greater degree of coordination between such groups – Robinson sought to mobilize activists behind a local franchise of the PEGIDA 'brand'.[27] In his autobiography, he states that PEGIDA's example of "calm, measured and mature" protests offered the opportunity "to create something more mainstream" in Britain,[28] though its launch at one of several coordinated European-wide rallies gained a small turnout.[29]

Far-right groups are also exploiting the opportunities provided by increasingly transnational political networks, especially those centered upon counter-cultural activities such as music, which play a crucial role in acculturating and socializing new adherents to militant political activism. Transnational networks have been an integral part of far-right activism for decades, often combining the personal and the political. Former BNP chairman Nick Griffin, ousted from the party he had led since 1999, has used his brief tenure as a member of the European Parliament as a springboard for reinventing himself as an activist on the international far-right stage. Under the banner of the *Alliance for Peace and Freedom* – an international 'third position' network with ideological roots and personal connections traceable to the early 1980s – Griffin has emerged in the vanguard of far-right activists vocally defending Putin's Russia[30] and Bashar al-Assad's Baathist regime in Syria;[31] a country Griffin has visited several times. While the ideological bedfellows might be new, such alignments are not; finding their echo in Griffin's earlier declaration of "the new alliance"[32] between Britain's far-right, Khomeini's Iran, Gaddafi's Libya and Farrakhan's Nation of Islam in 1988.

Patterns of the transnational diffusion of ideas and tactics are not, of course, a one-way street: conflicts abroad intersect with and impact domestic extremist activity, serving as a catalyst for further militant activity. While attention is focused, understandably, upon Islamist groups, far-right 'foreign fighters' have also gained the skills and experience that could, under certain circumstance, be translated into domestic action. Unlike their Scandinavian counterparts,[33] British far-right activists are not known to be serving with the *Azov Battalion*,[34] a neo-Nazi brigade fighting Russian separatists in Ukraine.[35] However, internationalized groupuscules such as the *Misanthropic Division*, active within Britain's far-right milieu, utilize the battalion's symbology as a means of mobilizing and indeed valorizing 'militant' activity in a scene already awash with militarized, survivalist rhetoric. Another notable feature of many far-right demonstrations and neo-Nazi gigs in recent years has been the presence of a cluster of *National Rebirth of Poland* (NOP)[36] activists living in Britain, whose presence bolsters the neo-Nazi scene's increased combativeness and connectivity.[37]

Such immigration brings with it further security challenges for the monitoring of the far-right and mitigating the impact it might have upon 'community cohesion'. This was underlined by Pavlo Lapshyn, a Ukrainian student on a work placement in Britain, who murdered an 82-year-old Muslim man within days of arriving in the country and then detonated improvised explosive devices outside three West Midlands mosques – actions that would, undoubtedly, have had more serious ramifications had Lapshyn been a more proficient bomb-maker.[38] Again, such patterns are not *new*: the importance of *émigré* activists for the development of the British far right represents a process of diffusion traceable to the aftermath of the Bolshevik revolution in 1917.[39]

Conclusion

While the far-right and anti-Muslim 'scenes' are currently politically marginal, they will not disappear. Indeed, this is not the first time in recent history that the milieu has drastically contracted only to remerge years later. The legacy of this wave of anti-Muslim militancy is impossible to predict but, given its durability, is likely to include a lasting, sustainable, networked social movement. Even if this network lapses into 'abeyance'[40] for several years, it could still provide future activists with a pool of ideological and organizational resources upon which they can draw, should the 'scene', in its broader sense, be reactivated as a result of a future and, as yet, unforeseen 'catalytic event' such as that which originally led to the mobilization of the EDL in 2009. Current patterns of fragmentized mobilization and networking at a local and transnational level should be seen in this context as providing the necessary wherewithal through which such modes of militant opinion and action will sustain and survive into the future.

Annotations

1 | BBC News (2010): Election 2010. In: BBC News, May 6, (http://news.bbc.co.uk/1/shared/election2010/results/), accessed June 10, 2016.
2 | Matthew Goodwin (2012): The BNP is Finished as an Electoral Force. In: The Guardian, May 4, (http://www.theguardian.com/commentisfree/2012/may/04/bnp-local-elections-electoral-force-finished), accessed June 10, 2016.
3 | Nigel Copsey (2008): Contemporary British Fascism: The British National Party and the Quest for Legitimacy. London: Palgrave.
4 | BBC News (2015): Election 2015. In: BBC News, May 7, (http://www.bbc.co.uk/news/election/2015/results), accessed June 10, 2016.
5 | It is officially called the *Conservative and Unionist Party*.

6 | Following the 'success' of 'Brexit', UKIP leader Nigel Farage resigned as head of the party.
7 | It should be noted that, although the EDL are hostile to 'Islam', the group's leadership and the majority of its activists also reject the 'fascist' politics of the BNP, particularly their anti-Black and antisemitic racism.
8 | Joel Busher (2016): Understanding the English Defence League: Living on the Front Line of the 'Clash of Civilisations'. In: The London School of Economics and Political Science (LSE) British Politics and Policy blog, (http://blogs.lse.ac.uk/politicsandpolicy/understanding-the-english-defence-league-life-on-the-front-line-of-an-imagined-clash-of-civilisations/), accessed June 10, 2016.
9 | Joel Busher (2016): The Making of Anti-Muslim Protest: Grassroots Activism in the English Defence League. Abingdon: Routledge, pp. 123-157 and also Hilary Pilkington (2016): Loud and Proud: Passion and Politics in the English Defence League. Manchester: Manchester University Press, pp. 180-2.
10 | BBC News (2013): EDL Leader Tommy Robinson Quits Group. In: BBC News, October 8, (http://www.bbc.co.uk/news/uk-politics-24442953), accessed June 10, 2016.
11 | BBC News (2014): Lee Rigby Murder: Map and Timeline. In: BBC News, February 26, (http://www.bbc.co.uk/news/uk-25298580), accessed June 10, 2016.
12 | On which see Busher (2016): The Making of Anti-Muslim Protest; Pilkington (2016): Loud and Proud.
13 | The 'counter-jihad' movement represents a diffuse transatlantic milieu of individuals, blogs, websites, think tanks, groups, parties and politicians loosely linked by a central belief that 'Islam', and *ergo* Muslims, pose a threat to Western civilization.
14 | Hope Not Hate (2016): Smaller but More Violent: The Far Right in 2015. In: Hope Not Hate, February 7, (http://www.hopenothate.org.uk/features/far-right-2015/), accessed June 10, 2016.
15 | Donatella della Porta (2013): Clandestine Political Violence. Cambridge: Cambridge University Press, p. 151.
16 | Liverpool Echo (2016): Exposed: Extremists Thought to Have Been Involved in Right Wing Liverpool Rally. In: Liverpool Echo, March 1, (http://www.liverpoolecho.co.uk/news/liverpool-news/exposed-extremists-thought-been-involved-10968899), accessed June 10, 2016.
17 | Damien Gayle (2016): Far-Right and Anti-Fascist Protesters Clash in Dover. In: The Guardian, January 20, (https://www.theguardian.com/uk-news/2016/jan/30/far-right-anti-fascist-protesters-clash-dover) accessed June 10, 2016.
18 | For an overview of this propensity towards violence, see Alex Carter in this volume.
19 | Europol (2015): European Union Terrorism Situation and Trend Report, p. 36, (https://www.europol.europa.eu/content/european-union-terrorism-situation-and-trend-report-2015), accessed June 10, 2016.

20 | Callum McCulloch (2016): "Hitler Was Right": 'Neo-Nazis' Protest by York Minster. In: The Tab, May 28, (http://thetab.com/uk/york/2016/05/28/neo-nazi-protest-york-10941), accessed June 10, 2016.
21 | Channel 4 News (2015): National Action's Zach Davies Guilty of Attempted Murder. In: Channel 4 News, June 25, (http://www.channel4.com/news/national-actions-zack-davies-guilty-of-attempted-murder), accessed June 10, 2016.
22 | See for example Alex Evans (2016): Far-Right Protesters and Counter-Demonstrations to Descend on Rotherham Today. In: The Star, September 5, (http://www.thestar.co.uk/news/far-right-protesters-and-counter-demonstrations-to-descend-on-rother ham-today-1-7445750), accessed June 10, 2016.
23 | Manchester Evening News (2013): Three Arrested as Far-Right Groups "Try to Storm Rochdale Town Hall" in Protest over Grooming Case. In: Manchester Evening News, January 21, (http://www.manchestereveningnews.co.uk/news/greater-manches ter-news/three-arrested-as-far-right-groups-try-688399), accessed June 10, 2016.
24 | Original name in German: *Patriotische Europäer gegen die Islamisierung des Abendlandes*.
25 | Cahil Milmo (2015): EDL Founder Tommy Robinson Addresses Pegida Anti-Islam Rally in Holland. In: Independent, October 12, (http://www.independent.co.uk/news/uk/politics/edl-founder-tommy-robinson-addresses-pegida-anti-islam-rally-in-hol land-a6691406.html), accessed June 10, 2016.
26 | Imogen Calderwood (2015): "Do Not Let Germany Be Dragged back to Chaos and Destruction": EDL Founder Tommy Robinson Speaks to 40,000 Strong Crowd at the Pegida Anti-Immigrant Rally in Germany. In: Daily Mail, October 20, (http://www.dailymail.co.uk/news/article-3279659/German-far-right-activists-accuse-Angela-Merkel-treason-hold-night-time-floodlit-rally-Dresden-mark-anniversary-anti-immi grant-group.html), accessed June 10, 2016.
27 | Jamie Bartlett (2015): Across Europe with Tommy Robinson: Inside the New Wave of Anti-Immigration Protest Coming Soon to Britain. In: The Telegraph, December 4, (http://www.telegraph.co.uk/news/uknews/immigration/12031679/Across-Europe-with-Tommy-Robinson-inside-the-new-wave-of-anti-immigration-protest-coming-soon-to-Britain.html), accessed June 10, 2016.
28 | Tommy Robinson (2015): Enemy of the State, Plymouth: Press News, pp. 320–322.
29 | Josh Halliday (2016): Pegida UK Supporters Stage Anti-Islam Silent March in Birmingham. In: The Guardian, February 6, (https://www.theguardian.com/uk-news/2016/feb/06/pegida-uk-supporters-stage-anti-islam-silent-march-birmingham), accessed June 10, 2016.
30 | Dmitry Lovetsky (2015): Far-Right Politicians Come to Russia to Support Putin. In: CBS News, March 22, (http://www.cbsnews.com/news/far-right-politicians-come-to-russia-to-support-vladimir-putin/), accessed June 10, 2016.
31 | Lamiat Sabin (2014): What on Earth is Nick Griffin Doing in Syria? In: The Independent, December 1, (http://www.independent.co.uk/news/world/middle-east/what-on-earth-is-nick-griffin-doing-in-syria-9895196.html), accessed June 10, 2016.

32 | For the declaration, see Community Security Trust (CST) (2010): Political Soldiers and the New Man – Part Two. In: CST blog, April 27, (https://cst.org.uk/news/blog/2010/04/27/political-soldiers-and-the-new-man-part-two), accessed June 10, 2016.

33 | For more on this topic, see Kacper Rękawek (2015): Neither "NATO's Foreign Legion" nor the "Donbass International Bridages:" (Where Are All the) Foreign Fighters in Ukraine? Polish Institute of International Affairs (PISM) Policy Paper, 6/108, March 30, (http://www.pism.pl/files/?id_plik=19434), accessed June 10, 2016.

34 | Original name in Ukrainian: *Полк Азов*, sometimes called *Azov Regiment*. See also Heiko Koch, Matthew Kott and Mathias Schmidt in this volume.

35 | Tom Parfitt (2014): Ukraine Crisis: The Neo-Nazi Brigade Fighting Pro-Russian Separatists. In: The Telegraph, August 11, (http://www.telegraph.co.uk/news/world news/europe/ukraine/11025137/Ukraine-crisis-the-neo-Nazi-brigade-fighting-pro-Russian-separatists.html), accessed June 10, 2016.

36 | Original name in Polish: *Narodowe Odrodzenie Polski*.

37 | Mark Townsend (2016): Foreign-Born Fascists "Helping to Radicalize UK Far-Right Movement". In: The Guardian, February 6, (https://www.theguardian.com/world/2016/feb/06/foreign-born-fascists-radicalise-uk-far-right-movement), accessed June 10, 2016.

38 | BBC News (2013): Mosque Bomber Pavlo Lapshyn Given Life for Murder. In: BBC News, October 25, (http://www.bbc.co.uk/news/uk-england-birmingham-24675040), accessed June 10, 2016.

39 | For the impact of the Russian Revolution upon political antisemitism in Britain, see Sharman Kadish (1992): Bolsheviks and British Jews: The Anglo-Jewish Community, Britain and the Russian Revolution, London: Frank Cass.

40 | For further discussion of this concept, see Verta Taylor (1989): Social Movement Continuity: The Women's Movement in Abeyance. In: American Sociological Review, 54/5, pp. 761–775.

But – Where Do These People Come From?
The (Re)Emergence of Radical Nationalism in Finland

Oula Silvennoinen

Trouble is brewing for the European Union – and in Finland as well, where the country-wide elections of 2019 will see several new, EU-hostile nationalist groups attempt to establish themselves on the political map. At the same time, Finnish neo-fascism is seeking to entrench itself and become normalized as a respected part of the political framework.

On the heels of growing disillusionment, the time appears to be ripe. As Heikki Hiilamo, professor of social policy at Helsinki University notes, Finland has been particularly hard hit by the most recent economic downturn. The middle and lower classes are seeing their expectations fade into uncertainty, as globalization is bringing new and intangible threats in the form of vanishing jobs. Finland is headed towards increasing social inequality, with the reality that the educated and the employed are drifting farther apart from 'globalization's losers'. With the lack of any self-evident owner, the accumulating political capital is attracting radical nationalist interest.[1]

THE DECLINE OF THE FINNS PARTY

Much is at stake in the next parliamentary elections: the major channel for political protest, the populist *The Finns Party*[2], may be falling apart, leaving its inheritance up for grabs. The party, which broke through with decisive success in the 2011 parliamentary elections, is an unstable coalition of traditional advocates for 'little people' – blue-collar conservatives seeking a labor movement without the left, and radical nationalists consciously riding on an anti-immigration platform.

Now under pressure, the constituent groups may start looking for other channels of protest. The party has so far been held together by its leader, Timo Soini; currently, however, his dazzlingly successful experiment in Finnish populism seems to be headed towards inevitable failure. A series of recent polls predict a sharp loss in support for the party, which has been unable to make good on its pre-election promises of pushing through decisive changes, especially in two crucial areas: the economy and immigration.[3]

CRISIS-INDUCED AUTHORITARIAN MOBILIZATION

The definitive backdrop for the current crisis of populism is the European refugee situation. In 2015, Finland admitted some 32,000 asylum-seekers, most of whom are still housed in immigration detention centers around the country. For a nation of 5.5 million, with a remarkably homogenous ethnic and cultural background, this figure is considered great, even far too great by many. Often, the only concrete symbol of the global community's intrusion into the local world is a detention center and its inhabitants, tossed into a locality, seemingly without considering the locals.

Even a brief glimpse at the Facebook group of Finland's anti-immigration movement, *Close the Borders*[4], lends support to Hiilamo's analysis: the socially underprivileged and undereducated are well represented among the members, many of whom suffer from unemployment or live on social benefits. Their resentment stems from several sources, but it is nearly unidirectionally aimed at asylum-seekers, typically referred to as 'invaders'. Fear is all-pervasive: the asylum-seekers are thought to present an acute threat to their surroundings, as they are believed to commit rape at any given opportunity. Many commenters regularly describe their country as facing an 'Islamic invasion' and being in danger of being 'Islamicized' within at most a few decades. The driving force behind this process of ultimate societal and cultural disintegration is seen to be the ruling elite, who, for some unfathomable reason, are promoting a reckless immigration policy to the benefit of 'dark-skinned honorary citizens'.

Many commenters revel in fantasies of a violent backlash: swear words, threats and sexual insults induce an atmosphere akin to hate-fests in comment threads, culminating in visions of a civil war between the self-attested 'patriots' and the estranged elite along with their supposed protégés, the immigrants. For most of the commenters, the group represents a safety valve through which individuals can vent their anger – few of the bloodcurdling threats have actually materialized. But, as many of them say: "How long before someone freaks out?"

FIFTH ESTATE: THE RISE OF THE FAKE MEDIA

A major factor driving the surge of radicalized nationalism has been the successful channeling of dissatisfaction towards the immigrants, especially the asylum-seekers. A key player in this process has been the 'fake media', publications disguising themselves as 'alternative' news outlets which harbor a propagandistic agenda. Fake media act free of any restraints of journalistic accuracy or accountability, recycling and rewriting stories acquired through real and not-so-real news services. The sole aim of fake media news is to generate moral outrage: stories about asylum-seekers receiving or demanding social benefits are designed to rouse the ire of the underprivileged; hostility directed at the EU, the USA and NATO is the norm.[5]

This agenda bears an uncanny resemblance with the political interests of Vladimir Putin's Russia; too close, in fact, to be mere coincidence. Fake media's ties to the Russian government have been under scrutiny by researchers, journalists and bloggers alike. While no conclusive proof of direct Russian involvement is available, the circumstantial evidence all points to Putin's government. Rather conspicuously, fake media do not criticize Russia or Russian policies, while also maintaining close ties to both radical nationalists and known pro-Russian advocates.[6]

Tellingly, fake media attack those who dare criticize either the fake media outlets themselves or their links to Russian interests. Here, the means of choice is a social media campaign through which the intended victim is publicly vilified and exposed to the rage of the masses. Thus, whether or not any individual actor is in direct Russian patronage, fake media de facto serve Russian interests by fostering divisive political rhetoric and undermining social trust. The aim seems to be the social destabilization of the EU and NATO member states, thus weakening their ability to present a united front against Russian power politics.

A FRAGMENTED FIELD OF WOULD-BE CAPITALIZERS

These developments have already come home to roost: both politics and social life are fragmenting and compartmentalizing, while trust and respect towards almost all traditional authorities are eroding. In an atmosphere of suspicion laden with conspiracy myths, the elites, the university, the church, trade unions, the media particularly the national broadcasting Company YLE) and even the once almost universally respected Finnish Red Cross have all fallen under suspicion. The political parties, without exception, have been hit the hardest, and the first victim, in a way of poetic justice, will be *The Finns Party*.

After the last parliamentary elections, a number of would-be political gainers have emerged. The most serious attempt to capitalize on resentment towards the EU and the fiscal policies of the Eurozone has been made by the nascent *Citizen Party*[7], led by the unsinkable political veteran, Paavo Väyrynen.

The next municipal and parliamentary elections will test the mettle of Väyrynen's political intuition and decide the fate of his new party.

Further down the spectrum of radicalized nationalism we find the newly-founded *Finland Democrats*[8], modeled after the much-more successful Swedish *Sweden Democrats*[9], and who already claim a number of local chapters. Its agenda is dominated by immigration, social grievances and opposition to the elites and the EU. *Finland Democrats* and the anti-Islamization *Finnish Defence League* are both members of the *European Liberty Coalition*, a loose grouping of north-European radical nationalist organizations. Another contender for party status, *True Finnish Blue*[10], styles itself as a 'popular movement'.

Surrounding these would-be parties are several organizations that do not aspire to party status. The *Finnish Resistance Movement* (SVL)[11] is an openly National Socialist organization, conspicuously promoting hero figures from Nazi propaganda and Finnish inter-war fascist movements on its webpage. It boasts that it is a branch within a Nordic network of similar movements, with sister groups in Sweden, Norway and Denmark. One recent development has been the attempt to create a social welfare organization, *Finnish Aid*[12], dealing out material help for those considered national comrades.

Another offspring is the *Soldiers of Odin Finland*, which has rapidly branched into a number of international sister organizations. The street-patrolling *Soldiers'* own claims to mass membership and support may be questioned:[13] their self-proclaimed level of activity seems to be inflated and their organizational and motivational endurance remains untested. While members of the *Soldiers* typically deny racist motivations and stress the unarmed nature and law-abiding intentions of their vigilantism, the organization is associated with known neo-Nazi activists from the SVL. The intent of patrolling in uniform is to create violent confrontation and challenge the authority of the police in maintaining public order and safety.[14]

Finnish Sisu[15] is the most successful of the radical nationalist organizations without aspirations of being a proper party. Founded in 1998, with a serving Member of Parliament as its chairman and several other active politicians among its supporters, the group can be considered a venerable veteran in the frenetic world of Finnish radical nationalism. *Sisu* is explicit in its yearning for the nationalist agenda of the inter-war period, cherishing the memory culture of the victors of the 1918 Finnish civil war. Its program can be described as fascist, with an emphasis on the threat of community decline. As an antidote, an 'organic national community' is envisioned as basis for a re-forged Finnish nation and state – a future Europe shall consist of culturally and ethnically independent nation-states.

WAITING FOR A LEADER

With the success of *The Finns Party* waning and no obvious heir to take its place, the current landscape is a battleground for would-be leaders, none of whom has yet proven charismatic enough to muster anything resembling mass popularity. Forming inclusive parties capable of sustained political activity has so far been the Achilles' heel of Finnish radical nationalism. Despite grandiose rhetoric, almost all of the radical nationalist 'popular movements' are mass movements in name alone. Comparisons to Finnish fascism during the inter-war era are obvious: again, political potential breaks down into a number of mutually suspicious and fratricidal groupings, which prevents the rise of an effective common front.

The nationalists' vision for Finland, and Europe, is essentially a negative one: obsessively concerned with security, defensive, nostalgic and isolationist. Successful policies consist of fending off perceived threats; actual success is only presumed to follow from a vaguely outlined national revolution. With Soini's party badly discredited, Finland's radical nationalists and fascists are waiting for their own Donald Trump to galvanize disaffection into authoritarian protest at the ballot box. While the electoral success may well fall short of enabling an actual political takeover as in Hungary or Poland, it may yet grant the radicals enough leverage to effect long-lasting influence in society and political life.

ANNOTATIONS

1 | Heikki Hiilamo (2016): Muukalaisvihamielisyys kumpuaa ahdistetusta keskiluokasta ja alistetusta köyhälistöstä [Wellsprings of Xenophobia in Beleaguered Middle Class and Suppressed Poor]. In: Helsingin Sanomat, February 14, (http://www.hs.fi/sunnuntai/a1455249808686), accessed June 23, 2016.
2 | Also called *True Finns*, original name in Finnish: *Perussuomalaiset*.
3 | Uutiset (2016): Puoluekannatusmittari: miten puolueiden kannatus on muuttunut vuosien saatossa? [Party Support Meter: How Has Party Support Changed with the Times?], March 31, (http://yle.fi/uutiset/puoluekannatusmittari__miten_puolueiden_kannatus_on_muuttunut_vuosien_saatossa/8778938#start=252), accessed June 23, 2016.
4 | Original name in Finnish: *Rajat kiinni*.
5 | I will not provide links to these sites, as they largely live from advertising income generated by web traffic. Those who nevertheless wish to have a closer look can check *MV-lehti*, *Magneettimedia* (also notable for its antisemitic content) or *Uberuutiset*, to name a couple.
6 | Saara Jantunen (2015): Infosota [Infowars]. Helsinki: Otava.
7 | Original name in Finnish: *Kansalaispuolue*.

8 | Original name in Finnish: *Suomidemokraatit*.
9 | Original name in Finnish: *Sverigedemokraterna*.
10 | Original name in Finnish: *Aitosuomalaiset Siniset*.
11 | Original name in Finnish: *Suomen Vastarintaliike*.
12 | Original name in Finnish: *Suomalaisapu*.
13 | Corey Charlton (2016): Fears Grow Over Finland's Far-Right Vigilante Group 'Soldiers of Odin' as the Country Struggles to Deal with Huge Influx of Migrants, in Daily Mail, January 13, (http://www.dailymail.co.uk/news/article-3397860/Anti-immigrant-Soldiers-Odin-raise-concern-Finland.html), accessed July 23, 2016.
14 | Uutiset (2016): Soldiers of Odin's secret Facebook group: Weapons, Nazi Symbols and Links to MV Lehti, March 16, (http://yle.fi/uutiset/soldiers_of_odins_secret_facebook_group_weapons_nazi_symbols_and_links_to_mv_lehti/8749308), accessed June 23, 2016.
15 | Original name in Finnish: *Suomen Sisu*. There is no appropriate translation for Sisu. Sisu basically means perseverance in the face of adversity, commitment to push things through despite any hardship and obstacles, expressing the historic self-identified Finnish national character.

The Far Right in Latvia
Should We Be Worried?

Matthew Kott

For quite some time now, far-right politics in Latvia have remained relatively stable and predictable. The current state of instability in Europe – with the Ukraine conflict, the refugee crisis, and, most recently, the 'Brexit' – has, however, prompted some developments that could turn into significant trends in the medium to long term.[1] These trends stand to have an effect on broader European politics, if left unchecked.

THE ETHNIC DIVIDE IN LATVIA'S FAR RIGHT

For much of the past 25 years since Latvia regained independence from the USSR, the main dividing line on the far right has been ethnic in nature, namely the tensions between radical Latvian ethno-nationalism and its post-Soviet Russian counterpart.[2] The main vehicle of ethnic Latvian political nationalism has been the party *For Fatherland and Freedom/Latvian National Independence Movement* (TB/LNNK)[3], which has its roots in the struggle for independence during the *Perestroika*-era. Throughout the 1990s and 2000s, this party absorbed radical start-ups and also survived radical schisms, eventually turning into a party of social and fiscal conservatism that mainly engaged in symbolic nationalist politics and populistic, anti-Russian sloganeering during election campaigns. This normalization and deradicalization took place as TB/LNNK was increasingly included in government coalitions – even providing the Prime Minister in 1997–98. At the same time, a semi-legal and semi-clandestine radical milieu of far-right groupuscules, including antisemitic, neo-Nazi and fascistic clusters, existed in symbiosis with TB/LNNK, particularly through nationalist youth organizations. One of the most notorious of these was the terroristic underground reincarnation of the inter-war *Thunder Cross Party*[4], whose members unsuccessfully tried to blow up the Soviet Victory Monument in central Riga.[5]

On the other side of the ethnic divide, Latvia's sizeable Russian-speaking community – feeling marginalized and discriminated by the nationalizing Latvian state – has had a complex relation with far-right ideologies due to the post-imperial legacy of the Soviet Union. For much of the post-Soviet period, 'Russian' parties, i.e., those rooted in the Russian-speaking community, have generally self-identified as being on the political left. A key element in the strongly pro-Soviet Baltic Russian identity is the victory over National Socialist Germany in the Second World War. Despite this strong anti-Nazi identity, a few Russian-speakers in Latvia have committed neo-Nazi hate crimes.[6]

Compared to these rare neo-Nazi skinheads, the more serious far-right political actors were the local branches of the main fascistic movements in Russia, the National Socialist *Russian National Unity* (RNE),[7] based around the city of Liepāja, and the syncretic, Eurasianist *National Bolshevik Party* (NBP),[8] primarily active in and around Riga and Daugavpils.[9] The former trained paramilitary cadres and gained legal legitimacy through a clever coup of entryism, in which they took over the registered Latvian ultra-nationalist *Latvian National Democratic Party*[10] from within, turning it into a legal RNE front. Their main rivals were the *National Bolsheviks*, a party whose ideology combines elements of Stalinism and fascism, and which succeeded in attracting non-ethnic Russians as activists. NBP activists engaged in highly visible provocations[11] and terrorism – a group of them occupied and threatened to blow up the steeple of Saint Peter's Church in central Riga[12]. After the latter act, the NBP was forced underground, and many fled to Russia. With time, a clandestine NBP network was rebuilt in Latvia and, following social unrest in the late 2000s, relaunched itself as a supposedly socialist popular protest movement in the wake of the economic downturn.[13]

New Ideologies and Strategies in the 21ST Century

In the early 2000s, a new far-right ideology appeared: political homophobia[14]. Originally based in a primarily Russophone charismatic revivalist Christian congregation, the phenomenon grew to include socially conservative clergy from the larger, predominantly Latvian-speaking Lutheran and Catholic churches. This resulted in the creation of new party, *Latvia's First Party* (LPP),[15] also colloquially known as the *Preachers' Party*, as a political vehicle for socially conservative and homophobic politics. From 2002 to 2007, this party achieved a significant degree of political influence at the municipal level and in the national parliament. During this period, the party had a number of ministers, including Nils Muižnieks as minister for societal integration from 2002 to 2004. Parliamentarians and local politicians from LPP have continued to promote homophobic political agendas – often inspired by similar policies from illiberal neighboring countries – even after their party disappeared in an amalgamation process in 2007.[16]

Another political expression of the far right arising around the time of Latvia's EU accession was the anti-globalization movement, featuring a steadily growing far-right ideological bent. With the financial crisis of 2008–9, the movement gained new momentum, with loose networks coalescing around the website *antiglobalisti.lv*. These activists, both ethnic Latvians and Russophones harboring conspiracy myths, arranged protests against government bailouts of failed banks, in which the iconography used on placards mixed populist anti-elitism, Euroskepticism and antisemitic iconography. Together with various far-right organizations in the neighboring Baltic states, they have participated in marches against the EU's alleged policies of 'zombification' and 'genocide' against the people.[17] Nevertheless, their influence in the broader public sphere – beyond the comments sections of internet news portals – was generally minimal.

FAR-RIGHT RESTRUCTURATION IN TIMES OF CRISIS

Regarding the ethno-nationalist far right, the early 2010s witnessed significant reinvigoration and consolidation. Most significantly, the ultra-nationalist movement *All for Latvia!*[18] became a major political player. Founded as a radical youth splinter group in the early 2000s, it had grown into a political party by 2006. A number of high-profile publicity stunts, such as a protest against the ratification of the border treaty with Russia, gained the group popularity and legitimacy from across the nationalist right. In 2010,[19] they entered an electoral alliance with TB/LNNK; this combination reinvigorated Latvian nationalism by not only bringing in new faces that differed from the tired old ones in TB/LNNK, but also by injecting ideological tendencies that reversed the aforementioned deradicalization process of the mainstream TB/LNNK. Within his cooperation, activists from *All for Latvia!* gained influence over much of the existing TB/LNNK party apparatus, particularly at the local, grassroots level. When the two parties were formally merged as the *National Alliance* (NA),[20] it represented a textbook case of successful far-right entryism. For almost the entire 2010s, the NA has been in the government coalition, and radical politicians from *All for Latvia!* have gained key roles in the state.[21]

A similar consolidation initially took place in the Russian far right. Burying their long-standing differences, the overwintered elements of the RNE and *National Bolsheviks* joined forces to form the lobby movement *For the Mother Tongue!* (ZaRYA) that turned into a political party.[22] Mobilizing all of their latent political capital, ZaRYA forced a constitutional referendum in 2012 to make Russian the co-official language.[23] During the campaign, the establishment 'Russian' parties were forced to take a position, lest they lose legitimacy to the radicals in the eyes of their voters. This led to an overall radicalization of the political discourse on ethnic relations in Latvia. Even though the referendum failed, it opened a channel for new political initiatives: the leaders of ZaRYA were also elected to the newly created Congress of Non-Citizens, the aim of which was to apply pressure for greater political rights for a significant number of Russophones without Latvian citizenship.[24]

Nevertheless, in contrast to the NA, the vested interests of the main 'Russian' party, *Harmony Center*,[25] proved resilient against the lure of radicalization. In elections, ZaRYA failed miserably in transforming its newfound prominence into seats at the local, national or EU levels. A rift developed in ZaRYA when the National Bolshevik leader, Vladimir Linderman, opted to spearhead an initiative for a new referendum, this time to ban 'homosexual propaganda', joining forces with Latvian radical nationalists and political homophobes.[26] The RNE faction in ZaRYA saw this as a betrayal of the Russian cause, and formed a new organization, *Russian Dawn*,[27] with a radical Russian ethno-nationalist position.[28] The events in Ukraine in 2014 further exacerbated the problems for the Russian far right in Latvia. While both groups came to support the annexation of Crimea and the Donbas separatists, their reactions were quite different. NBP activists from Latvia, most prominently the so-called Black Lenin, Benes Aijo,[29] actively participated in the political and military campaigns there;[30] a handful of other National Bolsheviks have also fought with the separatists in the Donbas.[31] In contrast, the RNE faction in Latvia seems to have limited participation in the Donbas conflict to engaging in pro-Russian propaganda activities.

THE CHANGING LANDSCAPE OF THE FAR RIGHT IN LATVIA

The Ukraine conflict also exposed a radicalization of the other major 'Russian' party, *For Human Rights in a United Latvia*[32]. The party's long-time member of the European Parliament, Tatyana Zhdanok, took part in the delegation of generally far-right organizations that acted as international observers to the Crimean Referendum in 2014.[33] Just prior to this, the party had changed its leftist-sounding name to the more ethno-nationalist *Latvian Russian Union*[34].

The Ukraine conflict also led marginal Latvian extremist groups to carry out recruitment drives for volunteers to join far-right militias[35], such as the *Azov Battalion*[36]; these actions, however, enjoyed minimal success. More worrying was the NA's ability – in the context of the Latvian government's general support for the post-Maidan government – to lend 'European' credibility to the far-right *Svoboda* party.[37] However, more extremist groups criticize the NA for not being radical enough: on March 16, 2016, at the annual commemoration of Latvians who fought in the *Waffen-SS* Latvian Legion during the Second World War, a representative of the *Azov Battalion* named 'Yaroslav' was in Riga at the invitation of former *Thunder Cross* leader Igors Šiškins. 'Yaroslav' got into a verbal debate with leading NA politician Imants Parādnieks, who considered the presence of the Nazi-inspired *Azov* banner as a "provocation" to discredit the commemoration event organized by the NA.[38]

The refugee crisis in 2015 has changed some of the rules of the game. The very idea of non-European refugees coming to Latvia has mobilized the far right. With racist and xenophobic attitudes towards Middle Easterners and Africans being common in Latvia, ethnic Latvian and Russian radicals, along with the reinvigorated anti-globalists, have found common ground in the discourse of 'endangered whiteness', of an EU and Muslim conspiracy of genocide against the 'white' peoples of Europe.[39] Old and new political entrepreneurs jockey for position, such as the *Guards of the Fatherland*,[40] an anti-immigration organization with a paramilitary profile, modelled on the inter-war front organization of the *Thunder Cross Party*.[41] On social media, this group portrays itself in much the same terms as the *Soldiers of Odin*[42] vigilante movement in the Nordic countries, which has recently also spread to Estonia.[43] Other parts of the far right in Latvia seem to be suffering from the shifting political topography, with Linderman recently announcing that ZaRYA will unregister as a political party and go underground[44] – whether this will lead to the dissolution or to radicalization of Latvia's NBP cadres remains to be seen.

Conclusion

Latvia is perhaps the only EU member state where the far right has been included in the government coalition for years, without significant condemnation from its European partners. As such, Latvia may end up helping far-right ideas seem more respectable in European politics, for example, that of political homophobia. At the same time, Latvia's geopolitical position and cultural makeup makes it an ideal entry point for ideological conflicts imported from further East: the Ukraine crisis has mobilized both Latvian and Russian ultra-nationalists, and it may yet destabilize the delicate societal balance. Latvia is also not immune to jihadism, as recent events have shown,[45] thus further fueling a public discourse that is hostile to Muslims and non-European refugees in general. The recent adoption of slogans and visual symbolism about 'white genocide' and Islamophobia borrowed from far-right movements in other countries – such as the crossed-out mosque sign first popularized by the "Pro-"campaigns in Germany – is a reminder that, just as in the 1990s, Latvia could be a 'growth market' for far-right positions imported from neighboring Western and Northern Europe, increasing the overall clout of these ideas in the EU.

Up to now, the NA in Latvia's government, along with the neo-fascists and anti-globalists on the street and on social media, have been able to normalize far-right ideas and politics in an EU member state without the same scrutiny or outcry that such developments have attracted in other countries. Indeed, Brussels directs less criticism at Riga than Moscow does in this respect – despite the fact that a potential policy interest exists for the Kremlin in Latvian society becoming more divided by ethnic tensions and rejecting common European values. If the legitimization of the far right in Latvia is allowed to continue, it may very well help to tip the political balance in the EU away from openness and cooperation, especially since the 'Brexit' victory in June 2016 threatens to put wind in the sails of far-right populists and ultra-nationalists across Europe. Thus, despite its relatively small size, Latvia and its various far-right groups may have a disproportionate role in the transmission of radical ideologies from East to West, and vice versa, particularly if disruptive regional actors such as the Kremlin pump (even more) money into some of these movements.

Annotations

1 | This article builds on some ideas presented in an overview published in Matthew Kott (2012): Rumsrena extremister, [Acceptable Extremists]. In: Expo, 2012/4, pp. 40–43.

2 | For a good summary of developments up to the early 2000s, see Nils Muižnieks (2005): Latvia. In: Cas Mudde (ed.), Racist Extremism in Central and Eastern Europe. London, New York: Routledge, pp. 101-128.

3 | Original name in Latvian: *Tēvzemei un Brīvībai/Latvijas Nacionālā neatkarības kustība*. TB/LNNK was an amalgamation of the parties TB and LNNK.

4 | Original name in Latvian: *Pērkonkrusts*. Following his release from jail for his role in the Victory Monument bombing (see below), Igors Šiškins renamed the group the Gustavs Celmiņš Center *(Gustava Celmiņa centrs)*, named for the inter-war *Thunder Cross* leader, Gustavs Celmiņš. For the inter-war party, see Matthew Kott (2015a): Latvia's *Pērkonkrusts*: Anti-German National Socialism in a Fascistogenic Milieu. In: Fascism: Journal of Comparative Fascist Studies, 4/2, pp. 169-193.

5 | BNS (2000): Radicals 'Perkonkrusts' Handed Prison Time in Blasts. In: The Baltic Times, June 6, (http://www.baltictimes.com/news/articles/383/), accessed June 20, 2016.

6 | LETA (2011): Three Skinheads Accused of Desecrating Jewish Graves. In: BNN October 12, (http://bnn-news.com/skinheads-accused-desecrating-jewish-graves-38892), accessed June 20, 2016; TBT Staff (2007): Skinheads Attacked Two Somali Refugees. In: The Baltic Times, January 5, (http://www.baltictimes.com/news/articles/17084/), accessed June 20, 2016.

7 | Original name in Russian: *Russkoe Natsional'noe Edinstvo*.

8 | Original name in Russian: *Nastional-bol'shevistskaia partiia*.

9 | On these parties in general, see Viacheslav Likhachev (2002): Natsizm v Rossii, [Nazism in Russia]. Moscow: Panorama.

10 | Original name in Latvian: *Latvijas Nacionāli demokrātiskā partija*.
11 | E. g. the assault on Prince Charles with a carnation, see BBC (2001): Schoolgirl Who Hit Prince Faces Jail. In: BBC News, November 9, (http://news.bbc.co.uk/2/hi/uk_news/1646735.stm), accessed June 20, 2016.
12 | Nick Coleman (2000): Russian Extremists Take St. Peter's. In: The Baltic Times, November 23, (http://www.baltictimes.com/news/articles/3423/), accessed June 20, 2016.
13 | Lenta.ru (2009): Natsbol Linderman sozdal v Latvii sotsialisticheskuiu partiiu, [National Bolshevik Linderman Founds a Socialist Party in Latvia]. In: Lenta.RU, 28 September, (https://lenta.ru/news/2009/09/28/party/), accessed June 20, 2016; RT.com (2012): Latvia Moves to Outlaw Pro-Russian Socialist Party. In: RT.com, October 30, (https://www.rt.com/politics/latvia-outlaw-pro-russian-socialist-570/), accessed June 20, 2016.
14 | Political homophobia is a strategy that involves a gendered reaction to perceived threats against masculine identity and the 'natural' patriarchal social order. It can be encountered in contexts of societies undergoing or having recently undergone traumatic political and economic transformations, where scapegoating 'gays' for all of societies' perceived ills – much in the same manner as political antisemitism blames everything on 'the Jews' – provides populistic and identity-based answers to complex social phenomena, such as the erosion of traditional male economic power in a globalized world. Often the literature focuses on cases of postcolonial societies, e. g., Ashley Currier (2010): Political Homophobia in Postcolonial Namibia. In: Gender and Society, No. 24, pp. 110–129. Political homophobia in post-Communist Eastern Europe would also need to systematically be researched.
15 | Original name in Latvian: *Latvijas Pirmā partija*.
16 | For examples, see Mozaika (2007): Homophobic Speech in Latvia: Monitoring the Politicians, Riga: Mozaika. ILGA-Europe, (http://www.ilga-europe.org/sites/default/files/Attachments/latvia_-_homophobic_speech_in_latvia_english.pdf), accessed June 20, 2016.
17 | For photos from their various demonstrations, see Antiglobālisti (no date): Piketi [Demonstrations]. In: antiglobalisti.org, no date, (http://antiglobalisti.org/piketi/), accessed June 20, 2016.
18 | Original name in Latvian: *Visu Latvijai!*.
19 | Central Electoral Commission (2010): Nacionālā apvienība "Visu Latvijai!": "Tēvzemei un Brīvībai/LNNK" 2010.gada 2.oktobra 10.Saeimas vēlēšanas, [National Alliance "All for Latvia!": "TB/LNNK", Elections to the 10th Saeima on October 2, 2010]. In: CVK, August 2, (https://www.cvk.lv/cgi-bin/wdbcgiw/base/komisijas2010.CVKAND10.kandid2?nr1=10), accessed June 20, 2016.
20 | Original name in Latvian: *Nacionālā apvienība*.
21 | For example, Jānis Iesalnieks, considered a radical ideologue and key promoter of fascistic ideas in the party, while not elected to parliament, sits on the board of the *National Alliance* and is the parliamentary secretary to the minister of justice. Iesal-

nieks gained international attention for a tweet in 2011 in support of terrorist Anders Behring Breivik: DPA (2011): Ermittlungen gegen lettischen Parlamentarier [Investigations against Latvian Member of Parliament]. In: Tageblatt, August 10, (http://www.tageblatt.lu/nachrichten/story/Ermittlungen-gegen-lettischen-Parlamentarier-30688344), accessed June 20, 2016.

22 | Original name in Russian: *Za rodnoi iazyk!*.

23 | The ZaRYA campaign video for the referendum presents NBP frontman Linderman and RNE leader, Evgenii Osipov, in a fascistic visual aesthetic: Rodnoi iazyk (2013), April 23, (https://www.youtube.com/watch?v=UeWohOjOBzg), accessed June 20, 2016.

24 | For a list of those elected to the "Parliament of the Unrepresented", see Kongress negrazhdan (2013): Deputaty Parlamenta nepredstavlennikh [Members of the Parliament of the Unrepresented]. In: Kongress negrazhdan, June 19, (http://www.kongress.lv/ru/material/348), accessed June 20, 2016.

25 | Original name in Latvian: *Saskaņas centrs*.

26 | A. U. (2014): A Minister Comes Out. In: The Economist, November 12, (http://www.economist.com/blogs/easternapproaches/2014/11/latvia-and-gay-rights), accessed June 20, 2016. Cf. Inga Spriņģe (2016): The Rise of Latvia's Moral Guardians. In: Re:Baltica, January 20, (http://www.rebaltica.lv/lv/petijumi/buvnieki_partijas_iepirkumi/a/1298/the_rise_of_latvias_moral_guardians.html), accessed June 20, 2016.

27 | Original name in Russian: *Russkaia Zaria*.

28 | Diena.lv (2014): Oficiāli reģistrēta krievu valodu kā valsts valodu rosinājusī Osipova biedrība Russkaya Zarya, [Osipov's Society Russkaya Zarya, which Proposed Registering Russian as a State Language, is Officially Registered]. In: Diena.lv, January 12, (http://www.diena.lv/latvija/politika/oficiali-registreta-krievu-valodu-ka-valsts-valodu-rosinajusi-osipova-biedriba-russkaya-zarya-14039723), accessed June 20, 2016.

29 | Mike Collier (2014): An Unlikely Revolutionary: Beness Aijo. In: LSM, July 31, (http://www.lsm.lv/en/article/features/an-unexpected-revolutionary-beness-aijo.a93076/), accessed June 20, 2016.

30 | Kieran Corcoran (2014): Heathrow Worker Who Left UK to Fight with Pro-Russian Rebels Says Ukraine and the West Shot down MH17 to Smear Russia. In: Daily Mail, July 20, (http://www.dailymail.co.uk/news/article-2698823/Beness-Aijo-Putins-British-disciple-UK-student-29-linked-pro-Russian-rebels-blamed-shooting-MH17-arrested-Latvia-leaving-UK-fight-Crazy-Ukrainians.html), accessed June 20, 2016.

31 | Eng.lsm.lv (2014): Donetsk Fighters from Latvia to Face Punishment. In: LSM, July 20, (http://www.lsm.lv/en/article/societ/society/donetsk-volunteers-from-latvia-to-face-punishment.a93050/), accessed June 20, 2016.

32 | Original name in Latvian: *Par cilvēku tiesībām vienotā Latvijā*.

33 | Anton Shekhovtsov (2014): Pro-Russian Extremists Observe the Illegitimate Crimean 'Referendum'. In: Anton Shekhovtsov's blog, March 17, (http://anton-shekhovtsov.blogspot.se/2014/03/pro-russian-extremists-observe.html), accessed June 20, 2016.

34 | Original name in Latvian: *Latvijas Krievu savienība*.

35 | See for example Imants Liepiņš (2014): Latvieši gatavi palīdzēt ukraiņiem, [Latvians Ready to Help Ukrainians]. In: NRA, March 3, (http://nra.lv/latvija/112571-latviesi-ga tavi-palidzet-ukrainiem.htm) accessed June 20, 2016; Ģirts Vikmanis (2015): Cīnījos par Latviju: Saruna ar latvieti, kurš karojis Ukrainas brīvprātīgo bataljonā, [I Fought for Latvia: A Conversation with a Latvian, who Fought in a Ukraine Volunteer Battalion]. In: Latvijas Avīze, March 3, (http://www.la.lv/latvietis-kurs-karojis-ukrainas-brivpratigo-b-ataljona-cinijos/), accessed June 20, 2016.

36 | Original name in Ukrainian: Полк Азов, sometimes called *Azov Regiment*. For the transnational composition of the Azov Battalion see Heiko Koch, Graham Macklin, and Mathias Schmidt in this volume.

37 | For example the National Alliance politician Einārs Cilinskis was photographed together with Oleh Tiahnybok of *Svoboda*: @EinarsCilinskis (2014): Tikšanās ar O. Tagņiboku un citiem frakcijas Svoboda deputātiem-LV jāveido ciešāka sadarbība ar demokrātisko Ukrainu, [Meeting with O. Tiahnybok and Other MPs of the Svoboda Parliamentary Group – Latvia Must Develop Closer Cooperation with Democratic Ukraine]. In: Twitter, February 23, (https://twitter.com/einarscilinskis/status/437675067552849920), accessed June 20, 2016.

38 | MixNews (2016): Instruktor batal'ona 'Azov' o Paradniekse: Rozha mne ego ne nravitsia!, [Azov Battalion Trainer on Parādnieks: I don't Like his Mug!]. In: MixNews.lv, March 16, (http://www.mixnews.lv/ru/exclusive/news/197433_instruktor-batalona-azov-o-paradniekse-rozha-mne-ego-ne-nravitsya-video/), accessed June 20, 2016.

39 | Matthew Kott (2015b): Becoming More 'European': In the Wrong Way. In: Baltic Rim Economies, No. 5, p. 25.

40 | Original name in Latvian: *Tēvijas sargi*.

41 | Cf. Kott (2015a): Latvia's *Pērkonkrusts*, p. 181. *Guards of the Fatherland* is not directly related to the aforementioned reincarnation of the *Thunder Cross* led by Šiškins.

42 | On the *Soldiers of Odin* in Finland, see Oula Silvennoinen in this volume.

43 | Janis Laizans/Joachim Dagenborg (2016): Anti-immigrant 'Soldiers of Odin' Expand from Finland to Nordics, Baltics. In: Reuters, March 2, (http://www.reuters.com/article/us-europe-migrants-vigilantes-idUSKCN0W411Z), accessed June 20, 2016.

44 | LETA (2016): Lindermana partija turpmāk darbosies 'pagrīdes režīmā', [Linderman's Party Henceforth to Go into 'Underground Mode']. In: TVNET, February 29, (http://www.tvnet.lv/zinas/latvija/598202-lindermana_partija_turpmak_darbosies_pagrides_rezima), accessed June 20, 2016.

45 | Eng.lsm.lv (2016): Security Police Moves on Two Persons over Going to War in Syria. In: LSM, March 2, (http://www.lsm.lv/en/article/societ/society/security-police-moves-on-two-persons-over-going-to-war-in-syria.a171739/) accessed June 20, 2016.

The Achilles' Heel of Bulgaria's Patriotic Front

Yordan Kutiyski

Ever since Bulgaria's admission to the European Union (EU) in 2007, the country's far right, although domestically weak, has managed to send its representatives to the European Parliament (EP). Prior to 2014, these members of the EP remained largely isolated, retaining a non-affiliated status. Initially, Volen Siderov's far-right party, *Attack*[1], the first of its kind in post-communist Bulgaria, won three seats in the legislative body in 2007. Formed in 2005, *Attack* quickly gained electoral support, conveying a strong xenophobic and anti-minority rhetoric combined with an emphasis on Orthodox Christian values and opposition to globalization. No other Bulgarian party has previously sought to attract voters using such a strategy. *Attack* participated in the short-lived *Identity, Tradition, Sovereignty* group in the EP. Further efforts to construct a lasting political grouping on the far right with the participation of Bulgarian parties proved futile, minimizing their influence on shaping debates and decision-making. Losing a seat in 2009, *Attack* remained outside of any recognized EP political group.

The situation changed in 2014, however, when the *Internal Macedonian Revolutionary Organization – Bulgarian National Movement* (VMRO-BND)[2] propelled Angel Dzhambazki to the EP and later to the soft Euroskeptic *European Conservatives and Reformists* (ECR) group. VMRO originated as an independence movement in the 19th century and was engaged in various political activities in the early 20th century, including terrorist attacks. Under communist rule, VMRO was allowed to exist as a cultural organization, resuming its organizational and political activities after 1989 under the name VMRO-BND, initially taking part in the democratic opposition, *Union of Democratic Forces* (SDS)[3]. As the party gradually moved rightwards, it left SDS to take part in a number of electoral coalitions, some of which led to parliamentary representation. VMRO-BND's rhetoric was less explicitly nationalist in the early years of Bulgaria's transition to democracy but became more and more so in the 2000s, especially with the success of *Attack*. In 2014, VMRO-BND founded the *Patriotic Front* (PF)[4] together with like-minded parties and formations. Contrary to *Attack*, this newly established far-right coalition has quickly gained prominence in both the European and Bulgarian political scene and is seen as an acceptable partner. However, PF's links to extreme right movements and activists could eventually negatively impact its reputation and credibility.

THE FORMATION AND RISE OF THE PATRIOTIC FRONT

Disillusioned by *Attack's* parliamentary support for a short-lived centrist minority coalition government at home, its electorate shrank by nearly 80 percent from one European election to the next, leaving the party empty-handed in 2014. Moreover, *Attack* gradually shifted its rhetoric and platform away from vehement opposition to the perceived 'Turkeyzation' and 'Gypsyzation' of Bulgaria towards advocating a statist economic policy and close cooperation with Russia – a move that did not bring much electoral benefit. This vacuum certainly contributed to the rise of VMRO-BND, which, in coalition with the centrist conservatives, *Bulgaria Without Censorship* (BBC)[5], won two seats in the EP, including one for Dzhambazki, who has attracted criticism for his radical views and controversial statements[6]. The electoral volatility brought about by the decline of *Attack* created space for political entrepreneurship on the far right; the *National Front for Salvation of Bulgaria* (NFSB)[7], led by former Siderov employer and media-mogul Valery Simeonov, joined forces with VMRO-BND prior to the early Bulgarian parliamentary elections in October 2014. Neither party managed to pass the four-percent threshold in 2013, with NFSB and VMRO-BND gaining 3.7 and 1.9 percent of the vote, respectively. In 2014, however, their collaboration project, the PF, became the fifth-largest party, gaining 7.3 percent of the vote and 19 seats in the national assembly. Simultaneously, *Attack* was relegated from the fourth to the seventh-largest political force, and, although it remained represented in parliament, the party lost more than half of its seats.

THE PATRIOTIC FRONT: AN ACCEPTABLE POLITICAL PLAYER?

Whereas *Attack* has been a political outsider at home and abroad – deprived of government participation domestically and unable to collaborate on the European level – the PF is largely viewed as an acceptable partner. The party does maintain a rather moderate profile: its 2014 program focused on national economic revival, modernization of the healthcare and education systems, and fighting corruption. With regard to its stances on ethnic minority issues, the PF acknowledges that all ethnic groups should have equal rights, granted that they profess a Bulgarian identity and adhere to Bulgarian legislation[8]. At the EU level, the party representative, Angel Dzhambazki, joined the ECR – a club of established parties, including Britain's incumbent Conservatives. At home, the PF joined a broad coalition government led by the center-right *Citizens for European development of Bulgaria* (GERB)[9], and obtained a share of governing positions, including those of deputy ministers. Thus, in a very short period, the PF proved to be a much more successful political project than *Attack* had ever been. Still, the two parties share a common background[10], while their voters have a very similar socio-economic and ideological outlook. It is therefore remarkable that the PF managed to rapidly integrate into mainstream politics, while *Attack* has remained isolated for years – especially considering PF's links to extreme right activists, who openly profess National Socialist ideology. These links may prove particularly problematic for PF's image abroad, as the VMRO-BND has persistently collaborated with the extreme right and even nominated immensely questionable personalities for office, who have been accused of committing various hate crimes and were apprehended by the Bulgarian judicial system. As none of the parties represented in parliament openly associates itself with National Socialism, such linkages need to be closely scrutinized and condemned in order to keep Bulgarian and European politics free from anti-democratic influence.

LINKS WITH THE EXTREME RIGHT

Angel Dzhambazki, arguably the most prominent representative of Bulgaria's far right, has been personally involved in numerous campaigns aimed at securing the release of individuals (currently no longer in custody) well-known in the Bulgarian neo-Nazi milieu, including Nikolai Yovev and Dimiter Lazarov.

Yovev, an extreme right activist from Bulgaria's south-west, was arrested in 2012 in relation to the murder of a security guard at a branch office of *EuroRoma*[11], a party promoting Roma rights, in the town of Sandandski. The guard died from the explosion of a bomb that was planted at the party office[12]. Previously known to the police on account of his involvement in an assault on a Roma family[13] in the aftermath of a protest that took place after the vehicular homicide of 19-year-old Bulgarian by a Roma man[14] in the village of in Katunitsa, Yovev is also well-known for the dissemination of National Socialist propaganda and for his involvement in the football hooligan movement. VMRO-BND has publically announced its support for Yovev, claiming that the accusations against him constitute "repression against nationalists"[15]. The party went as far as nominating Yovev as a Member of Parliament prior to the 2013 election in an attempt to secure his release[16], while Dzhambazki has attended several protests against his detention[17].

Glorified by the extreme right, Yovev remains a strongly controversial figure. It is rather surprising that an individual occupying the influential position of a member of the EP would publically voice support and provide assistance to a well-known neo-Nazi. Though it remains unclear to this day whether Yovev was involved in the murder, his open propagation of anti-democratic ideology is reason enough for those with a democratic mindset to distance themselves from such a questionable personality. Yet, despite this, Dzhambazki and VMRO-BND have rallied behind Yovev's candidature.

This has not been the only instance in which Dzhambazki and VMRO-BND have provided support for an arrested extreme-right activist. On their way to a demonstration against the detention of undocumented immigrants in 2010, a group of far-left activists were attacked and severely beaten[18] in a tram in Bulgaria's capital, Sofia. After the attack, the victims identified Dimiter Lazarov, a VMRO-BND member[19] with ties to neo-Nazi groups such as the militant white supremacist movement *Blood & Honour* and the organization of radical nationalists, *National Resistance*[20], as one of the perpetrators.[21] After Lazarov was detained in relation with the crime, VMRO-BND resorted to the same tactics, nominating the right-wing extremist for office prior the 2014 parliamentary election[22]. At the time of writing, the court has still not delivered a verdict on Lazarov's involvement. Rather than distancing himself from representatives of the extreme right, Angel Dzhambazki personally attended the trial and publically defended Lazarov[23].

Conclusion

The Bulgarian far right has only recently emerged as a credible political partner both at home and abroad. At the European level, any clear linkage between a member of the EP and the extreme right would easily impair or even destroy a political career. In Bulgaria, however, PF's role as a junior coalition partner is unlikely to be undermined within the current parliamentary configuration, given the close ties between the Prime Minister and the party's leadership. It remains to be seen whether PF's European partners will ever question Dzhambazki for his links to the Bulgarian neo-Nazi movement. These links may prove to be the Achilles' heel in the acceptance of Bulgaria's far right, destroying its international, if not domestic, credibility.

Annotations

1 | Original name in Bulgarian: *Атака*.
2 | Original name in Bulgarian: *Вътрешна Македонска Революционна Организация – Българско Национално Движение*.
3 | Original name in Bulgarian: *Съюз на Демократичните Сили*.

4 | Original name in Bulgarian: *Патриотичен Фронт*.
5 | Original name in Bulgarian: *България без Цензура*.
6 | Asa Bennet (2014): David Cameron's New 'Openly Racist' Brussels Ally Says Conchita Wurst Is 'Dangerous', June 29, (http://www.huffingtonpost.co.uk/2014/06/25/tories-ecr-brussels-conchita-wurst-mep_n_5528786.html), accessed June 26, 2016.
7 | Original name in Bulgarian: *Национален Фронт за Спасение на България*.
8 | Patriotic Front (2014): Political Program, (http://www.nfsb.bg/public/izbori_2014_HC/PF_PROGRAMA_2014_crivi.pdf), accessed June 26, 2016.
9 | Original name in Bulgarian: *Граждани за Европейско Развитие на България*.
10 | Ekaterina R. Rashkova/Emilia Zankina (2015): How Radical, How Much For Women? Examining the Gender Question in Radical Right Parties in Bulgaria. Paper prepared for presentation at the European Conference on Politics and Gender, Sweden: Uppsala, June 11–13.
11 | Original name in Bulgarian: *Евро Рома*.
12 | 24 hours (2012): Почина Малин Илиев, ранен при взрива пред офис"Евророма, [Malin Iliev, Wounded by Explosion at an EuroRoma Office, Has Deceased], July 29, (https://www.24chasa.bg/Article/1483846), accessed June 26, 2016.
13 | Blitz News (2012): Николай Йовев е единият от арестуваните за взрива в Сандански, [Nikolai Yovev Is One of the Arrested for the Explosion in Sandanski], July 1, (http://www.blitz.bg/news/article/144862) accessed June 26, 2016.
14 | Darik News (2011): Убийството на младеж в Катуница доведе до двудневни безредици, [The Murder of a Youth in Katunitsa Has Led to Two Days of Disorder], September 24, (http://dariknews.bg/view_article.php?article_id=780376), accessed June 26, 2016.
15 | VMRO-BND (2013): Политическите репресии над националисти продължават, [The Political Repressions against Nationalists Continue], May 1, (http://www.vmro.bg/politicheskite-represii-nad-natsionalisti-prodlzha/), accessed June 26, 2016.
16 | Sonya Kolchakova (2013): ВМРО готови с вкарването в листите си на обвинените за взрива в Сандански, [VMRO-BND has Finalized the Nominations of those Prosecuted for the Explosion in Sandanski], March 28, (https://news.bg/crime/vmro-gotovi-s-vkarvaneto-v-listite-si-na-obvinenite-za-vzriva-v-sandanski.html), accessed June 26, 2016.
17 | Info-net (2013): С протест поискаха свобода за арестанти – кандидат-депутати на ВМРО, [Protesters Demand the Release of Prisoners Nominated for Parliament by VMRO-BND], April 19, (http://infomreja.bg/s-protest-poiskaha-svoboda-za-arestanti---kandidat-deputati-na-vmro-11295.html), accessed June 26, 2016.
18 | Ivaylo Krachunov (2010): Неонацисти нападат трамвай, бият антифашисти [Neo-Nazis Beat up Anti-Fascists in a Tram Attack], June 6, (http://www.trud.bg/Article.asp?ArticleId=504351), accessed June 26, 2016.
19 | Dimiter Lazarov (2014): Фундаменталистки призиви заливат мрежата, ДАНС спи [Fundamentalist Appeals Are Flooding the Internet, while National Security Sleeps], September 24, (http://www.vmro.bg/лазаров-фундаменталистки-призиви-заливат-мрежата-данс-спи/) accessed June 26, 2016.

20 | Original name in Bulgarian: *Национална Съпротива*.

21 | Dnevnik (2014): Делото за побоя в трамвай 20 отново в съда, продължава през октомври, [The Trial for the Attack in Tram 20 in Court again, Continues in October], April 23, (http://www.dnevnik.bg/bulgaria/2014/04/23/2286530_deloto_za_poboia_v_tramvai_20_otnovo_v_suda_produljava/), accessed June 26, 2016.

22 | OffNews.bg (2014): Листите на Патриотичен фронт за парламентарните избори, [The List of Patriotic Front Nominees for the Parliamentary Elections], September 4, (http://offnews.bg/news/Politika_8/24-Listite-na-Patriotichen-front-za-parlamentarnite-izbori_383583.html), accessed June 26, 2016.

23 | Trud.bg (2012): Фалстарт на дело за бой в трамвай, [A Lawsuit for a Beating in a Tram Fails to Start], November 10, (http://www.trud.bg/Article.asp?ArticleId=1567661&fb_source=message), accessed June 26, 2016.

The Changing Faces of Neo-Nazism
Militant Far-Right Activism in Greece

Maik Fielitz

In Greece, far-right politics during economic crises have, until now, been inextricably associated with the spectacular rise of the neo-Nazi party *Golden Dawn* (XA)[1].[2] The evolution of XA into a serious challenger within Greek politics came as a surprise to many pundits, as support did not decline even when the party's crimes were revealed and put to trial.[3] In fact, the constellation of XA is unique in the European far right. Deriving from an intertwined network of far-right groupuscules, movements and parties, XA has adopted a genuine stance based on historical National Socialism for years and also engaged in violent street battles. Parties with such a militant record are generally relegated to the fringes of the political spectrum by analysts since they lack the integrity needed to attract mainstream voter segments.[4] Besides this, dissident actors such as the early XA consciously deny any compliance with rules and institutions of a perceived hostile political order and mainly articulate their anti-systemic stance through disruptive means such as political violence.[5]

Nowadays, XA's strategic opening[6] – in the light of its burgeoning success at the ballot boxes – has created a twofold dilemma: on the one hand, old bonds to neo-Nazi subculture and the image of a violent militia increasingly turn out to be an obstacle for greater integration with potential supporters from the moderate far right. On the other hand, proponents of the self-proclaimed *National Socialist Movement in Greece* criticize an alleged renunciation of the central values of neo-Nazism, as XA is allegedly shifting from militant activism towards mainstream politics.[7]

Delving into debates within the tense terrain of militant far-right activism, this study sheds light on the conflictive relations in Greek neo-Nazism and its recent re-constitution in Greece. In order to do so, it is vital to trace XA's trajectory from a pioneer of Greek neo-Nazism to a party that challenges liberal democracy in the electoral arena. At the same time, I argue that it is necessary to go beyond the unilateral focus on XA in order to understand the party's behavior and the scene-internal dynamics that operate in and beyond the group's structure.

Considering neo-Nazism a complex phenomenon within a larger far-right field of actors, this chapter grapples with the discourses and practices of the habitat from which XA emerged and from which it recruits. In a word, the chapter attempts to open the black box of Greek neo-Nazism and reveal patterns of changing interactions that help contextualize the rise of XA into far-right politics in Greece.

THE TRAJECTORY OF GOLDEN DAWN'S ASCENDANCE

If one sought to organize as a Greek neo-Nazi in the 1980s and 90s, there were hardly any alternatives to XA to choose from. Looking back on his political career of neo-Nazi activism, Ioannis Giannopoulos – a self-proclaimed 'veteran of Greek National Socialism' – explained that he had "no other choice"[8] than to join the ranks of XA to promote 'the cause of National Socialism'. Tracing the roots of organized Greek neo-Nazism, it is, accordingly, no exaggeration to see XA as its pioneer, combining (neo-)National Socialist ideology with a race-based understanding of Hellenism from the outset.[9] Concurrently operating as a closed ideological circle and violent militia, XA attracted action-oriented nationalist youths as well as fascist collaborators reminiscing about the anti-communist climate of the occupation and civil war period in the 1940s.

As self-proclaimed anti-systemic 'avant-garde of neo-Nazi activism' in the 1980s and 90s, XA initially denied any compliance with democratic rules, procedures and institutions. Considering party politics as a dirty business that stands opposed to its "pure National Socialist ideology",[10] the activities flourished in international neo-Nazi networks[11] and among national subcultures rather than aspiring to mass representation. Since the late-1990s, however, XA's strategy and style of politics has fundamentally changed. The acts of forming a political party in 1994, building a coalition with moderate far-right networks,[12] renouncing paganism, and gradually reframing its National Socialist ideology into "popular nationalism"[13] demonstrate the end of the "pure years"[14] and a long-term trend towards (strategic) moderation. Likewise, the ultimate goal of creating a race-based dictatorship and implementing violent tactics to exert spatial dominance remains in place.[15]

Fueled by a climate of political polarization and economic hardship in the late 2000s, XA capitalized on widespread xenophobia by building local strongholds in the center of Athens. Filling a gap after the leading far-right force *Popular Orthodox Rally* (LAOS)[16] lost credibility in right-wing circles for its participation in the interim 'Government of National Unity' under Loukas Papadimos,[17] XA entered the Greek parliament with 6.9 percent in 2012. Stabilizing its results in the European parliamentary elections in 2014 and in the national elections in January and September 2015, the party even managed to become the third political force in a transforming party landscape.[18]

TENDENCIES OF DECENTRALIZATION IN GREEK NEO-NAZISM

Influenced by an international diversification of neo-Nazi activism, XA's tactical defection of central characteristics of neo-Nazi ideology, along with its static structure and inflexible standing towards new far-right currents, provoked internal debates on the future of Greek neo-National Socialism. As a consequence, disillusioned activists formed spin-off networks organized in tiny regional collectives, which were strongly bound to subcultural activities, debates on neo-Nazi ideology and direct action. Those 'small political entities' (frequently meta-political, but never primarily party-political) – labelled as *grouspuscular right* in the academic literature[19] – were not significant in number but still managed to challenge, first and foremost, XA's claim to be the sole representative of the neo-Nazi milieu, and formed alternatives to the hierarchical model of XA.

Two main camps epitomize this trend of decentralization: in one, older veterans acted under the umbrella of the national-revolutionary *Black Legion*[20], which served as a last resort for classic neo-Nazi activism. The other is a nationwide *Network of Autonomous Nationalists*[21] comprised of younger activist. From the mid-2000s on, the latter acted as the spearhead for far-right autonomous activism in Greece, fueled by both a fierce antisemitism and a non-compromising rejection of liberal democracy and party politics. Understanding National Socialism as a 'leaderless grassroots ideology'[22], these activists advocate for decentralized structures that combine lifeworld orientations with political agitation and clandestine actions along with a strong aestheticization of violence, all of which is coupled with the brazen use of anti-fascist symbolism.[23]

Lacking organizational coherence, the *Network of Autonomous Nationalists* dissolved in 2012 and nurtured a number of independent groupuscules that had more determination. This resulted in a strong increase of clandestine right-wing crimes in Greece during the last five years.[24] Most incidents can be ascribed to a violent neo-Nazi network, the *Non-Conformist Meander Nationalists* (AME)[25], which meticulously documents its actions on the group's blog. Their repertoire comprises arson attacks against social centers and occupied houses, desecrations of Jewish cemeteries[26] and violent assaults on leftist party offices. Recently, activists of AME have operated under the label of *Combat 18 Hellas* (C18), mimicking the armed insurrection of tiny cells that act independently, with only three to five persons, according to the British role model.[27] The first actions making use of the symbol 'C18' included the desecration of the monument of Pavlos Fyssas – who was murdered by a XA representative on September 18, 2013 – and a Molotov cocktail attack against the *Pasamontana* social center in Korydallos.[28] Published texts and communiqués on other occasions explicitly refer to XA: while they dissociate their actions from XA's "tragic ideological transformation"[29], at the same time, they grant XA a prominent position by indicating a twofold message – declaring the continuation of XA's early work while simultaneously attempting to appeal to the militant wing of XA in order to (again) wage a militant struggle.[30]

GOLDEN DAWN IN THE MIRROR OF MILITANT FAR-RIGHT ACTIVISM

The inherent debate about XA harks back to the contested notion of what National Socialist activism means in the Greek context and how to strategically proceed in achieving its short- and medium-term objectives. Composed as a dissident ideology – "an absolute, irrevocable, and uncompromising fight against the very philosophical foundations of the entire ruling world order"[31] – the hard core of neo-Nazism demands an irrevocable confession to the foundation on a common normative basis. According to the early writings of XA, its spokesmen conceive far-right activism to be incompatible with engagement in a framework of liberal democracy.

Now that XA increasingly plays the card of strategic deradicalization[32], it is of particular interest to assess the notions of the organizational field that surrounds it in order to evaluate the political turn through an emic perspective. On the basis of a qualitative content analysis of the websites and journals of eight neo-Nazi groupuscules, online networks and subcultural forums,[33] four conflictive patterns are identified that establish a practically irreversible line between militant neo-Nazism and XA.

First, procedural criticism of static party hierarchies spread the notion of inner party corruption and self-enrichment structures. As it has not changed its internal hierarchy since the very outset, achieving higher positions in the organization increasingly depends on personal benevolence or even family bounds and less on political conviction or one's level of engagement.

Second, compliance with the rules of the perceived hostile political system has cultivated the notion that XA has become part of the political establishment. Thus, the populist slogan "scumbags, traitors, politicians" used by XA to capitalize on widespread disenchantment now turns against the group itself, which allegedly changed sides.[34] This culminates in the reproach aimed at XA that it has stabilized "a collapsing political system"[35] by taking the parliamentary path and renouncing its revolutionary ambitions.

Third, XA has recently been attacked for diluting the idea of National Socialism in Greece. The autonomous spectrum, in particular, endeavors to question XA's reputation on the scene by exposing policies, protagonists and practices that supposedly contradict the normative framework of neo-Nazi activism. Some matters prominently discussed include its affiliation to Christian orthodoxy, the integration of non-National Socialist 'careerists' within central party positions and the commemoration of right-wing nationalist anniversaries[36]. Instead, autonomous neo-Nazis aim to (re-)cultivate National Socialism as an ideology of steadfast dissent in contrast to the alleged dodging of XA's representatives who are described as "inhibiting factors for strengthening the National Socialist dynamic inside of 'Golden Dawn' and outside of it"[37].

Last, the increasing attraction of geopolitics and the unilateral support for the Russian government[38] – especially with regard to the conflict in Ukraine – provoked discord among militant neo-Nazi groups which strongly collaborate with the *Azov Battalion*[39], as is the case for the Greek groups *Black Legion* and *Ideapolis*.

Despite the criticism towards XA, there are positive opinions on how to estimate its electoral success from the perspective of party remote neo-Nazi activism: groups such as the AME (sharing a personnel overlap with XA) emphasize that they welcome the election results as windows of opportunity for grassroots activism[40] and basically stand in solidarity when it comes to legal prosecution and attack from leftist and anarchist opponents.[41] This instance once again shows that relations to XA remain in flux and highly depend on XA's performance and institutional responses.

Towards a Struggle for Hegemony in Organized Neo-Nazism?

Neo-Nazism in Greece is far more heterogeneous than any sole focus on XA might presume. Faced with electoral opportunities, the far right in Greece in general and the neo-Nazi wing in particular has to tackle a classic dilemma faced by far-right actors once they become influential: opening to bourgeois constituencies while at the same time maintaining internal consistency and peculiarity in a heterogeneous environment. As the brief analysis here has revealed, this situation has generated conflicts about the normative basis and the strategic approach which have constantly been renegotiated since neo-Nazism diversified in the 2000s. This fragmentation has complicated interactions among the central proponents of Greek neo-Nazism. While XA lost credibility due to its parliamentary turn, its position on the scene was bolstered by strong subcultural bonds to organized hooliganism and *White Power Music* networks, such as *Blood and Honour*.[42]

In sum, XA's transition from dissident grassroots activism to oppositional party politics created a space on the fringe of the far-right spectrum that points to further radicalization of militant milieus. Whereas XA is strongly criticized for its supposed ideological turn, it still remains a common point of reference for militant far-right activism. Despite inconsistencies in the position of current developments around XA, the reaction of organized neo-Nazis to XA's increasing adaptation is helpful in evaluating internal party realignments.

This obviously resulted in an internal review of the situation of the far right in Greece, ushering the struggle for sovereignty in neo-Nazi spectrum into a new era.

ANNOTATIONS

1 | Original name in Greek: *Χρυσή Αυγή*.
2 | See Daphne Halikiopoulou/Sofia Vasilopoulou (2015): The Golden Dawn's "Nationalist Solution": Explaining the Rise of the Far Right in Greece. New York: Palgrave Pivot.
3 | XA's leadership is accused of coordinating a criminal organization according to paragraph 175 of Greek penal law. Trying four different cases, the trial against 69 defendants was launched in April 2015. See Maik Fielitz (2015): (Morgen)Dämmerung vor Gericht, April 17, (http://www.sicherheitspolitik-blog.de/2015/04/17/morgendaemmerung-vor-gericht/), accessed July 12, 2016; Maik Fielitz (2015): From a Political Challenger to a Criminal Case: Prospects and Pitfalls in the Trial against Golden Dawn. Manuscript prepared for the Conference Legal Proceedings against Right-Wing Terrorism, University of Applied Sciences Düsseldorf, December 4; Dimitris Psarras (2014): Η Χρυσή Αυγή Μπροστά στην Δικαιοσύνη [Golden Dawn on Trial]. Rosa Luxemburg Foundation: Brussels.
4 | Piero Ignazi (2002): The Extreme Right: Defining the Object and Assessing the Causes. In: Martin Schain/Aristide Zolberg/Patrick Hossay (eds.): Shadows Over Europe: The Development and Impact of the Extreme Right in Western Europe. New York: Palgrave Macmillan, pp. 21-37.
5 | Cf. Christopher Daase/Nicole Deitelhoff (2014): Reconstructing Global Rule by Analyzing Resistance, International Dissidence Working Paper, No. 1, (http://dissidenz.net/wp-content/uploads/2016/04/wp1-2014-daase-deitelhoff-en.pdf), accessed July 10, 2016, pp. 11-13.
6 | João Carvalho (2015): The End of a Strategic Opening? The BNP's Window of Opportunity in the 2000s and its Closure in the 2010s. In: Patterns of Prejudice, 49/3, p. 285.
7 | National Socialist Movement of Greece (2015): Ανακοίνωση της Εθνικοσοσιαλιστικής Κίνησης Ελλάδος: Η 'Χρυσή Αυγή' οι εκλογές και η στάση των Ελλήνων Εθνικοσοσιαλιστών [Statement of the National Socialist Movement of Greece: The 'Golden Dawn', the Elections and the Position of the Greek National Socialists], January 19, (http://mavroskrinos.blogspot.de/2015/01/blog-post_94.html), accessed August 10, 2015.
8 | Black Legion (2014): Αποκλειστικό: Συνέντευξη του παλαίμαχου Εθνικοσοσιαλιστή Ιωάννη Γιαννόπουλου στον 'Μαύρο Κρίνο' [Exclusive: Interview with the National Socialist Veteran Ioannis Giannopoulos to the 'Black Legion'], July 2, (http://mavroskrinos.blogspot.de/2014/07/blog-post_2.html), accessed July 10, 2016.
9 | See Maik Fielitz (2015): Beyond the Fringe: Unfolding the Dynamics of Golden Dawn's Rise. In: Sebastian Goll/Martin Mlinarić/Johannes Gold (eds.): Minorities

Under Attack: Othering and Right-Wing Extremism in Southeast European Societies. Wiesbaden: Harrassowitz, pp. 257-275.

10 | Golden Dawn (1980): Η Εκδόσις Μας [Our Publication]. In: Chrysi Avgi, No. 1, p. 2.

11 | Maik Fielitz (2013): Goldene Morgenröte für Europas Extreme Rechte? Der Transnationale Einfluss der Griechischen Chrysi Avgi [Golden Dawn for the European Extreme Right? The Transnational Influence of the Greek Chrysi Avgi]. München: Fachinformationsstelle Rechtsextremismus München.

12 | Between 2005 and 2008, XA was organized in the electoral coalition, the *Patriotic Alliance* [Πατριωτική Συμμαχία], and even succumbed to the authority of moderate far-right entrepreneurs.

13 | See the programmatic and ideological text: Golden Dawn (2013): Λαϊκός Εθνικισμός Τώρα! [Popular Nationalism now!], August 1, (http://www.xryshaygh.com/enimerosi/view/laikos-ethnikismos-twra1), accessed July 10, 2016.

14 | According to the XA dropout Haris Kosoumvris, the "pure ideological years" persisted from 1980 and 1996. Haris Kosoumvris (2004): Γκρεμίζοντας τον Μύθο της Χρυσής Αυγής [The Revelation of the Golden Dawn Myth]. Athens: Erevos, p. 16.

15 | Dimitris Psarras (2012): Η Μαύρη Βίβλος της Χρυσής Αυγής [The Black Bible of Golden Dawn]. Athens: Polis.

16 | Original name in Greek: Λαϊκός Ορθόδοξος Συναγερμός.

17 | After the Prime Minister Giorgos Papandreou resigned his office in 2011, a tripartite interim government was installed (consisting of the social democrat *Panhellenic Socialist Movement*, the conservative *New Democracy* and the far-right LAOS) under the leadership of Loukas Papadimos. It was the first time that a far-right party participated in the national government. Cf. Antonis A. Ellinas (2013): The Rise of Golden Dawn: The New Face of the Far Right in Greece. In: South European Society and Politics, 18/4, p. 547.

18 | See Antonis A. Ellinas (2014): Neo-Nazism in an Established Democracy: The Persistence of Golden Dawn in Greece. In: South European Society and Politics, 20/1, pp. 1–20.

19 | Roger Griffin (2003): From Slime Mould to Rhizome: An Introduction to the Groupuscular Right. In: Patterns of Prejudice, 37/1, p. 30.

20 | Original name in Greek: *Μαύρος Κρίνος*.

21 | Original name in Greek: *Δίκτυο Αυτόνομων Εθνικιστών*.

22 | This is discussed in the central booklet for Autonomous Nationalists in: Network of Autonomous Nationalists (2011): Νοσταλγοί του Μέλλοντος [Nostalgics of the Future], a copy is available at: https://scribd.com/document/113523707/Νοσταλγοί-του-Μέλλοντος, accessed August 2, 2016.

23 | See also Jan Schedler/Alexander Häusler (2011): Autonome Nationalisten: Neonazismus in Bewegung [Autonomous Nationalists: Neo-Nazism on the Move]. Wiesbaden: VS Verlag für Sozialwissenschaften.

24 | Besides the surge of racist and homophobic violence in the Greek city centers between 2011 and 2013 that can mainly be attributed to XA, see Maik Fielitz (2015):

Beyond the Fringe, p. 270, arson attacks on alternative projects spread since early 2015.

25 | Original name in Greek: *Ανέναχτοι Μαίανδριοι Εθνικιστές*.

26 | Central Board of Jewish Communities in Greece (KIS) (2015): Announcement for the Desecration of the Athens Jewish Cemetery, October 23, (http://www.kis.gr/en/index.php?option=com_content&view=article&id=603:announcement-for-the-desecration-of-the-athens-jewish-cemetery-&catid=12:2009&Itemid=41), accessed June 26, 2016.

27 | The far-right militant organizations *Combat 18* (sometimes in cooperation with AME) claimed the responsibility for at least nine attacks that were meant to cause severe harm but missed their target. For further information on *Combat 18* see Nick Lowles (2001): White Riot: The Violent Rise and Fall of Combat 18. Bury: Milo Books. See also Alex Carter in this volume.

28 | Giannis Baskakis (2015): Ανάληψη ευθύνης για τη βεβήλωση του μνημείου Φύσσα [Claim of Responsibility for the Desecration of the Fyssas Monument], March 4, (http://www.efsyn.gr/arthro/analipsi-eythynis-gia-ti-vevilosi-toy-mnimeioy-fyssa), accessed July 10, 2016.

29 | Ristorante Verona (2013): Δηλώσεις του Μιχαλολιάκου στον ΣΚΑΪ [The Statements of Michaloliakos on SKAI], May 20, (http://ristorante-verona.blogspot.de/2013/05/1952013.html), accessed August 2, 2015.

30 | Combat 18 (2015): "Αναρχικό-Αντιεξουσιαστικό" Στέκι Αντόπνοια/C18 Hellas - A. M. E. ['Anarchist-Antiauthoritarian' Hangout Antipnoia/C18 Hellas – AME], June 12, (http://combat18hellas.blogspot.gr/2015/06/blog-post.html), accessed August 2, 2015.

31 | Povl H. Riis-Knudsen (1987): National Socialism: The Biological Worldview, a copy is available at: https://archive.org/details/NationalSocialismTheBiologicalWorldview, accessed July 8, 2016, p. 2. See also the Greek translation by the edition of XA: Povl H. Riis-Knudsen (1989): Εθνικοσοσιαλισμός. Η Βιολογική Κοσμοθεωρία [National Socialism: The Biological Worldview]. Chrysi Avgi: Athens, p. 8.

32 | Anton Shekhovtsov (2015): How the European Far Right Became Mainstream: Strategic 'Deradicalization' Is the Key to Winning Euroskeptic Votes, Politico, April 22, (http://www.politico.eu/article/euroskeptics-far-right-became-mainstream/), accessed July 4, 2016. See also Lotte Laloire in this volume.

33 | Those were: The periodicals *Patria* and *Blood and Honour*, the blogs of the aforementioned groups *Non-Conform Meander Nationalists* (AME), *Combat 18 Hellas* and *Black Legion*, the neo-Nazi news platform *Altermedia Hellas*, the subcultural coined websites of *Ristorante Verona* and *Ideapolis*. These are the most active and influential print and online media resources of neo-Nazi and far-right militant activism in Greece.

34 | Altermedia (2013): Η 'Χρυσή Αυγή'... Είναι Το Πιο Συστημικό Κόμμα Της Βουλής [Golden Dawn is the Most Systemic Party of the Parliament], January 12, (www.altermedia.info/hellas/2013/01/12/c-nooth-aoath-assiae-oi-dhei-ooocieei-euiia-ocoaioetho/), accessed August, 8, 2015.

35 | Aristotelis I. Kalentzis (2014): Ο Αριστοτέλης Ηρ. Καλέντζης για τον Νίκο Ρωμανό [Aristotelis I. Kalentzis about Nikos Romanos], December, 3, (http://mavroskrinos.blogspot.de/2014/12/blog-post.html), accessed July 18, 2016.

36 | Golden Dawn recently took a positive stance towards the August 4th regime by Ioannis Metaxas (1936–1940) who repealed the Italian threat to occupy Greece in 1940 and the latter tripartition of Greece by the fascist axis. This is today commemorated by the so-called *Oxi* holiday. XA's participation in those commemorations is highly exposed due to the implicit anti-national socialist character, referring to the multiple national socialist groups in the Greek inter-war period that strived for a coalition with the German regime.

37 | National Socialist Movement of Greece (2015): Ανακοίνωση της Εθνικοσοσιαλιστικής Κίνησης Ελλάδος [Statement of the National Socialist Movement of Greece], January 19, (http://mavroskrinos.blogspot.de/2015/01/blog-post_94.html), accessed July 19, 2016.

38 | Maik Fielitz (2014): Byzantinische Verhältnisse? Golden Dawn und die Eurasische Doktrin, July 27, (http://www.sicherheitspolitik-blog.de/2014/07/29/byzantinische-verhaeltnisse-golden-dawn-und-die-eurasische-doktrin/), accesessed July 2, 2016; Sofia Tipaldou (2015): The Dawning of Europe and Eurasia? The Greek Golden Dawn and its Transnational Links. In: Marlène Laruelle (ed.): Eurasianism and the European Far Right: Reshaping the Europe-Russia Relationship. Lanham: Lexington Books, pp. 193-218.

39 | Original name in Ukrainian: Полк Азов, sometimes called *Azov Regiment*. On the transnational reach of the regiment, see also Heiko Koch, Matthew Kott, Graham Macklin, and Mathias Schmidt in this volume.

40 | AME (2012): Μετεκλογικά Συμπεράσματα και Εκλόγιμες Αλήθειες [Post-Election Consequences and Eligible Truths], June 19, (http://maiandrioi.blogspot.de/2012/06/blog-post_19.html), accessed July 15, 2016.

41 | AME (2013): Το Κομμουνιστικό Κόμμα τι Γνωρίζει; [What does the Communist Party know?], June 19, (http://maiandrioi.blogspot.de/2012/06/blog-post_19.html), accessed July 18, 2016.

42 | Sofia Tipaldou (2012): Rock for the Motherland: White Power Music Scene in Greece. In: Paul Jackson und Anton Shekhovtsov (ed.): White Power Music: Scenes of Extreme Right Cultural Resistance. Scenes of Extreme Right Cultural Resistance: Searchlight Magazine. (Mapping the Far Right), pp. 47–55.

List of Contributors

Tamir Bar-On is a researcher on the French *Nouvelle Droite* and completed a Ph. D. in Political Science on this subject at McGill University in 2000. He is the author of *Where Have All the Fascists Gone?* (Ashgate, 2007) and *Rethinking the French New Right: Alternatives to Modernity* (Routledge, 2013). He currently works as a research professor at Tecnológico de Monterrey (Campus Querétaro) in Mexico.

Samuel Bouron is an associate professor at the University of Paris-Dauphine. His work focuses on the relationship between the far right and the media. He coordinated (in co-operation with M. Drouard) the special issue *The Beautiful Neighborhoods of the Extreme Right* (Agone 54, 2014, in French), in which he wrote a chapter on the training of *Identitarian Bloc* activist leaders and the professionalization of their communications.

Alex Carter is a Ph. D. candidate at Teesside University. He received his Bachelor's degree in Politics from Kingston University and his Master's degree in Nationalism and Ethnic Conflict from Birkbeck College, University of London. Alex is affiliated with Teesside University's Centre for the Study of Fascism, Anti-Fascism and Post-Fascism.

Liz Fekete is the director of the London-based Institute of Race Relations and head of its 'European Research Program'. She writes and speaks extensively on aspects of contemporary racism, refugee rights, far-right extremism and Islamophobia across Europe and is author of the study *Pedlars of Hate: The Violent Impact of the European Far Right*.

Maik Fielitz is Ph. D. candidate at the Cluster of Excellence 'The Formation of Normative Orders' and is associated with the Chair for International Relations and Theories of Global Orders at Goethe University Frankfurt am Main. His current research interests include far-right activism in Europe with a particular focus on Greece. He is affiliated with the research program 'International Dissidence'.

Caterina Froio is a postdoctoral researcher at the Centre d'Études Européennes of Sciences Po, Paris. Her research deals with political parties, far-right organizations, party government and agenda-setting dynamics in comparative perspective. She published *Fascists of Another Millennium? Crisis and Participation in CasaPound Italia* (Bonanno, 2014, in Italian) together with P. Castelli Gattinara, G. Bulli, M. Albanese.

Halina Gąsiorowska is a Ph.D. candidate at the Institute of Applied Social Sciences at the University of Warsaw and at the Faculty of Arts and Social Sciences at SWPS University of Social Sciences and Humanities. In her research, she focuses on processes of forming personal and group identity in various social movements. She is interested in sociocultural perspectives on identity.

Daniel Koehler is the director of the German Institute on Radicalization and De-Radicalization Studies (GIRDS) and co-founder of the *Journal for Deradicalization*. He built the first database of right-wing terrorism in Germany. He recently published the monograph *Right-Wing Terrorism in the 21st Century* (Routledge Series on Fascism and the Far Right, 2016).

Matthew Kott is a historian at the Centre for Russian and Eurasian Studies at Uppsala University in Sweden. His research interests include historical and contemporary manifestations of fascism and extremism, along with racism and xenophobia in Northern Europe. Latvia is his particular country of expertise.

Angélique Kourounis is a French-Greek filmmaker who has produced various documentaries on Greece in the condition of crisis – primarily for French and Swiss broadcasts. She is committed to feminist and migrant struggles in Greece and beyond.

Yordan Kutiyski received his M.Sc. in Political Science from the VU University Amsterdam and holds an M.A. in Latin American Studies from the Centre of Latin American Research and Documentation (CEDLA) at the University of Amsterdam. His research interests include electoral behavior, European politics and Latin American politics.

Laura Lotte Laloire is pursuing her M.A. in International Studies/Peace and Conflict Studies at Goethe University Frankfurt am Main and Technical University Darmstadt. She works at the Peace Research Institute Frankfurt (PRIF) and is a freelance journalist. She is conducting research on the relationship among the ideologies, strategies and political violence of social movements, with an empirical focus on Turkey.

Graham Macklin is a senior lecturer in History at Teesside University in England where he researches fascist and extreme right-wing politics and activism in Britain, North America and Europe along with political violence and terrorism. He is currently completing a monograph on White Racial Nationalism in Britain and also co-edits *Routledge Studies in Fascism and the Far Right*.

Holger Marcks is as a research associate at the Chair for International Organizations at Goethe University Frankfurt am Main. As part of the project 'Transnational Escalation Mechanisms of Violent Dissidence', he is conducting research on political violence in historical anarchism. He is also interested in aspects of nationalism and has published on the advancement of right-wing extremism in Hungary.

Oliver Saal studied History at Freie Universität Berlin. He resides in Berlin and works as an author, writing for *Netz gegen Nazis*, among others. Most of his writings deal with European far-right politics in historical and contemporary perspective.

Mathias Schmidt received his Master's in Political Science and Sociology from Leipzig University. His research interests are Eastern Europe, political theory and analyses of power. He currently works on a project that is researching identity, power and conflict in post-socialist countries.

Oula Silvennoinen is an adjunct professor of European History at the University of Helsinki. He earned his Ph.D. with a work on the co-operation between the Finnish and German security police in 1933–1944. He authored the book *Fascism in Finland: Heralds of the Black Dawn* (WSOY, 2016, in Finnish) together with M. Tikka and A. Roselius. His research interests include radical nationalism and the history of the Holocaust.

Mihnea-Simion Stoica is a Ph.D. candidate and researcher at Babeș-Bolyai University in Cluj-Napoca, Romania. He holds an M.Sc. in Comparative Politics from VU Amsterdam and he is the director of the Dutch Cultural and Academic Centre in Cluj. He is on the editorial board of the *Journal for the Study of Religions and Ideologies* and his research interests revolve around political communication.

Natascha Strobl and **Julian Bruns** are (with Kathrin Glösel) authors of the following books on the New Right in Austria and Europe: *The Identitarians: A Handbook on the New Right's Youth in Europe* (Unrast, 2014, in German) and *Cultural Revolution of the Right: Who and what is the New Right these days?* (VSA, 2015, in German). Natascha is a researcher in the field of right-wing extremism and also an anti-fascist activist. Julian is a researcher and Ph.D. candidate specialized in fascist literature in the inter-war period of Northern Europe.

Stijn van Kessel is a lecturer in Politics at Loughborough University. He obtained his doctoral degree (D.Phil.) at the University of Sussex. His current research mainly focuses on populism in Europe and radical right party discourse. He is the author of the monograph *Populist Parties in Europe: Agents of Discontent?* (Palgrave Macmillan, 2015).

Bernhard Weidinger monitors the Austrian far right at the Documentation Centre of Austrian Resistance (DÖW) in Vienna. He is a member of the 'Research Group on Ideologies and Politics of Inequality' (FIPU) and is the author of a standard work on German-nationalist student fraternities and politics in Austria after 1945: *In the National Defense Struggle of the Borderland Germans* (Böhlau, 2015, in German).